BRING ON THE BOOKS

FOR EVERYBODY

Jim Collins

DUKE UNIVERSITY PRESS   Durham and London 2010

BRING ON THE BOOKS FOR EVERYBODY

How Literary Culture Became Popular Culture

Duke University Press gratefully acknowledges
the support of the Institute for Scholarship in
the Liberal Arts, College of Arts and Letters,
University of Notre Dame, which provided
funds toward the production of this book.

A portion of chapter 2 appeared previously as
"Of Books, Lattes, and Class Distinctions:
Superstores and the New Quality Consumerism,"
Harvard Design Magazine (winter–spring 2000): 55–66.

for
William Collins
and
Virginia Collins
(1930–2008)

CONTENTS

ACKNOWLEDGMENTS

I would like to thank my colleagues at Notre Dame and at other institutions for graciously volunteering to read parts of this manuscript and offering crucial advice—Kim Middleton, Dudley Andrew, Peter Holland, James Naremore, Pam Wojcik, Steve Fredman, and Tom Schatz. I also thank the students and faculty at the University of Copenhagen, the University of Melbourne, the Chicago Film Seminar, and the College of St. Rose, where I was invited to present parts of this book and received extremely useful suggestions.

I owe the deepest thanks to Angela Ndalianis at the University of Melbourne, who read, most meticulously, the entire manuscript in various incarnations. Her invaluable insights had the most profound effect on this book, and I doubt that I will ever be able to return such an enormous favor. I know no better close reader, or truer friend.

I would like to thank the Institute for Scholarship in the Liberal Arts, College of Arts and Letters, at the University of Notre Dame for its support of this entire project.

I also want to thank Ken Wissoker at Duke University Press, who lived up to his reputation as an editor extraordinaire. Courtney Berger, Leigh Barnwell, Amy Ruth Buchanan, Katie Courtland, Fred Kameny, and Pam Morrison have also been a delight to work with, as they have provided kind and careful guidance throughout the publication of this book. In addition, I express my sincere appreciation to the reviewers and copy editor of this manuscript, because their suggestions were consistently insightful and improved the finished product.

Finally, I want to thank my family for boundless emotional support. My parents, William and Virginia, were, as they have always been, the foundation of my support. My wife, Stephanie, and my daughters, Ava, Nell, Sophia, and Gabriela, have all made essential contributions. They will find themselves within this book, appearing at various places, because my life as an educator begins and ends with them.

INTRODUCTION

*Digital Books, Beach Chairs,
and Popular Literary Culture*

This book about the changes that have occurred in literary culture in the United States within the past decade began with cup of coffee and a vacant stare in a strip mall store in Mishawaka, Indiana. The coffee was a Starbucks latte and the store was Barnes & Noble, where I sat with my daughters as they downed their Italian sodas and argued about which *Harry Potter* movie was really the best. Already all too familiar with this particular debate, I stared off into space, first at the façade of the Outback Steakhouse across the parking lot, and then upward, where I encountered another café scene in the mural that wrapped around us along the ceiling.

The mural presented a tableau of Great Authors — Henry James, Virginia Woolf, Jane Austen, Edith Wharton, and company — all seated at adjacent

1. Authors Mural, Barnes & Noble store, Mishawaka, Indiana, 2008

tables in an imaginary Literary Café Valhalla. I was initially struck by the absurdity of the tableau, since we were, after all, in a chainstore in a suburban development that had been a cornfield only a few years before, and the people at the tables adjacent to mine weren't talking about the subtleties of literary craft—one woman sat alone reading an issue of *Martha Stewart Living*, two teenagers talked about much they hated having to read *A Separate Peace* and wondered why their English teacher wouldn't let them talk about something interesting like *William Shakespeare's Romeo +Juliet* or *Shakespeare in Love*, while another couple talked about Oprah's Book Club. I followed their gaze to the front of the store, where I saw the table that featured the current Oprah Selection. I looked back down at my table, where the course packet for my "Postmodern Narrative" course was sitting next to my latte. I'd brought it along to prep the next class, to give myself something to do while the kids did their Barnes & Noble routines. At that moment, I was overwhelmed by the absurdity not of the store's décor but of my presuming to teach my students anything about contemporary literature without taking superstores, blockbuster film adaptations, and television book clubs into account, not just as symptoms of the current state of the *culture industry* but as the sites, delivery systems, and forms of connoisseurship that formed the fabric of a *popular* literary culture.

The first article in that course packet was John Barth's essay "The Literature of Replenishment" (1980), in which he laid out a provisional definition for what the postmodern writing of the future should be, arguing quite vehemently that it must somehow expand the audience for literary fiction. He identified what he considered to be the most pertinent differences between modernist and postmodernist writing as he set his agenda for replenishment, namely, a reconnection between the literary novelists and the broad-based audience that had been commonplace in the premodern period. According to Barth, this loss of audience was attributable to the "difficulty of access" that was one of the chief distinguishers of modernist writing, and directly responsible for the unpopularity of modernist fiction outside of intellectual circles and university curricula. His ideal postmodernist author should try to recover that lost audience: "He may not hope to reach and move the devotees of James Michener and Irving Wallace, not to mention the great mass of television addicted non-readers. But he should hope to reach and delight, at least part of the time, beyond the circle of what Mann called the Early Christians: professional devotees of high art" (203).

If we fast-forward twenty-some years, the literary world Barth describes in that essay now seems antique. The ideal postmodern novel he hoped would appear did indeed materialize, in the form of novels such as Salman Rushdie's *Midnight's Children* (1981), Graham Swift's *Waterland* (1983), Julian Barnes's *Flaubert's Parrot* (1984), Don DeLillo's *Libra* (1988), and Jeanette Winterson's *Sexing the Cherry* (1989); and by now those novels have become canonical and are regularly taught in courses on postmodern fiction. But something else happened in the meantime that redefined the entire notion of accessibility. Writers of literary fiction such as Amy Tan, Ian McEwan, Toni Morrison, Jhumpa Lahiri, Margaret Atwood, and Cormac McCarthy have the brand-name recognition once enjoyed by writers of bestsellers like Michener. Their popularity depends upon a great mass of reading-addicted television watchers and a culture industry ready and eager to bring them together through book clubs, superstore bookstores, and glossy high-concept adaptations that have dominated the Academy Awards for the past decade. Michael Ondaatje's *The English Patient* (1992) was a Booker Prize–winning example of Canadian postmodern fiction, but it also became a hugely successful film by Miramax, winning nine Oscars, including Best Picture of the Year in 1996, at which point it became the subject of an episode of *Seinfeld* and was later voted "Most Romantic Film of the Decade" by the readers of *Romance Times* magazine (the bible of the romance genre industry). Popular literary culture, in a variety of new incarnations, now appears to be everywhere you look—at the multiplex, driving down the strip, floating through the mall, or surfing the Net. And over the course of those twenty years, those early Christians—the professors of literature—ran amuck, allegedly refusing to hold up their end of the conversation as they spoke in High Theory and killed off authors on a regular basis before some returned, eager to connect with addicted readers, who congregated enthusiastically online and on television, to share fiercely held opinions about books. Apparently, the love of literature can now be fully experienced only outside the academy and the New York literary scene, out there somewhere in the wilds of popular culture.

The most profound change in literary America after the rise of postmodern fiction wasn't the next generation of cutting-edge novelists; it was the complete redefinition of what literary reading means within the heart of electronic culture. The really significant next new thing wasn't a matter of radical innovations in literary craft but massive infrastructural changes in literary culture that introduced a new set of players, locations, rituals, and use values for reading literary fiction. Within the past decade media critics have argued that film viewing has changed so thoroughly that we need to reconsider the power of images since most visual entertainment is no longer enjoyed in the confines of the darkened theater but on screens that come in a seemingly endless variety of formats and locations, from iPods to laptops to theme park sensory extravaganzas. The private dream state that used to be considered the very bedrock of film-viewing pleasure no longer seems quite adequate for describing the multiple-choice gestalts of contemporary visual culture. New technologies of exhibition have reshaped the pleasures and practices that now define what *going to a movie* might mean. Yet I would argue that the experience of literary reading has been transformed to an even greater extent, since who reads it, how it is read, where it is read, and even what is read under the heading of literary fiction have all changed in fundamental ways.

What used to be a thoroughly private experience in which readers engaged in intimate conversation with an author between the pages of a book has become an exuberantly social activity, whether it be in the form of actual book clubs, television book clubs, Internet chat rooms, or the entire set of rituals involved in "going to Barnes & Noble." What used to be an exclusively print-based activity—and fiercely proud of it—has become an increasingly image-based activity in which literary reading has been transformed into a variety of possible literary experiences. Of course you like Jane Austen—but how do you take your Austen? In novel form? As a television adaptation with Colin Firth, or as a film adaptation with Kiera Knightly? As a fictionalized account of reading Jane, as in *The Jane Austen Book Club*? If so, in novel form complete with reader's guide, or the movie adaptation with Emily Blunt playing the character who reads *Persuasion* so passionately? Or as any and all of the above, at any given moment, as you surf through the possible Austen experiences?

How and where those audiences appreciate literary fiction has changed profoundly, but so has the literary fiction written for those passionate readers who watch television book clubs, cruise Amazon, or take their literature in cinematic form at the local multiplex or via Netflix. The refunctioning of literary experiences is a matter of how you read them, but it's also a matter of how you write them. The use value of reading quality fiction—what we read it *for*—has become a central issue in novels that insist on their ability to perform a vitally important function in the lives of those reading-addicted television viewers, whether it be the delivery of essential information about acquiring significant others and material goods, or the delivery of a "pure" aesthetic experience that is intended to transcend the realm of mere consumerism (and is aggressively marketed as such). In either case, we find literary fiction insisting on its therapeutic value in everything from Melissa Bank's *The Girls' Guide to Hunting and Fishing* to Nick Hornby's *A Long Way Down* to Zadie Smith's *On Beauty* to Alan Hollinghurst's *The Line of Beauty*.

Hilma Wolitzer's novel *Summer Reading* (2008) exemplifies just how explicit this refunctioning project has become. One of the three main characters is Angela, a retired English professor who leads a local reading group in discussions of Anthony Trollope's *Can You Forgive Her?*, Flaubert's *Madame Bovary*, and Charlotte Brontë's *Villette*. The discussion begins ambitiously: "What is the function of literature? Angela had posed the question at the beginning of the meeting, before they'd even mentioned Trollope" (27). That a novel written by a respected literary author who has taught creative writing at places like the University of Iowa Writers' Workshop and Columbia University would pose the question that literary critics have been mulling over for centuries isn't really that surprising, but the critical blurb on the cover of the paperback suggests a radical relocation for that discussion: "A Hamptons vacation, trophy wives and characters who dig books . . . Bring on the beach chair — *People*."

Trollope and Flaubert at the beach? Twenty years ago the very idea would have sounded like a Woody Allen parody in *The New Yorker*. Trollope on *Masterpiece Theatre*, of course, but never at the beach, the most notoriously nonintellectual location within American culture, where one is supposed to read only for pleasure. When the most popular lifestyle magazine in North America recommends a novel as ideal summer reading because it brings together the Hamptons (the favorite playground of the celebrity news industry) and people who talk avidly about books by Trollope, Flaubert, and Brontë, and then suggests that the function of literature should be pondered from the vantage point of beach chairs filled with readers of *People* magazine who evidently also really *dig books*, then literary reading is no longer what, or where, it used to be.

Accessing *Madame Bovary* at the beach involves two interdependent developments that are equally profound in terms of how literary reading has been transformed in the United States at the beginning of the twenty-first century. I can have a copy delivered to my beach chair "in under a minute" via Amazon on a Kindle digital reader, and if I have any qualms about buying a Kindle that will hook me up with Flaubert almost instantaneously, I can watch video testimonials at Amazon featuring not only CEO Jeff Bezos but also the Nobel Prize–winning novelist Toni Morrison telling me what a wonderful device it is for really avid readers—and she too will tell me that it's great if you want to read "in the yard, at the beach, on a plane." Yet taking Flaubert to the beach involves another kind of empowerment in addition to new forms of digital downloadability; it depends every bit as much on amateur readers feeling perfectly comfortable taking on books that were formerly thought to be fully accessible only to professionalized readers. The beach in this case signifies a geographic space, but also a figurative space where there used to be no confusion about the differences between pleasure reading and literary reading. In other words, of course, you can get an order of Flaubert more easily from your beach chair than an order of fried clams, but why would readers of *People* magazine think of *Madame Bovary* as a good read, intended for people just like them? Because their English teacher recommended it once upon a time? Or because it was the novel that the book club read in Tom Perrotta's novel *Little Children* (also available in under a minute)? Or because it was the novel Kate Winslet's character identified with so fiercely in the film version of *Little Children*? Or because books about readers reading passionately have themselves become bestsellers and are supposed to be taken to the beach, at least according to an advertisement from the Random House Publishing Group that appeared in the *New York Times*.

The first of the books featured in this advertisement, Azar Nafisi's *Reading Lolita in Tehran*, details the book club she formed with a handful of students and how their discussions become vital transformative experiences when they make the novels that they read into narratives about their *own* lives (*Lolita* also available in under a minute, if I feel more like Nabokov than Flaubert that particular afternoon). The promotion of this book alongside Lorna Landvik's *Angry Housewives Eating Bon Bons* (2004) and Matthew Pearl's novel *The Dante Club* (2004) reveals a great deal about the imagined readership, especially since Pearl's novel features America's first Dante scholars (Henry Wadsworth Longfellow, James Russell Lowell, J. T. Fields, and Oliver Wendell Holmes) solving heinous murders in post–Civil War Boston. Why have the adventures in interpretive reading undertaken by erudite, scholarly readers like Nafisi, Lowell, and company suddenly become bestselling entertainment for those readers in beach chairs?

2. "Hit the Beach," advertisement in *New York Times Book Review*, June 2004

How do we begin to get a handle on this robust popular literary culture fueled by such a complicated mix of technology and taste, of culture and commerce? Some of its infrastructural features are directly attributable to the conglomeration of the publishing industry—the ever-expanding number of titles, the ubiquity and velocity of delivery systems in the form of superstores and online book sales; the increasing synergy among publishing, film, television, and Internet industries; and the exponential increase in targeting quality consumers. But a number of other factors are the result of changes in taste hierarchies—the radical devaluation of the academy and New York literary scene as taste brokers who maintained the gold standard of literary currency, the collapse of the traditional dichotomies that made book reading somehow naturally antagonistic to film going or television watching, and the transformation of taste acquisition into an industry with taste arbiters becoming media celebrities. And perhaps the most fundamental change of all: the notion that refined taste, or the information needed to enjoy sophisticated cultural pleasures, is now easily accessible outside a formal education. It's just a matter of knowing where to access it, and whom to trust.

I have no interest in judging the ultimate effects of that interplay in a unilateral way. This is not a bumper sticker book, e.g., *Honk If You Think Culture Is Going to Hell in a Handbasket* or *My Literary Values Aren't Dead, Sorry about Yours*. My goal in this book is to trace the contours of a particular "media ecology" shaped by the increasing convergence of literary, visual, and material cultures. The phenomena that I examine in detail—Barnes & Noble superstores, Amazon, book clubs (actual, virtual, and fictionalized), adaptation films, and literary bestsellers—all merit book-length studies individually, but I think they are best understood as interdependent components of a popular literary culture that has its own ways of identifying a literary experience as such, with its own way of "talking the talk" of passionate reading, its own modes of circulation and access, and its own authorities to sanction what sort of pleasures are to be enjoyed there. This is not to suggest that I intend to merely describe that interplay as a detached observer, complete with digital pith helmet and clipboard. This is a highly opinionated account, but not a blanket condemnation or celebration. I teach courses in postmodern literature but also contemporary Hollywood, as a member of both an English department and a film department. This experience has given me a keen understanding of the intricacies of style as well as the complexities of the entertainment industry. I think it has also given me a healthy ambivalence about both, repulsed equally by rapacious greed and insufferable sanctimony. So, if you hope this will be an exposé of the Evils of the Culture Industry, or a snappy remix of "I Sing the Culture Electric," go no further, because this book just isn't for you. Think of these first few pages as the thirty-second sample of a song you get to hear at iTunes—if you don't like it so far, you're going to hate the rest of it. If, on the other hand, you want something that does more than simply reaffirm all of the old prejudices as it tries to identify the moving parts and interconnections of the popular literary culture you're surrounded by, you might want to continue.

The Literacy of Infinite Personalization

The increasing accessibility of literary fiction obviously involves a host of issues concerning the status of "the book" and the nature of literacy at the beginning of the twenty-first century. In a cover story in the *New York Times Magazine* (May 14, 2006) entitled "Scan This Book!" Kevin Kelly argues that because of exponential increases in accessibility "everything we thought we knew about books is going to change." He focuses on the decision by Google in 2006 to digitize the contents of five major research libraries into one vast universal library, thereby creating an unprecedented degree of access to books:

> Might the long-heralded great library of all knowledge really be within our grasp? Brewster Kahle, the archivist overseeing another scanning project says that the universal library is now within reach. "This is our chance to one-up the Greeks!" he shouts. "It really is possible with the technology of today, not tomorrow. We can provide all the works of humankind to all people of the world. It will be an achievement remembered for all time, like putting a man on the moon." And unlike the libraries of old, which were restricted to an elite, this library would be truly democratic, offering every book to every person. (44)

This desire to take books to the people of the world on a grand scale is not restricted to Google, since it is also the principal goal of Barnes & Noble, Borders, Amazon.com, and Oprah Winfrey's Book Club—a project epitomized by the charge she gave her "book elves" as they hand out hundreds of copies of *The Good Earth* to her studio audience at the end of her *Anna Karenina* show: "Bring on the books for everybody!" Kelly's analysis of the ramifications of the scanning of books is a key text for understanding the revolution in accessibility, but so is the *O: The Oprah Magazine*—"Our First Ever Summer Reading Issue" (July 2006), which offered to its millions of readers advice from Toni Morrison and Harper Lee about the pleasures of books, along with featured articles with titles such as "How It Begins" and "How to Read a Hard Book." Kelly argues compellingly that the basic contours of what constitutes a book have been changed by a digital revolution. The "Summer Reading Issue" in many ways confirms this, since it features on "The O List" ("A few things I think are great"—Oprah) a portable digital library, the Sony Librie ("Download up to 80 of your favorites—hundreds more with a memory card"), as well as a "special deal just for you" on twenty of the recommended titles: "This issue is so full of books you're going to want that we asked the nice people at Amazon to do us a favor and give you a break. Just go to www.amazon.com/oprahmagazine." Kelly focuses on the technological dimensions of this universal accessibility, emphasizing the shifting relationships between copy and copyright and how "digital bits" will change notions of authorship. Taking books to the people on the grandest of scales involves a number of other questions: What happens to literary reading when it becomes a sophisticated form of self-help therapy? What prompts this need to get some kind of aesthetic *fix*, in all senses of that word? Who functions as an expert? And what sort of literary fiction is being written for this passionate readership?

In order to gain a better understanding of "the book" in the age of digitized accessibility, we need to pursue the questions Kelly frames so incisively but situate them in reference to a specific culture of reading. This culture may indeed rely on twenty-first-century technologies of scanning, storage, and downloadability, but it also draws on early-nineteenth-century notions of reading as self-transformation, filtered through late twentieth-century discourses of self-actualization, all jet-propelled by state-of-the-art forms of marketing "aesthetic experience." In other words, literary reading in the age of universal access to the universal library is an uneven development, shaped equally by contemporary information technologies, Romantic-era notions of the self, and late Victorian conceptions of aesthetic value. The reality of a universal library is indeed upon us, thanks to Google, and Amazon.com can make individual titles appear in less than a minute. But those books come to us through a thriving popular literary culture, which invests the literary text—whether experienced on the page, or on the screen, or on a laptop—with a variety of *use values*, some of which are just as unprecedented as those scanning technologies. We can begin to make sense of "the book" and what constitutes "literacy" within this reading culture only when we seize on those contradictions and resist the urge to generalize unilaterally about the effects of increased access.

I want to offer just one cautionary example. John Updike expressed profound doubts about Kelly's article in a *New York Times Book Review* editorial entitled "The End of Authorship" (June 25, 2006). He was troubled by Kelly's celebration of this "huge, virtually infinite wordstream accessed by search engines and populated by word snippets," because it will mean the end of reading as "an encounter between two minds." He concludes:

"The book revolution [that] from the Renaissance taught men and women how to cherish and cultivate their individuality, threatens to end in a flurry of word snippets. For some of us, books are intrinsic to sense of personal identity" (27). Updike obviously hadn't gotten his copy of *O*'s "Summer Reading Issue" when he penned his countermanifesto, because if he had, he would have seen that this ideology of reading as intrinsic to a sense of personal identity is the central organizing principle for the entire issue. In her final word to her readers, "What I Know for Sure," Oprah says: "What I know for sure is that reading opens you up. It exposes you and gives you access to anything your mind can hold. What I love most about reading: It gives you the ability to reach higher ground. A world of possibilities awaits you. Keep turning the page" (224). When Oprah brings books to everyone, everyone is encouraged to make their reading intensely personal—what's the point of reading otherwise? Consider the quotations about reading scattered throughout the magazine. A page of perforated punch-out bookmarks features a series of quotations about the joys of reading from the likes of Jorge Luis Borges ("I always imagined Paradise to be a sort of library") and Margaret Walker ("When I was about 8, I decided that the most wonderful thing, next to a human being was a book"). The monthly "Calendar" feature is also studded with the same type of quotations that confirm Updike's sentiments: "Writing and reading is to me synonymous with existing" (Gertrude Stein) and "My home is where my books are" (Ellen Thompson). Interestingly, the most explicit invocation of Updike's notion of reading as intrinsic to a sense of personal identity comes in the introduction to an article entitled "Comfort Zone: Book Keeping": "Your books are your autobiography. They map your history, reflect your tastes, hold your emotional moments between covers. On these pages, intelligent designs for sharing space with the literature you love." This text is superimposed on the proper set for all this reading, with the following suggestions:

> Curling up with an absorbing story is as crucial to your well-being as leafy greens or sunshine. And it's especially restorative if you have a corner dedicated to the printed word, with all the comforts: say a cool linen-covered chaise longue (Interieur); plump embroidered pillows ($184 each, Historically Inaccurate Decorative Arts); a cashmere throw ($325, Calypso Christiane Celle); and "good lamp" ($1,050, Regeneration Furniture) as well as lots of natural light. Of course you'll have well stocked shelves within reach (teak bookcase, $2,200, Regeneration Furniture).

This clean, well-lighted, *Elle Decor*-style space for intensely personal, transformative reading suggests that this reading culture depends on the downloadabilty of books but also on easy access to expertise about how to read even "hard books" from an informed position, and about the right sort of reading space. The text for this feature introduces the "*t* word" avoided by most academic critics, as well as these famous authors — *taste*. The idea that literary reading is an expression not just of some nebulous inner wisdom but of one's personal taste, and that it can be fully articulated only by a series of interconnected purchases, suggests that this reading culture is a hybrid of information technology and self-help discourse, fueled by high-octane Romantic humanism, all made possible through the generous sponsorship of quality consumerism.

We can't begin to appreciate how this interplay works without looking closely at the way new delivery systems make a reading culture possible in the first place, but we can't really discern the impact that this increasing accessibility has on "the book" unless we have a fine-grain understanding of the sort of "literacy" that is required to appreciate them. Delivery systems provide not just the books but also the sites, the talk, and the sense of belonging to a community of readers. Amazon delivers the goods, but it is also a breeder reactor of reading communities, just as Barnes & Noble provides the books and the locations for thousands of local book clubs. The technologies of accessibility do not function in a unilateral way — some may lead in the direction of wordstreams and digital bits, but others only sanctify the most traditional forms of authorship. Consider the ways in which technologies of storage and access enable passionate listeners to enjoy experiences of music that are anything but uniform. iTunes makes over a million songs available, and by ripping and burning them on my iBook, or downloading them on my iPod I can make play lists or compilation mixes to my heart's content, organized according to the most personal listening agendas, any of which would diminish the singular intentions of the original authors of that music. On the other hand, "digital technology" can valorize, even fetishize, that singularity like never before. Consider the CD Collectors Editions boxed sets such as *The Complete Columbia Recordings: Miles Davis with John Coltrane, 1955–1961*, in which listeners get, in addition to all of the original albums, dozens of alternate takes from record label archives; or the *London Calling: Legacy Edition* boxed set, which includes the original Clash album, another disk of alternate takes, and a DVD of footage shot during the recording of the material. In much the same way, Google's universal library will enable burning and ripping of favorite bits from books, but another kind of effect is achieved by the DVD edition of *The Hours*, which includes extensive commentary tracks by its director Stephen Daldry and the novel's author, Michael Cunningham, along with hours of special features about Virginia Woolf, in which noted scholars offer insights about the Author, her novels, and Cunningham's appropriation of *Mrs. Dalloway* within his novel. The inclusion of those special features blurs the line between what is intended for amateur and professionalized readers since it converts the DVD edition of *The Hours* into something resembling a Norton Critical Edition of literary masterpieces used for decades in college English classes, in which the reader gets the integral text of the novel, copiously footnoted, followed by a collection of essays that contextualize the novel from a variety of different perspectives. In each case, the singularity of the masterpiece as product of the Great Author is the organizing principle of the entire enterprise, whether that Great Author is Virginia Woolf or The Clash.

This complicated interplay of early-twenty-first-century forms of digital storage and early-nineteenth-century conceptions of individual genius played out across a variety of media formats exemplifies what Henry Jenkins has referred to as *convergence culture*. According to Jenkins, the initial theorizing about the digital revolution, which was supposed to produce sweeping transformations that would render all previous forms of media instantaneously antiquated (books as "dead-tree" technology), has recently given way to far more subtle investigations of the ways in which old and new media now coexist synergistically: "Cinema did not kill theater. Television did not kill radio. Each old medium was forced to co-exist with emerging media. That's why convergence seems more plausible as a way of understanding the past several decades of media change than the old digital revolution paradigm had. Old media are not being displaced. Rather their functions and status are shifted by the introduction of new technologies" (14). I think this essential point can be taken further in regard to the popularization of literary reading, since it involves more than the convergence of old and new media—it depends, just as fundamentally, on the convergence of antique and emergent notions of access, artistic genius, reading pleasure, and personal taste.

The digital technologies that make downloadable universal libraries possible have one hugely important thing in common with the sort of traditional book talk spoken by Updike and all the various voices in the "Summer Reading Issue" of *O*—both are devoted to the immediate personalization of literary reading. In the next chapter I will focus on the way in which Amazon *rehangs* the site for each customer based on previous purchases, so that upon each subsequent visit all is cut to the measure of what appears to be an intensely individualized taste profile. Updike may have been concerned about the loss of the personal dimension of reading, but one of the chief distinguishing characteristics of the popular literary culture is the hyperpersonalization that empowers the reader, marketer, and reader/novelist to take any liberties needed to ensure that pleasure. While the "Summer Reading Issue" was on the newsstand and Updike's editorial appeared in the *New York Times Book Review*, Jennifer Kaufman and Karen Black's novel *Literacy and Longing in L.A.* (2006) was a bestseller advertised in that same *New York Times*. This novel about a passionate reader concludes with a lengthy list of the main character's favorites books, which she refers to throughout the course of the action, at which point the novel becomes a kind of hybridized combination of fictional narrative and personal guide to literary reading. While I will be talking about this novel at greater length in chapter 6, I want to reflect here on the title of this novel, because it has everything to do with the reading culture of the popular literary: Why this *longing* for the literary experience within an audience of amateur readers? What sort of personalized literacy circulates within this novel and across its readership? And why does that personalization make literary reading such a vital form of popular culture?

My determination to explore this popularization may seem like a puzzling move to some readers, since the National Endowment for the Arts published a report in the fall of 2004 entitled *Reading at Risk: A Survey of Literary Reading in America*, which insisted that the reading of books has been declining in the United States within the past decade and that it's all attributable to the evil influences of electronic media. While many of the assumptions made in that report involve highly debatable interpretations of its statistical data, none is more troubling, or more limiting, than its central theme—that reading books and viewing electronic media are mutually antagonistic experiences that take place in incommensurate, hermetically sealed cultures. That television and computer technologies are to blame was not an earth-shaking conclusion, since it was such predictable reiteration of the traditional attack on mass culture as the ruination of genuine culture by providing all those easy, promiscuous pleasures: "Reading a book requires a degree of active attention and engagement. Indeed, reading itself is a progressive skill that depends on years of education and practice. By contrast, most electronic media such as television, recordings, and radio make fewer demands on their audiences and indeed often require no more than passive participation. Even interactive electronic media, such as video games and the Internet, foster shorter attention spans and accelerated gratification" (vii).

The report details, in an elaborate associated-tastes argument, how literary readers are much more likely to attend museums, concerts, and so on but assumes that electronic media are consumed by some great Other composed of unwashed nonreaders. Yet upon closer inspection of the data, certain points emerge that undermine that sweeping central argument. In table 13, "Average Number of Hours per Day Watching TV, U.S. Adults," we learn that while nonreaders may watch television 3.1 hours per day, those who read literature watch 2.7 hours per day. The authors of the report begin by insisting that what they consider "frequent readers" (twelve to forty-nine books a year) watch less TV (2.4 hours) than nonreaders; but they also found that really "avid readers" (fifty or more books a year) watched more (2.6 hours), leading them to the grudging conclusion that "overall, . . . frequent readers watch only slightly less TV per day than infrequent readers. The SPPA (Survey of Public Participation in the Arts) results cannot show whether people who never read literary works would do so if they watch less TV, or whether they would use this extra time in other ways" (15). The authors of the report then make a rather surprising admission, given their central argument: "In some cases, TV watching may have a positive effect on literary reading. Authors regularly appear on TV to promote their books, and some TV book clubs have been extremely popular. In fact, in the spring of 2002 most book publishers were very disappointed when Oprah Winfrey cancelled the book club related to her talk show. The effects of mass media, particularly television, movies and the Internet, merit further scrutiny" (16).

Indeed they do. Interestingly, when the NEA issued another report on reading in January 2009, *Reading on the Rise*, it found a significant increase in literary reading, but it was unwilling to reconsider the relationship between literary reading and electronic media. In his preface to the report, Dan Gioia argues:

A significant turning point in recent American cultural history. For the first time in over a quarter-century, our survey shows that literary reading has risen among adult Americans. After decades of declining trends, there has been a decisive and unambiguous increase in virtually every group measured in this comprehensive national survey. . . . Combined with general population growth, these higher reading rates have expanded literary readership by 16.6 million, creating the largest audience in the history of the survey.

This increase is due to the forces he congratulates: "Legions of teachers, librarians, writers, parents, public officials, and philanthropists who helped achieve the renascence." He also cites the Big Read projects and a widespread awareness that something had to be done about the decline in literary reading.

While all of those parties did indeed contribute mightily to the cause, the report attributes nothing to the massive transformation in the culture of reading that has occurred over the past decade in terms of where and how readers now access their literary experiences (in a variety of different interdependent media), why they feel empowered to make literary reading *their own*, or why they would be drawn to literary reading as a favorite leisure-time activity. Teachers and librarians merit the heartiest of congratulations for their steadfast efforts, but anyone who has waited with a few hundred other parents and supercharged thirteen-year-old readers in the middle of the night in a strip mall store for the release of a vampire novel knows that other forces have been at work. We weren't there because the local librarian thought it was a good book we should make every effort to read. I'm not referring here just to the power of conglomerate publishing, even though bestselling books are now regularly talked about in the media in terms of opening-weekend grosses and how they compare to other blockbuster book releases. The more important point is that those readers knew that this vampire novel was written for *them*, and they knew exactly where to go to get their copy, because they had already become habituated readers and habituated customers at that bookstore. The largest audience for literary reading in the history of the NEA survey is attributable to the work of teachers and librarians, but also to superstore chains, and adaptations films at the multiplex down the strip, and Amazon communities, and television book clubs, and digital books, and all of those beach chairs.

One of the main goals of this book is to challenge the argument regarding the relationship between literary reading and electronic culture that is central to both of those NEA reports. I have no interest in measuring the effects of the mass media on reading as some kind of instrumental tool that might increase the number of readers in the United States a few percentage points. That sort of approach, in which mass media becomes a good thing if they lead viewers to genuine cultural pleasures, would only perpetuate all the old dichotomies between mass culture and high culture that grow ever more antiquated. In their conclusion to the *Reading at Risk* report, the authors set forth "questions for a research agenda and national conversation on literature participation," but they begin with a question that would only push further research in exactly the wrong direction, because they continue to position literary reading and electronic media in an antagonistic relationship: "How does literature, particularly serious literary work, compete with the Internet, popular entertainment, and other increased demands on leisure time?" (30). Why *compete*? A far more productive question might be, How has the experience of literary work become a form of popular visual entertainment? And how can we hope that the habit of literary reading will survive if it doesn't?

What I hope to do in this book, then, is provide a fine-grain analysis of popular literary culture where mass media and literary reading are not mutually opposed but interdependent experiences, crucial associated tastes that tell us more about how people who consider themselves readers actually come to their literary experiences, which are no longer restricted to the solitary act of reading a book. The NEA report uses the term "literary reading" liberally but attempts no such fine distinctions, preferring to use it as an all-encompassing category, "including popular genres such as mysteries, as well as contemporary and classic literary fiction. No distinctions were drawn in the quality of literary work" (2). Yet within popular literary culture, qualitative distinctions are relentlessly drawn in regard to both marketing and connoisseurship. The adaptation films that have dominated the Academy Awards have been winners of Man Booker, PEN Faulkner, and Pulitzer Prizes and advertised as such—anything but the mere genre fiction that serves as the basis for action pictures based on novels by the likes of John Grisham or Robert Ludlum. Those qualitative distinctions depend on a very particular sort of "literacy." The uses of this word are obviously wide-ranging and polyvalent, from relatively "neutral" conceptions of literacy defined as the ability to read, to highly charged conceptions of the term that make literacy into a kind of shorthand for a particular theory of education. Debates have swirled around E. D. Hirsch's notion of cultural literacy since the eighties, but the battles that raged over literary canons have in recent years given way to an even wider struggle over the question of a "national curriculum." The conflicts between opposing definitions of what constitutes cultural or critical literacy continue to invest the word "literacy" with a host of preconceptions about what should or shouldn't be learned, by practically everyone, at virtually any age level. I want to come at the question of literacy from another angle—what does the transformation of certain forms of literary reading into popular culture suggest about popular literacy, specifically in terms of what readers are now lead to believe they need to know in order to be culturally literate, not by E. D. Hirsch and company, but by television book clubs, superstore bookshops, mall movie adaptations, and literary bestsellers? In her seminal work on early childhood literacy, Lillian Katz argues compellingly that we need to focus on what shapes the *disposition to be a reader* if we hope to get a clearer picture of what animates lifetime reading. In much the same way, I believe we need to develop a far more sophisticated understanding of what shapes the disposition for literary reading among readers who don't have to, the postcollegiate or noncollegiate readers who read passionately, without a syllabus. What does popular literary culture offer as a payoff for such reading? "The joys of reading" doesn't really answer the question. If literacy ultimately depends on a set of assumptions about what is worth knowing, what does popular literary culture promise to deliver, since it provides not just the books for everybody, but the reasons for having a literary experience for everybody, in whatever format it may be encountered?

Who Really *Loves Reading?—The Discrediting of the Academy and Empowering Amateur Readers*

Bringing good books to a mass audience outside the academy is hardly a new development in and of itself. Ambitious public lecture systems and various bookselling gambits thrived during the 1890s, and then became even more elaborate with the introduction of the Book-of-the-Month Club in the late 1920s. The popularization of literary culture that begins in the 1990s, however, involves a far more extensive redefinition of what constitutes a quality reading experience. In *A Feeling for Books* (1997) Janice Radway meticulously details the ways in which the Book-of-the-Month Club brought a new delivery system, direct-mail marketing, to the selling of books and, in the process, challenged existing notions of literary authority as this aggressively "middle-brow" phenomenon scandalized official literary culture. Yet to conceive of Barnes & Noble, Amazon.com, Miramax, and Oprah Winfrey's Book Club as merely further expansions of middle-brow culture is to fail to recognize just how fundamentally cultural life in the United States has changed during the past decade. The Book-of-the-Month Club had to engage in elaborate rhetorical maneuvers to legitimize its authority in reference to an academy that still reigned supreme as broker of literary value. Radway makes the key point that as she was growing up she read featured selections from the Book-of-the-Month Club that were decidedly noncanonical: "good reads" exemplified by *To Kill a Mockingbird*, *Marjorie Morningstar*, and *Gone with the Wind* that formed a category unto itself, not to be confused with high-brow literary fiction. While she defends these club selections that made such an impression on her at the time, she adds that they had no place in her college English classes, where "the only female authors I read were the Brontës, Jane Austen, Emily Dickinson, and Edith Wharton" (349). Radway argues convincingly that "the book club wars were, in sum, a specifically American version of what we now call the mass culture debate" (4). But the "Other" that is mass culture has shifted profoundly within the past decade in terms of its location and, just as important, in terms of who now has the venue and the power to make those brow designations.

Where the Book-of-the-Month Club depended on the identification and promotion of a new class of fiction that could be offered as *good reads* distinctively apart from literary fiction, popular literary culture refunctions the literary novel as a *good read*, insisting that the appreciation of top-shelf fiction, whether it be canonical or contemporary, is possible for the general reader—it's all in how you read them, or, more precisely, what you read them *for*. By the late nineties, literary taste brokers outside the academy could present themselves as superior to an academy that could now simply be ignored, because the priesthood of literature allegedly minted only counterfeit forms of cultural capital that were valueless to real readers in search of a good book unless they could learn to express their expertise in the discourse of passionate reading. Within a thoroughly destigmatized popular literary culture no longer haunted by the original sin of consumerism, those readers could access both the books and the information needed to really appreciate them as aesthetic experiences with a degree of ease that made direct-mail marketing seem antique, and with a degree of confidence that made the academy seem irrelevant.

The popularization of literary reading depends as much on shifts in cultural authority as it does on changes within culture industries. In other words, popular literary culture came into being not just because Barnes & Noble, Amazon, and the Oprah Book Club appeared on the scene. They did indeed provide new contexts for passionate readers to talk about literary books and form reading communities that didn't feel intimidated by the traditional discourses of literary appreciation. But the robust self-confidence enjoyed by amateur readers could only have occurred during a time when there was a profound loss of faith in professional readers, a loss of confidence in traditional literary authority to say much of anything useful about the joys of reading. According to John Barth, the difficulty of access that distinguished modernist fiction was responsible for "the engenderment of a necessary priestly industry of explicators, annotators, allusion chasers, to mediate between the text and the reader" ("The Literature of Replenishment," 210). Whatever was wrong with modernist fiction, it was taken for granted that professors of English (what he called the Early Christians) and writers of literary fiction were bonded together, engaged in a kind of sacred dialogue in which each confirmed the value of the other.

The use of religious tropes to characterize the exchange between writers and critics exemplifies a longstanding tradition of marking off culture as a transcendent experience within a profane society, an experience that could be enjoyed only by restricting access. Carol Duncan's account of the sacralization of art in nineteenth-century America details the genesis of the rituals that were deemed necessary for a genuine cultural experience to transpire (*Civilizing Rituals*). The museum had to be separated somehow from the marketplace, ideally in a park, in a classical building that signified a temple of the arts, complete with long staircases and lions guarding the grand entrance. Once inside, the appreciation of art was a matter of learning the proper cues and rituals; culture was framed not just by this grandiose structure but by a way of speaking about art that allowed one to converse with it. Duncan cites Benjamin Ives Gilman's *Museum Ideals of Purpose and Method* (1918) as the most influential statement of this doctrine, which insisted that works of art, once they were put in museums, existed for one purpose only—to be looked at as things of beauty.

> As he expounded it (sounding much like William Hazlitt almost a century earlier) aesthetic contemplation is a profoundly transforming experience, an imaginative act of identification between viewer and artist. To achieve it, the viewer "must make himself over in the image of the artist, penetrate his intention, think his thoughts, feel with his feelings."

The end result of this is an intense and joyous emotion, an overwhelming and absolutely "serious pleasure" that contains a profound spiritual dimension. Gilman compares it to the "sacred conversations" depicted in Italian Renaissance altarpieces — images in which saints who lived in different centuries miraculously gather together in a single imaginary space to contemplate the Madonna. With this metaphor, Gilman casts the modern aesthete as a devotee of who achieves a kind of secular grace through communion with artistic geniuses of the past — spirits which offer a life-sustaining sustenance. (16–17)

The proper appreciation of literature depended, not surprisingly, on a similar separation from the marketplace, a comparable set of rituals and cues, and a specialized language in order to talk the talk of appreciation of books. The priesthood of English professors Barth refers to performed their duties within the academy, a world just as marked off in spatial terms — the campus as cultural park, featuring its own requisite architecture (various forms of Gothic and neoclassical architecture) for bona fide temples of learning. This priesthood instructed the uninitiated in ritual practices and sophisticated languages needed to express genuine appreciation. This combination of sanctioned sites and appropriate manners of speaking, which had to be learned before one could enter into the sacred conversation, was, in Foucauldian terms, a discursive formation, because it set both the limits and the modalities needed to distinguish between informed and uninformed ways of talking about an aesthetic experience. What distinguished literary works from mere genre fiction was not just a refinement of style, but also the refinement of a certain class of readers who observed the protocols of appreciation, protocols unnecessary for the enjoyment of popular fiction. In other words, the appreciation of literature necessitated a literary culture that stabilized just who could participate, which rituals would serve as the preconditions for the exchange, and which values would serve as the foundation for this community of readers.

The sacred literary conversation, then, was founded on a restriction of access, even as it was seemingly offered to all comers like the masterpieces in the public museum. But the popularization of the literary conversation has depended on the expansion and redefinition of literary culture far beyond its former confines, just as the museums of the late twentieth century and the early twenty-first have labored to significantly reduce the restrictive nature of the aesthetic conversation by making museums ever more user-friendly, in their search of a broader audience that needed to be reassured that it too could take part in genuine aesthetic experience. The prologue to Harold Bloom's bestselling *How to Read and Why* (2002) exemplifies how literary conversation is now supposed to be conducted. In order to be what Bloom calls an "authentic reader," an academic initiation process is no longer necessary, because "the way we read now partly depends upon our distance, inner or outer, from universities, where reading is scarcely taught as a pleasure, in any of the deeper senses of the aesthetics of pleasure" (22). The villains in this piece are professors, characterized here as a priesthood run amuck, "campus Puritans" who have only deprecated aesthetic values in pursuit of social moralism. Their greatest fault, however, appears to be the insularity of their critical discourse: "Since the universities have empowered such covens as 'gender studies' and 'multiculturalism,' [Samuel] Johnson's admonition becomes 'Clear your mind of academic cant'" (23).

In opposition to these covens, Bloom offers a genuine, rather than pagan, spirituality, founded on the opening of oneself to great literature: "Reading well is best pursued as an implicit discipline; finally there is no method but yourself, when your self has been fully molded. Literary criticism, as I have learned to understand it, ought to be experiential and pragmatic, rather than theoretical" (19). The conversation, though still conceived of as sacred, has become all-embracing: "We read Shakespeare, Dante, Chaucer, Cervantes, Dickens, Proust, and all their peers because they enlarge life. Pragmatically, they have become the Blessing, in its true Yahwistic sense of, 'more life into a time without boundaries.' . . . There is a reader's Sublime, and it seems the only secular transcendence we can ever attain, except for the even more precarious transcendence we call 'falling in love.' . . . Read deeply, not to believe, not to accept, not to contradict, but to learn to share in that *one nature* that writes and reads" (29, emphasis mine). This notion of a oneness that is accessible to all (or at least all who read Bloom) rejects the need for a priesthood and replaces it with the critic who serves as channeler of the Author's voice, who speaks directly, or almost directly, to readers who have opened themselves sufficiently. Reading the classics in this way becomes a veritable museum without walls, because Bloom, as celebrity medium, turns reading into an aesthetic form of self-help therapy: "Reading well is one of the great pleasures that solitude can afford you, because it is, at least in my experience, one of the most healing of pleasures" (14).

Once it has been wrested away from the covens of academe, reading literature is accessible to all, a point made abundantly clear by the celebrity style magazine *Vanity Fair*. In a regular feature entitled "Night Table Reading," in which celebrities divulge what they have been reading recently, movie star Sally Field had this to say about Harold Bloom's *How to Read and Why*: "Bloom is a brilliant writer. Reading this book is like taking a class in comparative literature" (340). The fact that Field doesn't just like Bloom, she really, really likes him, suggests that the wider audience has indeed been found. Talking the talk of a literary experience requires only a self willing to be opened and the expert channeler who can show you how to improve that self. It's like a class in comparative literature, but it's taught by Bloom, a priest who has leapt over the wall and now offers bestselling lessons in reading down at Barnes & Noble. Does this mean that genuine literary culture has begun to develop within the heart of the popular, since even Harold Bloom, or a piece of him, has gotten into bed with movie stars?

What is crucially important here is that Bloom does not begin his advice book with a homily about the joys of reading and then follow up with a list of suggested readings; he begins with this diatribe against professors of literature in order to present personalized reading as the only legitimate authority. For Bloom, loving literature means you must first reject the idea that the theory-besotted academy might retain any kind of authority whatsoever when it comes to knowing why we should read literary works. Within this scenario, amateur and professional readers cannot simply coexist, each in pursuit of their reading pleasures. Literary authority is a zero-sum game—apparently amateur, personal reading cannot lead to transcendent experience as long as the academy retains any shred of validity. It cannot be judged merely misguided; it must be completely invalidated, a coven that must be avoided at all costs.

I want to examine the recurring versions of this zero-sum game scenario in some detail, because the discrediting of the academy as ultimate arbiter of literary value was a key factor in the legitimizing of the popular literary. I have no desire to present an extensive point-by-point account of the polemical debates between the practitioners of High Theory and the avenging Bloomites. As James Shapiro says so eloquently in his review of Frank Kermode's book *Pieces of My Mind* (2003): "With the passage of time revisiting battles over narrative theory or whether French thinkers should be treated as allies or enemies offers all the thrill of a World War I regimental history. Granted, if you fought back then, there's some nostalgia value. If not, however grateful you are for the bravery of others, the trench warfare of English professors seems remarkably pointless" (10). Yet those battles were not just conducted within the academy. They were also fought throughout the nineties in the trenches of novels by very prominent British and American writers who specialize in the novel of ideas—A. S. Byatt in *Possession* (1990), Richard Powers in *Galatea 2.2* (1995), and Philip Roth in *The Human Stain* (2001). I think it's useful to look at the fictionalizations of this great struggle, since readers of literary fiction were encouraged to believe that nothing less than the future of literary reading depended on who won this Great War. Together they provide a kind of time capsule sampling of the literary culture of the early nineties, before the advent of popular literary culture.

This rage against professors of literature who failed to hold up their end of the sacred conversation was nowhere more obvious, or more strident, than in Byatt's *Possession*. As winner of the Booker Prize and a literary best-seller, it would appear to be the perfect incarnation of what Barth called for a decade before: quality fiction that appeals beyond the realm of the priest-hood. As Byatt herself described it: "It's like the books people used to enjoy reading when they enjoyed reading." Yet this restoration of pleasure to the act of reading depends on a thoroughgoing indictment of the professors of English who must learn the errors of their ways before the novel can come to rest. By pairing two sets of lovers, one featuring Victorian poets (Randall Ash and Christabel LaMotte), the other involving late-twentieth-century academics (Maud Bailey and Roland Mitchell), Byatt could hardly have made the opposition between creative and theoretical writing more explicit. In the opening chapters the reader is presented with a panorama of what is alleged to be academic life, complete with scheming professors and sexual cads who specialize in literary theory, exemplified by Fergus Woolf, and grotesque American feminist scholars, such as Leonora Stern, who write articles with such titles as "White Gloves: Blanche Glover: Occluded Lesbian Sexuality in LaMotte." But Byatt was not merely content to lampoon—this operation rescue demanded a conversion process. As Maud and Roland learn about the hidden love story between the Victorian poets through their literary detective work, they become increasingly uncomfort-able with themselves as devotees of high theory, especially when they dis-cover that their reading of their work, which is so animated by the politics of gender and sexual preference, appears to be so wrong—an old-fashioned heterosexual romance was the great mystery behind it all.

The reason they get it so wrong, according to Byatt, is that their training has blinded them to the truth: "They were children of a time and culture that mistrusted love, 'in love,' romantic love, romance in toto, and which nevertheless in revenge proliferated sexual language, linguistic sexuality, analysis, dissection, deconstruction, exposure" (458). When Roland eventually comes to realize what his training has blinded him to, he resolves to write differently: "He was writing lists of words. He was writing lists of words that resisted arrangement into sentences of literary criticism or theory. He had hopes—more intimations of imminence—of writing poems but so far had got no further than lists. These were, however, compulsive and desperately important" (467).

To love, and to love literature for the *right* reasons, become completely interdependent in *Possession*. The narrator offers the following intervention late in the novel:

> There are readings—of the same text—that are dutiful, readings that map and dissect, readings that hear a rustling of unheard sounds, that count grey little pronouns for pleasure or instructions and for a time do not hear golden or apples. There are personal readings, which snatch for personal meanings, I am full of love, or disgust, or fear, I scan for love or disgust or fear. There are—believe it—impersonal readings—where the mind's eye sees the line move onwards and the mind's ear hears them sing and sing. Now and then there are readings that make the hairs on the neck, the non-existent pelt, stand on end and tremble, when every word burns and shines hard and clear and infinite and exact, like stones of fire, like points of stars in the dark—readings when the knowledge of that we *shall know* the writing differently or better or satisfactorily, runs ahead of any capacity to say what we know, or how. (511–12)

Readings animated by theory then are merely dutiful, whether they be structuralist (the counting of grey little pronouns) or poststructuralist (the rustling of unheard sounds). The distinction between personal and impersonal demands greater scrutiny, because it reveals what sort of power relations need to be in effect for Byatt's sacred conversation between author and reader to be restored. Personal readings are rejected as too dependent on the mood swings of the reader. Impersonal readings, on the other hand, are fundamentally a matter of surrendering to the author and letting the writing overwhelm the reader, who is swept away, enraptured by knowledge that runs "ahead of any capacity to say what we know, or how." Whether Maud and Roland's readings are dutiful (as academics it's all part of their job) or personal ("I read as a committed feminist") they are both *mis*readings. Yet this mini-essay on reading is itself profoundly academic, and raises no hairs on any pelts, existent or nonexistent. While she may avoid, or use only dismissively, the words she associates with feminist and poststructuralist theory, Byatt's Romance is in many ways a fictionalized academic essay about the need for romance and an "impersonal" reader of the novel who will care deeply about such debates. The model reader (in Umberto Eco's sense of the term: the reader who gets all the jokes, recognizes the intertextual references, and can perform the interpretive work called for in a text) remains, despite all of the passionate activity to the contrary, an *academic* impersonal reader, who approves of this idea of hairs rising on the backs of heads and appreciates why the author is laboring so furiously to restore the once and future sacred conversation.

In *Possession* Byatt does not desacralize the literary experience but resacralizes it in profoundly nineteenth-century terms. The authentic literary experience is a sacred conversation between romantic author and the reader, here defined as pious listener, helped along by the novelist/critic as ventriloquist/channeler. To read is to surrender to the author, at which point the religious tropes begin to take on overtly erotic aspect. This belief that the author must be surrendered to absolutely for genuine literary experience to be consummated is also the foundation of Richard Powers's novel *Galatea 2.2*. Powers sets his novel on a university campus overrun by theory-poisoned academics who no longer love literature. Its main character is a novelist (named Richard Powers) serving as a humanist-in-residence in a Center for the Study of Advanced Sciences at an American university. When one of the other resident scholars, a cognitive neurologist, suggests that people must envy him, because, as a novelist he must be "king of the cats," he replies: "You're joking. Were maybe. A hundred years ago. It's all movies and lit crit now" (24). For Powers, the primary adversary in this cultural struggle is not Hollywood, however, but what he calls the "litcritter," a point that becomes most obvious when he visits the English Department: "I watched them up close, the curators of the written word. I moved about them, a 'double agent.' I listened around the mail-boxes, in the coffee room. Criticism had gotten more involuted since I was away. The author was dead, the text-function a plot to preserve illicit privilege, and meaning an ambiguous social construction of no more than sardonic interest" (191). While at the center, Powers becomes intrigued by computer-generated neural networks and a young master's student named A., who is preparing to take the English Department's comprehensive exam. These twin obsessions begin to interlace when he constructs a sophisticated neural net (a kind of artificial intelligence) that could take the same comprehensive exam that A. will be attempting to pass. His programming of this neural network (which he names Helen) becomes a project in intellectual autobiography as he recounts stories of his father and a favorite professor who taught him how to love literature. Helen as programmable neural net becomes a stand-in for the wished-for A., as well as a projection of his own sensibility, since he has absolute control over what he reads into her. Because A. is besotted with theory, she remains well beyond Powers's control, unlike Helen, who can only be entranced by what Powers chooses to read to her. Literary theory keeps A. from being able to really love literature, and by extension, this novelist. When he fantasizes about a life with A., Powers muses: "We could buy a house. She'd never have to worry about making a living again. I could call New York, tell them I had another book in me after all. She could spend her day living, recovering the pleasure of the text" (255). Here then, as in Byatt's *Possession*, a successful love affair depends on the ability to read for pleasure, which can be accomplished only if youth forsakes the false promises of French poststructuralism.

It does not take a French theorist, or a militant feminist critic, to see a pattern here—novelists insisting on the need to rescue literature from evil critics by asserting the power of the author, to whom readers must submit absolutely if they ever want to really love literature or another human being. This pattern takes on an even more grotesque cast in Philip Roth's *The Human Stain* (1999). Here in another campus novel, the main character, Coleman Silk, is a classics professor at Athena, a small New England college. Silk is forced into retirement when he is accused of making a racist comment in class. The misunderstanding snowballs into full-scale character assassination, and Silk leaves Athena, shamed and furious about this miscarriage of justice. The real villain of the novel is, however, a French poststructuralist named Delphine Roux, a feminist critic who embodies all the evils of literary theory. In an extended chapter entitled "What Maniac Conceived It?" Zuckerman delves into Delphine's psyche. She is a well-published academic and the walking-talking embodiment of poststructuralist theory, but she too has a guilty secret—she actually hates the stuff, ashamed by "the discrepancy between how she must deal with literature in order to succeed professionally and why first she came to literature." Roth frames that self-betrayal in terms of how she feels about Milan Kundera, whom she saw lecture in France:

Kundera's intention in his lectures was to free the intelligence from the French sophistication, to talk about the novel as having something to do with human beings and the *comédie humaine*; his intention was to free his students from the tempting traps of structuralism and formalism and the obsession with modernity, to purge them of the French theory that they had been fed, and listening to him had been an enormous relief, for despite her publications and growing scholarly reputation, it was always difficult for her to deal with literature through literary theory. (276)

These indictments of the academy all depend on a profound sense of nostalgia for what literary culture *used to be*—a time when professors and writers were bonded together, sharing the same values, respecting the sanctity of the words of the author. In short, these books attempt to restore the literary culture of the sixties, a time before the fall into theory perhaps, but also the period Barth describes in terms of exhaustion and insularity, the very period when the writing and reading of literary fiction was becoming so dangerously self-enclosed that Barth believed it had no future unless the readership of literary fiction could be opened up to a far broader audience. In the scenarios dramatized with such gusto by Byatt, Powers, and Roth, critics and authors try to kill each off in the center ring, but amateur readers don't even enter the picture, except as an abstract concept one needs to endorse from time to time—those little people out there somewhere, who just love to read. By now, this scenario seems like ancient history.

"Readers Are Artists Too, You Know": The Empowerment of Amateur Readers

The pleasures of the literary experience in the contemporary period are not confined to a one-on-one relationship between author and reader, no matter how eroticized that relationship is imagined to be by these novelists. The most substantial difference between then and now is not that the old mutual admiration society broke down because professors of literature no longer wanted to engage in the same sacred conversation. The turmoil that resulted from that breakdown did indeed result in a loss of confidence in those professional readers to identify the really good books and determine what the goals of reading literary fiction should be. Yet the most profound difference between the current situation and what Byatt and company thought of as the good old days is the rejection of the sacred conversation altogether; a new *secularized* conversation about books has changed the power relations within the triangular relationship between author, critic, and reader far more expansively than any of the internecine warfare within traditional literary culture, because in this conversation readers are capable of becoming authors of their own reading pleasure (assuming the right sort of instruction).

Within this radically secularized conversation, the new cast of curators and readers talk about books in ways that are meaningful to amateur readers and have the media technologies at their disposal to make their conversations into robust forms of popular entertainment in the form of television book clubs, the Listmania scene at Amazon.com, or a new wave of guidebooks for amateur readers authored by university professors and literary critics: Thomas C. Foster's *How to Read Novels Like a Professor* (2008), Edward Mendelson's *The Things That Matter: What Seven Classic Novels Have to Say about the Stages of Life* (2006), John Mullen's *How Novels Work* (2006), John Sutherland's *How to Read a Novel: A User's Guide* (2006), Arnold Weinstein's *Recovering Your Story: Proust, Joyce, Woolf, Faulkner, Morrison* (2006), and John Wood's *How Fiction Works* (2008). These guidebooks all promote a highly pragmatic approach to literary reading and address an audience of passionate amateur readers by staking out a new cultural space where a different kind of book talk takes place. The author in these new conversations is paradoxically both enormously important and an algebraic function. On the one hand, authors are seemingly restored to their former glory as literary gods, nowhere more vividly than in literary bio-pics like *Shakespeare in Love*, *Finding Neverland*, and *The Hours*, or in literary bestsellers like *Author, Author* and *The Master*. On the other hand, they also function as this month's "x," furnishing the *pre*text to the *really* important conversation conducted by readers, who are encouraged to give them significance in their *own* lives, or as the *pre*text to spectacular film or television adaptations that really visualize the pleasures of the written word, or as a *pre*text to contemporary novels of manners that update Austen or James or Forster.

The popularization of literary reading hinges on forms of personalization that were unimaginable within traditional notions of reading-as-personal-journey, because they impose a new set of power relations that make adaptability and incorporation the highest priorities. Just how different these power relations are within this new triangular relationship between Author, Critic, and Reader is exemplified in paradigmatic form by a comment made by Robert Hamlin, one of the English professors who served as a resident advisor for Oprah's Book Club during "A Summer of Faulkner." In "Faulkner 101," in an entry entitled "Make the Story Your

Own," Hamlin offers the following advice: "Faulkner prizes active, not passive readers. And what a compliment Faulkner's novels pay to the energetic reader, intelligent, enthusiastic readers! 'Join me as a partner in creativity,' he says. 'Help me discover and order and understand the story. Think of these characters and actions what you will. Interpret the story for yourself. Write your own ending.' Readers are artists, too, you know."

Readers have indeed become artists in the popular literary, and the ascription of these sentiments to the Author who needs, and welcomes, *our* help in creating the story suggests a shift in authority, at every corner of that triangle. This power to function as cocreator has to be authorized by a new sort of cultural authority who can extend the franchise of genuine aesthetic appreciation to amateur readers. Hamlin, as resident academic critic, is not busy killing off authors—he is a spokesman for the author but, just as important, an advocate for amateur readers. They are made to feel essential, because within this critical discourse the experience of great literature cannot be completed without their very personal readings. One can hardly imagine Byatt, Powers, or Roth conceiving of their readers as their "partners"—ventriloquist's dummies, maybe, but certainly not cocreators free to write their own endings. Had I suggested to the professor who taught the modern fiction course I took as an undergraduate that Faulkner needed me to complete *The Sound and the Fury*, she would have probably called Campus Security, convinced that I was criminally insane. When it comes to making meaning in literary texts, the "politics of the personal" has begun to resonate in very different ways across the lines that used to distinguish professional from amateur readers. The fact that very prominent literary authors now issue public statements that affirm the power of the amateur reader is exemplified quite vividly by the title of the article Toni Morrison contributed to the "Summer Reading Issue" of *O: The Oprah Magazine*—"The Reader as Artist": "The words on the page are only half the story, says Toni Morrison. The rest is what you bring to the party" (174).

This fluidity in regard to just who is responsible for making texts meaningful is, of course, hardly a relevation. Ironically, one of the central tenets of the demonized French theory was that the pleasure of the text was not there in the "work itself" but was produced by the act of reading—the reader was an equal player in making the text meaningful and pleasurable. Roland Barthes's articulation of this dynamic process in *The Pleasure of the Text* was enormously influential within the academy, but the reader in question was Barthes himself, professional reader extraordinaire, and the rarefied nature of that pleasure was never in doubt. Over the next three decades scholars working within the realm of reception studies greatly expanded both range of readers involved and the sorts of meanings they generated, particularly in regard to romance novels or popular television series. But within popular literary culture, the empowerment of the reader is not a critical project undertaken by critics attempting to uncover what has hitherto been ignored by literary criticism. The fully empowered reader is a given—why else would they be passionate readers if they weren't making books meaningful, and pleasurable, on their own terms?

The title of Arnold Weinstein's *Recovering Your Story: Proust, Joyce, Woolf, Faulkner, Morrison* (2006) epitomizes the degree to which this empowerment depends on redefining the relationship between author and reader in a new sort of special—but not sacred—conversation. The authors could hardly be more prominent in the title, but the "your" in *Your Story* belongs to the reader. Weinstein says in his preface that these novels are essential to him: "I need great books, have always needed them, for it is in these novels (that I read and teach and write about) that I find my own voice. . . . I realize ever more clearly that these novels tell my story as much as tell theirs. . . . In them you will encounter, in ways that you could not have anticipated, versions of yourself, enactments of your own story." This book about how these masterpieces of modernist literature should be read is "a guidebook of sorts, a personal tour of these rich and varied fictional worlds and it is meant to open them up, to make you realize how intimate and hospitable and mirror-like they are—rather than how daunting or inaccessible they may appear" (x). For it to succeed as a guidebook to the pleasures of reading novels that we have been led to believe are opaque to the uninitiated, the triangular conversation must do more than make them more hospitable: "How, then, can I be surprised that these writers speak me every bit as much as I speak them? In writing this book, in reflecting consciously on the personal hold these novels have on me, I have wanted to make that special conversation—between them and me, between the book and the reader— audible" (xii).

Appreciating why this new special conversation must be made "audible," resonating far beyond solitary reading or classroom discussion is the key to understanding popular literary culture, because it is only when it becomes robustly audible that reading literary fiction can thrive as a form of mass entertainment. For Weinstein, making it audible is a matter of articulating the unsaid in order for the amateur reader to appreciate the insights these novels offer, but making those lessons audible is also a matter of giving value to another way of reading literary fiction that acquires validity only when it is audible on a grand enough scale to overcome any doubts about its superiority in accomplishing the real purpose of reading.

The various outreach strategies that museums throughout the world have utilized so vigorously may take art to the people, but taking literary fiction to the people involves a different set of cultural transactions. Where the art museum may reach out, the art stays on the premises. It may go home in the form of refrigerator magnets, mouse pads, or umbrellas, but there's no doubt about where the original has to remain. The gift shops may grow ever larger, but the consumer space remains more or less distinct from the gallery space. Taking literary books to the people is a more complicated process, because once they begin to circulate outside the temples of learning, outside the "gallery" space of the classroom and the *New York Times Book Review*, literary novels circulate through places like Barnes & Noble superstores, Amazon Web sites, television book clubs, and the local multiplex, where there are no hard-and-fast boundaries between cultural space and consumer space. The "art" and the "paraphernalia" sit side by side, and since the outreach comes from outside, its strategies and ultimate impact are harder to assess. This is not to suggest that taste distinctions are no longer made within those locations. On the contrary, the absence of physical boundaries has led to the creation of elaborate taste distinctions sanctioned by authorities who, to use Pierre Bourdieu's term, *consecrate* certain forms of consumer activity as cultural pleasures. His account of the ways in which traditional literary culture distinguished itself from what he calls the public at large provides an extremely useful template that can be modified to account for the hybridization of those categories within popular literary culture. Just how dichotomous those categories were formerly imagined to be is exemplified by his distinction between *restricted* and *large-scale* cultural production:

> In contrast to the field of large-scale cultural production, which submits to the laws of competition for the conquest of the largest possible market, the field of restricted production tends to develop its own criteria for the evaluation of its products, thus achieving the truly cultural recognition accorded by the peer group whose members are both privileged clients and competitors. . . . From 1830 literary society isolated itself in an aura of indifference and rejection towards the buying public, i.e., towards the

"bourgeois." By an effect of circular causality, separation and isolation engender further separation and isolation, and cultural production develops a dynamic autonomy. (115)

It is significant that the progress of the field of restricted cultural production towards autonomy is marked by an increasing distinct tendency of criticism to devote itself to the task, not of producing the instruments of appropriation . . . but of providing a "creative" interpretation for the benefit of the creators. And so "mutual admiration societies" grew up, closed in upon their own esotericism, as, simultaneously signs of a new solidarity between artist and critic emerged. (116)

Thus it also includes the objective relations between producers and different agents of legitimation, specific institutions such as academies, museums, learned societies[;] . . . these authorities consecrate a certain type of work and a certain type of cultivated person. These agents of consecration may, moreover, be organizations which are not fully institutionalized: literary circles, critical circles, salons, and small groups surrounding a famous author or associating with a publisher, a review, or literary or artistic magazine. (121)

To recast Bourdieu's distinctions in reference to the current situation, popular literary culture depends on the development of another field *between* restricted and large-scale production, in which the delivery systems for literary experiences become increasingly large-scale, but the mechanisms of taste distinction appear to grow ever more intimate as reading taste becomes ever more personalized. The increases in scale secured by conglomeration allow for an unprecedented interdependency of the publishing, film, and television industries, which can reach that "public at large" wherever it may be with ever greater proficiency, but that culture also has its own "agents of legitimation," its own authorities, which consecrate the buying of books and the viewing of film and television adaptations as a genuinely literary experience distinct from mere consumer experience. All of this depends on new mutual admiration societies that revolve around cultivated, *ordinary* readers, whose love of the literary experience, in whichever media they encounter it, now serves as the basis for a new form of cultural production, positioned squarely between the academy and the conglomerate entertainment industry, and is shaped massively by both.

The promotion for Mary Ann Shaffer's and Annie Barrow's *The Guernsey*

Literary and Potato Peel Pie Society (2008) exemplifies this phenomenon neatly. The novel details what happens when a well-known author begins corresponding with members of a rural literary society following the Second World War, and a quotation from one of their letters is featured in bold print on the dust jacket: "Perhaps there is some secret homing instinct in books that brings them to their perfect readers." There were evidently more than enough of these perfect readers to make this novel a surprise literary bestseller, but how did potential readers know if they were the perfect readers for this novel? If they went to Amazon to find out more about this unusual title and checked out the customer reviews to see if the readers talking about the book in ways that made them feel as if they too were one of those perfect readers, they would have encountered a review entitled "For Lovers of Literature and Life" by Susan Schooniver, a customer review from the Amazon Vine™ program. By clicking on "What's This?" I learned a great deal about how consecration worked for this reading community at Amazon, particularly in terms of how a mutual admiration society of ordinary readers thrives, and how culture and commerce are configured accordingly:

> Amazon Vine™ is a program that enables a select group of Amazon customers to post opinions about new and pre-release items to help their fellow customers make educated purchase decisions. Customers are invited to become Amazon Vine™ Voices based on the trust they have earned in the Amazon community for writing accurate and insightful reviews. Amazon provides Amazon Vine™ members with free copies of products that have been submitted to the program by vendors. Amazon does not influence the opinions of Amazon Vine™ members, nor do we modify or edit their reviews.

The goal here is the "educated purchase decision," a distinction made possible only through the agency of select readers who have earned the trust of a community of like-minded readers and are thereby empowered to consecrate accordingly, with some help from Amazon, which makes it possible for these reader/customers to find one another. These crucial distinctions are apparently untainted by commodity relations, yet that expertise is used to promote a literary bestseller about the joys of deeply personalized reading, for a global market.

Sanctioning particular forms of book buying, blockbuster film viewing, and television chat show watching as aesthetic experiences depends upon intermediaries who can talk the talk of loving literature within that arena and enforce those distinctions while promoting their own rhetoric of quality. That conversation, however, doesn't just spontaneously occur somewhere out there beyond the sacred groves of academe where literary reading, self-discovery, information technologies, and consumerism all just spontaneously intersect. Those "secret homing instincts" get a lot of help. Tracing the permutations of this popular curatorship will be one of the central concerns of the next two chapters, but that discussion rests on another messy, unruly question that must be posed, because it goes straight to the heart of popular literary culture. This passionate reading, this longing for literacy, is obviously animated by some sort of self-cultivation project, because it isn't compulsory homework—but where does this urge come from, and how can we begin to describe it in ways that go beyond banal generalizations? And if all this occurs outside the realm traditionally sanctioned for the proper appreciation of things aesthetic, just where does it take place? And how have the publishing, television, film, and computer industries transformed that desire for self-cultivation into an extremely lucrative market?

Part I

THE NEW

INFRASTRUCTURE

OF READING

Sites, Delivery Systems,

Authorities

1

THE END OF CIVILIZATION
(OR AT LEAST CIVILIZED READING)
AS YOU KNOW IT

Barnes & Noble, Amazon.com,
and Self-Cultivation

How well do you remember that, say, six-hundred-pager the *Times* assured you was destined to become a classic? You know. The "monumental work of fiction" that you were supposed to run, not walk to the nearest bookstore to purchase, the book that was going to change your life, that you must read this year if you read nothing else . . . *Winner of the National Book Award*. . . . We sell these babies for fifty cents apiece, or try to, seven years after they come out. We sell them because no one has checked them out for four years.
—Jincy Willett, *Winner of the National Book Award* (2003)

They're gonna hate us at the beginning, but we'll get them in the end. . . . In the meantime, we might as well put up a sign, Coming Soon: a Fox Books Superstore, the End of Civilization as You Know it.
—Nora Ephron, *You've Got Mail* (1999)

At least, she thinks, she does not read mysteries or romances. At least she continues to improve her mind. Right now she is reading Virginia Woolf. . . . She, Laura, likes to imagine (it's one of her most closely held secrets) that she has a touch of brilliance herself, just a hint of it, though she knows most people probably walk around with similar hopeful suspicions curled up inside them, never divulged. She wonders, while she pushes a cart through the supermarket or has her hair done, if other women aren't thinking, to some degree or other, the same thing: Here is the brilliant spirit, the woman of sorrows, the woman of transcendent joys, who would rather be elsewhere.

—Michael Cunningham, *The Hours* (1998)

I begin this chapter with these three quotations, one drawn from a best-selling novel featuring a librarian as its narrator, one from a popular film about a romance between bookstore owners, and another from a bestselling prize-winning novel turned into an extremely successful film, because they reveal so much about conflicting but interdependent aspects of popular literary culture in the United States. In the first, a self-professed, "omnivorous reader" summarily rejects the authority of America's premier taste-making newspaper, the New York literary culture that it embodies, and the entire taste culture responsible for determining what is, and isn't, *significant* fiction. Yet this novel is far from a simple "let them read what they like" rant, since this librarian is full of advice about what should be read, and all too aware of the relationship among reading, literary value, and the book market, a point made quite vividly by the title of the novel, which literalizes that interdependency— *Winner of the National Book Award.* If the award signifies achievement *and* marketability, why not make the sticker on the front cover into the title of the novel? At this point, just what constitutes significant fiction appears to be up for grabs—is it in the craft of the fiction, or the way that it has been evaluated and promoted within a particular taste culture? The business of literary taste production and the business of selling books appear to be thoroughly interdependent, because, according to this particular *Winner of the National Book Award*, buying the book is buying into the authority of an evaluative system that can no longer be trusted when it comes to the pleasures of reading.

If avid readers can no longer trust the *New York Times* about what to read, where they go to actually buy books has become just as problematic. The bookstore has been undergoing a highly visible image change in recent years within the public imagination. In *You've Got Mail* (1999), characters played by Tom Hanks and Meg Ryan manage to fall in love despite the fact that they own rival bookstores, and in *Notting Hill* (2000) two more "A-list" movie stars, Julia Roberts and Hugh Grant, manage to somehow do the same, despite the fact that she's a Hollywood megastar and he owns a modest little bookshop. Struggling but devastatingly attractive bookstore owners seem to have replaced the starving young artist as the epitome of romantic cultural chic, embodying a sweet, but nonetheless, comical earnestness in their disdain of the marketplace for the pursuit of higher cultural ideals. That two such high-profile films should make bookstores one of their primary locations for falling in love suggests that bookstores now fulfill different cultural functions for a mass audience. Yet there is trouble in paradise—the bookstore may have acquired a degree of sexiness that has heretofore escaped the notice of the public at large, but they are also a battleground where the forces of legitimate and illegitimate culture clash by night, and day, or at least from 9:00 A.M. to 11:00 P.M., seven days a week. The proliferation of Barnes & Noble and Borders superstores has been widely reported in the press and roundly denounced as the ruination of smaller "real" bookstores, which have either already gone out of business or live in constant fear of eventual annihilation. So important are these real bookstores to the sanctity of a genuine literary experience that even the character played by Tom Hanks (the owner of the bookstore chain that is clearly modeled on Barnes & Noble) acknowledges the resistance his new superstore will encounter when it opens on the Upper West Side of Manhattan, admitting that such stores signal the end of civilization within this notoriously literary neighborhood in Manhattan. But why should a bookstore, of all things, signal the end of *civilization*?

The quotation from *The Hours* (1998), which describes what the "incessant reader" Laura Brown hopes to achieve in her reading, suggests something else—despite the runaway commercialization of bookselling and the loss of faith in traditional literary authority, there is still a persistent need to experience some kind of aesthetic pleasure that only literary fiction offers, even to nonprofessional readers. Cunningham's characterization of Laura as *driven* reader (which echoes so neatly the ethnographic accounts of actual reading group members discussed below) is paradigmatic—she is not a genre reader, she is in search of self-cultivation hoping to improve her mind, and her reading allows her to separate herself from mind-numbing quotidian concerns even while immersed in them at the supermarket. She experiences her own brilliance as she reads, because she senses that she and Woolf are kindred spirits, their shared sensibility allowing her to occupy a "twilight zone of sorts: a world composed of London in the twenties, of a turquoise hotel room, and of this car, driving down this familiar street. She is herself and not herself. She is a woman in London, an aristocrat, pale and charming, a little false: she is Virginia Woolf; and she is this other inchoate, tumbling thing known as herself, a mother, a driver, a swirling streak of pure life like the Milky Way . . ." (187). The three main characters in Cunningham's novel—Laura Brown, Virginia Woolf, and Clarissa Vaughan—all share remarkably similar perceptions and emotions, but what is particularly significant in this regard is that Laura, as the incessantly reading suburban housewife, shares the same rarified sensibility as the great Author and the New York literary editor. Reading is as formative and *trans*formative for Laura, the amateur reader, as writing and editing are for the professional literary types—the sensitivity of the reading makes it coequal with the sophisticated production of those words.

As such, Laura Brown may well serve as a kind of patron saint for the millions of nonacademic readers who form the rank and file of the contemporary popular literary culture, but with an essential caveat. She represents the prehistory of the popular literary because she is a solitary reader, adrift in a suburban wasteland, desperate to "only connect," but able to find kindred spirits only in Woolf and her character Mrs. Dalloway. The Laura Browns of the contemporary literary scene are a well-targeted audience, catered to aggressively by divisions of the publishing, television, and film industries, who are desperate to connect with her, eager to provide her with the means by which she can connect with armies of like-minded readers circulating in those same supermarkets and superstores. Laura could only connect with Mrs. Dalloway via her local library copy of the book; contemporary readers can become one with Laura by buying Cunningham's novel, but they can also become one with an imagined community of like-minded passionate readers if they buy *Bookclub-In-A-Box Discusses the Novel The Hours by Michael Cunningham*. Laura Brown floated through stores in the suburban America of 1947 trying to anesthetize herself to the banality around her; the Laura Browns of the early twenty-first century float through suburban discount stores like Target, where they encounter *The Hours* on Recommended Books end-cap displays. Within this consumer environment, literary books obviously occupy a very different place, but their appearance as featured books in the discount store points to an established audience, which itself suggests a widespread desire for an aesthetic experience, which is dramatically apart from the very space where you buy the book.

Taken together, the three quotations at the start of this chapter are representative of the changing infrastructure of popular literary culture and the fact that those changes have become the subject *of* popular culture. On the one hand, they suggest that widespread changes are under way in terms of who, or what, counts as an authority on the pleasures of reading and where those pleasures are to be found. While they reflect significant contestation about how this popular literary culture should define itself, outside the confines of the academy, the New York literary scene, and *real* bookstores that used to serve as its outposts across the rest of the country, the need to find a specific type of cultural fix appears undeniable for individuals who describe their reading in terms of an addiction for that which is ultimately civilizing. Laura Brown's reading is driven by a desire to improve her mind through her amateur reading, which would seem an unassailable virtue, but these self-cultivation projects pursued outside the academy have met with as much condemnation as celebration, nowhere more obviously in the wildly differing accounts of the benefits of the Oprah Winfrey Book Club, which I will explore in greater detail in the next chapter. How indeed do these changes mark the end of civilization as we know it, in regard to what civilization might consist of as process of self-cultivation, and in regard to how we come to know it or, more specifically, how we come to know how to acquire it?

The goal of this chapter is to gain a more subtle understanding of those readers who used to be called common readers but are more often called avid or passionate readers, now that they are defined in terms of the intensity of their desire rather than their lack of refinement. These readers may be described, with equal accuracy, as a target audience, a reading community with its own interpretive protocols, and a reading formation. I believe it is only by incorporating all three of these alternative definitions that we can learn just who is doing this reading, for what purposes, talking what sort of literary talk, catered to by what new delivery systems, and guided by which cultural authorities. In her ground-breaking work on reading groups (1992), Elizabeth Long stresses the social infrastructure of reading, arguing that "the ideology of the solitary reader suppresses recognition of the infrastructure of literacy and the social and institutional determinants of what's available to read, what is 'worth reading,' and how to read it" ("Textual Interpretation," 193). In her interviews with members of a variety of different book clubs she found that contemporary literary fiction and the classics were the most frequent choices, because they had the greatest potential for discussability, but their discussions were animated by a different kind of evaluative criteria, their own way of *talking the talk* of books.

Their independence flows from their "uses" of literature. Because these readers incorporate books into their lives primarily as special life-experiences, they often judge them according to their non-literary lives. While literary critics have, at least until recently, aspired to pure or disinterested aesthetic judgment, reading group members are "interested" readers: they are looking for not only a "good reading" but meaningful and pleasurable experiences from books and literary discussions. Thus "discussability," the very term that gears most reading groups into a traditional evaluative framework, also distances them from it. ("The Book," 312)

That "interested" readers would consider "discussability" the preeminent criterion for selecting books reveals just how tightly imbricated personal and social pleasures are within popular literary culture. To return to the distinctions made by A. S. Byatt in her novel *Possession*, which were discussed in the introduction, these are relentlessly personal readings, in the sense that books take on value only when they are introjected into the lives of readers, not the impersonal readings she prefers, where readers surrender themselves to the voice of the Author and check their personal lives at the door before entering. But "personal" does not mean solitary, or isolated. Because of their relative independence from the academic modes of literary analysis, these textual communities, then, are also distinct interpretive communities that give reading literary fiction a particular use value. Janice Radway has argued convincingly that this term (first developed by Stanley Fish to describe the ways that different literary critics could produce radically divergent interpretations of the same poems depending on the critical approach or community they were affiliated with) can be used to describe the *variable literacies* that give different values to reading inside and outside the academy ("Interpretive Communities"). But where the readers of romance fiction that Radway interviewed developed their own sort of literacy to enjoy *non*literary genre fiction on its own terms, the pleasures that nonacademic readers derive from reading literary fiction involves another kind of variant literacy, one that is shaped by elements drawn from reading protocols of both academic and popular interpretive communities.

These reading communities do not magically coalesce out of thin air—finding the titles worth reading, knowing how to talk about them, even knowing if you are a reader intended to read this sort of book all depend on an infrastructure. Tony Bennett's notion of a *reading formation* is particularly useful for understanding how all these factors coalesce to form something more than just a community of like-minded readers who have somehow managed to find one another and the sort of books they like to talk about together: "By reading formation I mean a set of discursive and intertextual determinations which organize and animate the practice of reading, connecting texts and readers in specific relations to one another by constituting readers as reading subjects of particular types and texts as objects-to-be-read in particular ways" ("Texts in History," 7). The community, then, is not just an audience or a community but a set of interconnections in which the desire for a certain kind of reading pleasure becomes hardwired into a literary culture. The Laura Browns of 2004 could "talk directly" to author Michael Cunningham if they signed up for his online course "A Home at the End of the World," at the University of Barnes & Noble. This connection between reader and author is made possible by the conflation of retail store and institution of "higher learning." At this point, the role of the superstore bookstore, publishers' reading guides, and television book clubs all become vital constitutive elements of an extended reading community that is simultaneously a target audience, consolidated as much by the type of questions posed in book club courses at the University of Barnes & Noble as by the "Customers Who Bought *The Hours* Also Bought" appeals at Amazon.com.

Any investigation of the sites that are provided to reading communities so they may proliferate online and via superstores necessarily involves a parallel investigation of their "architecture" and of the new forms of connoisseurship that circulate there. Steven Johnson has used the term "curatorial culture" to describe the importance of the chooser/repackager within the world of online music file accessing, the refined sensibility that sorts through the excess and is able to deliver what "they know you'll like": "Historically, the world of commercial music has been divided between musicians and listeners, but there's a group in the middle: people with great taste in music — the ones who made great that brilliant mix for you in college that are still listening to you. They're curators, not creators, brilliant at assembling new combinations of songs rather than generating them from scratch." To pursue this analogy within traditional literary culture, once there were authors and readers and official critics who were sanctioned to make the right choices for you, only now that sensibility is regarded with disdain because so many avid readers no longer trust the *New York Times Book Review*, any more than they would an allegedly theory-besotted academy to find them a good read. Other sorts of master curators have entered the picture, not surprisingly since knowing what you like—to drink, eat, wear, sit on, watch, decorate—has become a thriving form of popular culture in virtually every arena of what used to be thought of as elite taste. Accessing books depends every bit as much on accessing the expertise needed to read books from an informed position outside the realm of the classroom. Is this search for the necessary expertise just a traditional form of connoisseurship, being made available by emergent information technologies, or is this a twenty-first-century form of connoisseurship that depends on new technologies of access and new technologies of taste acquisition that empower amateur readers, listeners, and viewers to assume the role of curators of their own archives?

Since the taste arbiters who can be trusted by passionate amateur readers are found outside the academy, popular literary culture depends upon the convergence of literary and consumer experiences, an encounter that has generated widespread debate about the possible outcome of such a dalliance between partners who formerly kept a reproachful distance from each other. The pleasures of reading have traditionally been set in direct opposition to consumerism and the various forms of "mass culture" that emanate from it. The posters that used to hang in my local public library crystallize this dichotomy perfectly: one read "Fight Prime Time—Read a Book." To read was to educate oneself; to watch advertiser-driven television was the antithesis of that pure experience unsullied by the concerns of the marketplace. The vestiges of such purity, the very apartness of reading as private communion of mind and fine literature, have become a distinguishing feature of the popular literary, since the pleasures it offers must be distinguished somehow from the emptiness of *mere* consumerism, even while the accessibility of those pleasures is due to the increasing commodification of high-end cultural experiences. On the face of it, the superstore, the Web site, and television book club would appear to have replaced, or at least significantly diminished, the power of the public library and librarian as sources of pure knowledge about books. Yet the successful hybridization of aesthetic and consumer pleasures has been realized by introducing a *library factor* within the marketplace—the impression that popular curators, and even the bookstore chains, are determined to deliver the *goods* of genuine culture (goods in terms of the items themselves, as well as the benefits they contain) as a kind of public service, either without vested interests or with the most admirable vested interests, which serve that public good. In order to appreciate the complexity of this interplay between financial and cultural profit motives, we need to reexamine the taken-for-granteds in this age-old dichotomy, because the acquisition of culture—where and how we get it, and why we should want "it" in the first place—has an extremely complicated history, which reveals many of the central tensions that have shaped American culture over the past two centuries.

Acquiring Culture in the Marketplace: The Back Story

In her landmark study *The Making of Middle-Brow Culture* (1992), Joan Shelly Rubin seizes on the value of self-cultivation and details how it became such a widespread cultural disposition. She begins by citing a letter written to the *Ladies Home Journal* in 1906, in which the reader asked how she might "start to obtain culture." The woman wrote, "I have plenty of time and a good library at my disposal, but no money to employ teachers." Their resident critic, Hamilton Wright Mabie, responds: "Read only the best books." Rubin identifies the crucial assumptions at play in this exchange: "[That] culture could be dissociated from wealth, that it could be acquired; that the process of doing so entailed reading certain books and avoiding others; that becoming cultured required time; that cultured individuals commanded deference from those who timidly 'ventured' to join their company" (1). She argues compellingly that until the early nineteenth century, "not only was genteel culture compatible with wealth, it depended on it—because the pursuit of refinement was expensive." This interdependency of cultivation and wealth made culture into something inherited, like property. Extending the old adage "A gentleman never buys furniture, he simply brings something down from the attic," "culture" worked in much the same way—it came with the patrimony, and who could afford to buy quality furniture anyway, except the genteel class? The acquisition of cultivation that became possible for a rapidly expanding middle-class audience in the nineteenth century depended on making culture into commodity forms that could be purchased by the people who, in effect, had no attics—to become cultured inevitably meant becoming a consumer of cultural goods one didn't already possess. In his masterful study of this period, *Selling Culture: Magazines, Markets and Class at the Turn of the Century* (1996), Richard Ohman details the complex transactions that occurred, arguing that "a central need of people who became readers of *Cosmopolitan*, the *Ladies Home Journal* and the rest was to fix their bearings in the new fluid social space of that moment, and to do so to their social advantage" (220).

This balance between cultural and consumer experience was complicated by the increasing tendency to associate genuine cultivation with *inner virtue* and to set this new pairing in direct opposition to materialism. This uncoupling of wealth and cultivation led to profound suspicions about the rampant materialism generated by the Industrial Revolution. Once uncoupled from inherited wealth, the acquisition of culture had to be monitored according to a moral economy that could allow for consumerism but only by recasting it within the terms of a self-cultivation project grounded in the pursuit of "character" untainted by the demands of the marketplace. The chief advocates of this ideology of cultivation were the Harvard moral philosophers (Andrew Norton, William Channing) and the New Haven scholars circulating around Yale College (most especially the college presidents Theodore Dwight Woolsey and Noah Porter). Channing used the term "self-culture" to describe this cultivation in pursuit of virtue, which would counter the base desires and appetites that came from unbridled materialism—an ideal that quickly became hardwired into the liberal arts education within the American academy. Widespread cultivation became increasingly possible by the 1840s, because publishing was becoming an industry with national scope during this decade, due to the introduction of new printing and paper-making technologies that coincided with dramatic improvements in the transportation of goods. Self-cultivation had become a popular phenomenon by the middle of the century because of two interdependent booms—one in publishing and the another in the dissemination of knowledge needed to realize their potential use value, whether it took the form of books about the value of reading the right books, or an elaborate public lecture system that put public oratory in support of this search for character. The concept of self-culture could admit consumerism if it was a carefully guided consumerism that attempted, as Rubin phrases it so succinctly, "to harmonize one's possessions with one's nature."

While this notion of cultivation as pursuit of character held sway until the beginning of the twentieth century, it begins to undergo significant reformulation with the rise of modern consumer culture in America, particularly during the 1920s when, as Rubin argues, *personality* replaces character, and cultivation is uncoupled from moral development. At that point, the academy continues to advocate the value of an education committed to the development of moral character, counterposed to materialism, and becomes the guardian of what Bourdieu calls "legitimate culture," ready and eager to play sacred to consumerism's profane. But the demonization of the marketplace becomes even more pronounced with the rise of modernism, when financial concerns are seen as directly antithetical to the creation of a sophisticated literary culture. Self-cultivation, by the turn of the century, was becoming a mass audience phenomenon fueled by a literary marketplace just as eager to furnish a broad readership with the requisite cultural goods. Yet this audience in search of cultivation was perceived to be even more a threat to all that was good about genuine culture than the mob in search of pulp fiction. Lawrence Rainey, in *The Institutions of Modernism* (27), makes the crucial point that the first reported usage of the term "middlebrow" was in 1906, a clear indication not just of the stratification of reading publics but the perceived need to construct new hierarchies of taste that could delineate quality cultivation from mere book buying. Quality self-cultivation was increasingly conceptualized in modernist terms, primarily because its advocacy of aesthetic autonomy made taste something that could not simply be purchased. A new set of distinctions regarding the acquisition of culture emerged, which recoupled cultivation and inherited wealth in order to avoid what were alleged to be the disastrous effects of the marketplace on the quality of both the books and the readers who consumed them.

The complicated relationships that developed among authors, presses, and readerships as modernist literary culture began to take shape has been explored in compelling ways in Kevin Dettemar's and Stephen Watt's collection, *Marketing Modernisms* (1996); Ian Willison's, Warwick Gould's, and Warren Chernaik's *Modernist Writers and the Marketplace* (1996); Lawrence Rainey's *The Institutions of Modernism* (1998); and Sean Latham's *Am I a Snob?* (2003). All these studies shed an enormous amount of light on one hitherto ignored question in the history of modernism. There was indeed a very high premium placed on stylistic innovation, which demonstrated, with varying degrees of defiance, a desire to make serious literary work independent of the tastes of a general readership—*but who paid for it?* Dettemar and Watt describe this situation quite succinctly: "According to the models by which most of us were taught modern literature, the title of this volume, *Marketing Modernisms*, seems almost oxymoronic. That is to say, critical accounts of modernism and modernist writing frequently excavate, or are theorized across a chasm or 'great divide' between modernism, however multifoliate its ambitions and productions, and the larger marketplace" (1). How did Joyce, Eliot, Woolf, and company actually survive as writers before they were assumed into academic heaven? What sort of infrastructure served as the financial foundation for literary production that so gleefully rejected bourgeois reading pleasure and everything that catered to it?

Paul Delaney ("Who Paid for Modernism?") argues that two interdependent developments in the last two decades of the nineteenth century laid the foundation for a modernist mode of literary production that could be disdainful of commercial interests—the major restructuring of the literary marketplace, and the establishment of what he calls "*rentier* culture," in which the relationship between inherited wealth and cultivation reemerges within a new patronage system. The near universal literacy achieved in Britain by the end of the 1890s produced a mass market, but other factors made for significant differentiation within that "reading public."

> By the 1890s, a huge expansion of the reading public had swept aside the dominant literary formation of the previous fifty years. . . . Other changes in the literary marketplace included: the recognition of British copyright by the US in 1891; the rise of literary agents in 1890s; the shift from outright sale of literary property to payment by royalty; the fragmentation of novelistic form after the end of the three-decker; and the relaxation of censorship in consequence of the decline of the circulating libraries. These shifts worked together synergistically to create a new literary system, one that conditioned the creative impulses of all literary people and produced complex secondary effects. It is against the background of this new system that we can best understand Pound's project; not just to "make it new" at the level of the individual work, but also to construct a fully articulated *counter*-system for modernist literary production. (336)

This new system depended on the patronage of the rentier class—a population of individuals of "private means" who lived off the accumulations of previous generations and numbered nearly half a million adults by 1911—certainly large enough, and moneyed enough, to sustain a literary culture unto itself. According to Delaney,

> Rentier culture distinguished itself from market-sensitive art by elaborating an ethic of refinement. . . . The art novel assumed a certain leisured sensitivity both in its readers and the characters it represented. Rentier

artists were more likely to have roots in mercantile or financial sectors of the economy; their inherited incomes absolved them from active struggle in the marketplace, but neither were they responsible for a landed estate or local community. Their separation from the market was expressed in the common Victorian term for them, the "independent classes." (337)

This modernist patronage system is also detailed extensively by Rainey, who, like Delaney, concentrates on the need to create a countersystem outside commodity relations but still somehow involved within it. He argues that "modernism, poised at the cusp of that transformation of the public sphere, responded with a tactical retreat into a divided world of patronage, collecting, speculation, and investment, a retreat that entailed the construction of an institutional counter-space securing a momentary respite from the public realm increasingly degraded, even as it entailed a fatal compromise with precisely that degradation" (*The Institutions of Modernism*, 5). That compromise necessitated a complicated set of commodity relations for literary works. Rainey insists that, rather than conceiving of modernism as a simple rejection of commodification in pursuit of aesthetic autonomy, "it may be that just the opposite would be the more accurate account: that modernism, among other things is a strategy whereby the work of art invites and solicits commodification but it does so in such a way that it becomes a commodity of a special sort, one that is temporarily exempted from the exigencies of immediate consumption prevalent within the larger cultural economy, and instead is integrated into a different economic circuit of exchange" (3).

This notion of literary work as a *commodity of a special sort*, whose self-professed dismissal of commodity relations functions, as it were, as its major selling point, will have a great deal of relevance for my analysis of the literary bestseller in chapter 6, but I want to pursue here this modernist ambivalence toward the book market at the beginning of the century in order to better understand the vestigial force of that countersystem within the popularization of literary culture a century later. In *Am I a Snob?* Sean Latham concentrates on exactly that ambivalence in his analysis of the different sorts of literary snobbery that developed at the end of the nineteenth and beginning of the twentieth century. His examination of the various ways Virginia Woolf positioned herself in regard to both the literary marketplace and modernist literary culture reveals a complicated, conflicted relationship toward both. He provides abundant evidence of Woolf's determination to link artistic autonomy and aristocratic sensibility, arguing that "Woolf manages to blur the boundaries between the aristocrats of birth and the aristocrats of art, thereby cleverly effecting her own entry into the world of the beau monde. Imagining herself as a member of a small literary nobility constantly under assault by the forces of modernity, she confesses to Lady Ottoline Morrell that 'I am an aristocrat in writing'" (93). That only the enlightened aristocrat can be free from the taint of the marketplace is consistently elaborated throughout her novel *Orlando*, most obviously in her condemnation of the writer Nick Greene as a middle-brow writer devoted only to acquiring money and fame through his writing, and then even more vehemently in her characterization of Sir Nicholas Greene, now a twentieth-century middle-brow publisher concerned only with what will sell. The character of Orlando incarnates the interdependency of aesthetic sensibility and aristocratic freedom from the marketplace.

Latham finds this same class-specific conception of a genuine literary sensibility in Woolf's essay "A Room of One's Own," since Woolf's famous call for three hundred pounds a year and a room of her own for aspiring writers "imagines that this money and this room will only be granted to women of Woolf's own social class. The female children of the upper middle class, who had seen their brothers sent off to public schools and the hallowed halls of Cambridge and Oxford, possess in Woolf's mind a native sense of autonomy and taste. . . . [T]hey alone possess the ability to record the moment of true freedom when the artist's mind is suddenly severed from the world about her" (111). That this intelligence is *native* to a specific class, rather than acquired, results in deep reservations about the upwardly mobile middle-class intellectual who is unable to distinguish between genuine and counterfeit forms of cultural capital. She was deeply disappointed in Sackville West, her model for Orlando, when she devotes too much time to dreary women who were "earnest middle-class intellectuals." This Virginia Woolf would have been horrified by the presumptuousness of a Laura Brown, who imagines as she is reading that she somehow *becomes* Virginia Woolf, since she exemplifies exactly the sort of middle-class intellectual bent on self-improvement that Woolf considered a threat to all things truly literary. (I'm Virginia Woolf, and *you're not*.) According to Latham, "Woolf employs the aristocratic language of inheritance to describe her own obsession with the fine details of social distinction: 'The social side is very genuine in me. Nor do I think it reprehensible. It is a piece of jewelry I inherited from my mother'" (65).

Woolf in effect could bring the jewels down from the attic — she didn't need to acquire cultivation any more than she needed to buy jewelry and could live in a world of ideas unsullied by commodity relations.

Despite, or because, of this celebration of an inherited cultured sensibility, *Orlando* became a bestseller, outselling any other title published by Hogarth Press, a concern she ran with her husband, the author Leonard Woolf. While Woolf may have condemned the vulgarity of the marketplace as she advocated aesthetic autonomy in her writings, her ownership of the press made that autonomy possible in material terms. In her essay on Virginia Woolf and the press, Laura Marcus argues: "Hogarth Press represented work that cut out the middle-man and escaped literary commodification, it gave Woolf a way of negotiating the terms of literary publicity and a space somewhere between the private, the coterie, and the public sphere" (145). The elimination of the middleman as publisher seeking only profit, in the style of Sir Nicholas in *Orlando*, allows for a more rarefied exchange, in which quality fiction is written with the goal of publication and cold hard cash is laid down for books, but the taint of commodified culture is removed, since authors produce literature for book *collectors* who want to add them to their private libraries. The semantic distinctions that served as the foundation for such exchanges only barely conceal the taste ideology that legitimates the exchange as an authentic cultural experience rather than brute consumerism. This imperative to remove the taint of the marketplace in the early-twentieth-century literary culture was shaped by the convergence of century-old distinctions concerning the need to keep art somehow apart from the market, and modernist notions of avant-garde purity that were fueled by a complicated, internally contradictory amalgamation of neoaristocratic and socialist values that demonized the marketplace as the root of all evil. To return to Rubin's letter-writer who asks the *Ladies Home Journal* in 1906 how she might obtain culture, acquiring culture was becoming an increasingly risky activity by the twenties, despite the growth of popular presses ready and eager to provide her with the literary goods, because buying books (even the best books) from the wrong sources, with the wrong intentions, invalidated the entire cultivation process.

If culture was to be acquired by more than a coterie audience, a genuine cultivation process would have to be sanctioned that could incorporate the modernist agenda yet somehow give its neoaristocratic dimensions a more populist cast. The academy, and more specifically English departments, managed to fashion a cultivation project that was both elitist and populist at the same time, celebrating the values of modernist literary culture but proclaiming it as somehow available to all. According to Latham, the Leavisites in Great Britain and the New Critics in the United States "fashioned artifacts drawn from an imaginary aesthetic autonomy, purged of what they believed to be the market's poisonous taint" (216). John Guillory sums up the situation quite neatly: as students came to understand that literature was intrinsically difficult, "they also discovered at the same moment why it needed to be studied *in the university*" (*Cultural Capital*, 172). One didn't have to inherit culture like family jewelry—it could be acquired, but only within the university, where it could be properly taught outside the realm of commodity relations. In his account of the transformation of the study of English as academic discipline during this period, Terry Eagleton stresses that "English" as an academic subject was first institutionalized not in the great universities but in the Mechanics Institutes and extension lecturing circuits and was therefore considered "the poor man's classics—a way of providing a cheapish, 'liberal' education for those beyond the charmed circles of public school and Oxbridge." As women began to enter the realm of higher education, it was a "convenient sort of non-subject to palm off on the ladies, who were in any case excluded from science and the professions" (*Literary Theory*, 28). The professionalization of English, as a field suitable for the best and the brightest male scholars was spearheaded by Leavis and his journal *Scrutiny*, in which the rigorous study of English necessitated a new way of talking the talk of literary analysis and a new hierarchy of taste that would allow it to clear a space for itself next to classics, but far above popular British fiction. Only a certain type of writing would be judged English. Eagleton argues:

> *Scrutiny* was not just a journal but a moral and cultural crusade: its adherents would go out to the schools and universities to do battle there, nurturing through the study of literature the kind of rich, complex, mature, discriminating, morally serious responses (all key *Scrutiny* terms) which would equip individuals to survive in a mechanized society of trashy romances, alienated labour, banal advertisements and vulgarizing mass media. . . . The *Scrutiny* case was inescapably elitist; it betrayed a profound ignorance and distrust of the capacities of those not fortunate enough to have read English at Downing College. "Ordinary" people seemed acceptable only if they were seventeenth-century cowherds or "vital" Australian bushmen. (33)

This regendering of the *study* of English as a properly masculine pursuit exemplifies one of the central tenets of the modernist culture (articulated in detail by scholars such as Andreas Huyssens (*After the Great Divide*, 1986), Tania Modleski (*Loving with a Vengeance*, 1989) and Patrice Petro (*Joyless Streets*, 1989). Avant-gardist writing was a difficult, rigorous affair and therefore framed in masculine terms, while mass culture was rejected as easy, promiscuous, and altogether feminine. Pulp fiction in its various forms was all that the study of English had to define itself over and against, but there was no more disreputable "other" than popular fiction addressed to women. To return to Rubin's example of the woman who could not afford to pay teachers but who wanted to buy good books, all the good books in the world weren't going to make any difference, because genuine cultivation could be secured only through proper instruction in how to really read, which could be acquired only within the academy. The woman was looking for cultivation in all the wrong places—the *Ladies Home Journal* was the last sort of place she should be going to for advice, because it represented all that was the enemy of the academy, a popular publication addressed to ladies who remained home instead of attending college.

Once the study of English was stabilized within the academy, the tensions between cultivation on a mass scale and the still persistent coupling of literary taste and inherited class privilege became successfully hybridized in a form of intellectual class snobbery. Just as the literary novel was a commodity of a special sort whose appeal depended on its avowedly anticommodity status, this intellectual taste formation was snobbery of a special sort, snobbery that defined itself as antisnobbery, at least of the financial kind. Like thousands of other students descended from immigrant stock with no inherited cultivation whatsoever to our names, I acquired certified cultivation, in my case, in the English and film departments at the University of Iowa, the "Athens of the Prairie," where I learned to talk the talk of modernist aesthetics and became a blue-blood intellectual snob. During this initiation process I learned to sneer, with equal fervor, at class distinctions based on inherited wealth, and at all of the forms of popular culture that my family had enjoyed as I was growing up. The most important lesson that I learned during my apprenticeship was that what really separated ordinary from extraordinary readers was not a matter of who loved literature passionately and who didn't. The crucial distinction, which an entire institutionalized practice of reading endlessly reiterated, was between those who knew how to read *closely* and those who merely read, passionately or otherwise. Untutored reading might lead to pleasure but certainly not to insight, which could be found only with the right operating instructions.

The professionalization of English (like the professionalization of film studies in the seventies, which I will discuss in the next chapter) was predicated on intensive differentiation. Reading, and reading professionally, seemed on the surface, at least, to be so similar that radical differentiation was required, and academic reading wasn't the sort of thing that anyone should try to do at home. Just as medicine labored in the eighteenth century to differentiate itself from alchemy when the two appeared, to the uninformed eye, to be more or less the same thing, reading within the academy had to turn reading outside the academy into the equivalent of alchemy—an unsystematic hodge-podge of opinion guided by irrational goals with no way of evaluating the results. Yet the very closeness of the tutored and untutored that necessitated differentiation also greased the wheels for the rapid return of the repressed, especially when the authority of the academy was thrown into question and a new set of sites and tour guides appeared to offer lessons in the *pleasures* of a new kind of authorized reading.

McBooks, or Carnegie Superstores?

Given this conviction that literary culture and genuine self-cultivation both had to function as countersystems apart from consumerism, the popularization of both throughout the past decade within the very heart of the marketplace required a new-taste cartography to provide legitimacy where none could have possibly existed before. The vestigial force of both the modernist ideal of aesthetic autonomy and the concomitant sanctioning of only certain forms of cultivation is nowhere more obvious than in the demonization of the superstore bookstore—they do indeed signal "the end of civilization as we know it," or at least as we were taught to know it within traditional literary culture. The debates about the effects of the superstore have been accompanied by a steady stream of articles that have focused on the impact of the superstore phenomenon, most of which echo Nora Ephron's account of the bookstore wars by emphasizing only the destructive effects of Barnes & Noble and Borders. The controversy boils down to a collision between two opposing notions of how one acquires cultivation—"genuine culture requires specialized sites and the proper initiation process" (because it cannot simply be purchased if it is to have any beneficial value) versus "culture should be accessible to all" (and if commerce makes that

possible, the benefits certainly justify the means). The former is exemplified by André Schiffrin's book *The Business of Books* (2000), which presents a
thoroughgoing indictment of corporate publishing: the superstore is only
a cog in the conglomerate machine, which, in its all-consuming obsession
with profit "leaves little room for books with new controversial ideas or
challenging literary voices." The latter position, in which accessibility of
culture can be seen as only a positive value in a democratic society is set
forth in no uncertain terms by Brooke Allen in her article "Two—Make
That Three—Cheers for the Chain Bookstores" (2001):

> What if fifteen years ago someone had suggested a nationwide network
> of gigantic bookshops, carrying about 150,000 titles each, staying open
> until 11:00 P.M. or midnight, and offering cafes, comfortable chairs, and
> public restrooms? And what if these sumptuous emporia were to be found
> not only in the great urban centers but also in small cities and suburbs
> all across the country in places like Piano, Texas; Knoxville, Tennessee;
> and Mesa, Arizona? Wouldn't we have thought that sounded like pure,
> if unattainable, heaven? Well that is what the superstore chains—Barnes
> & Noble; Borders; and Books-A-Million, based in Birmingham, Ala-
> bama—have brought us. Why, then, this chorus of disapproval from the
> cultural elite? Why the characterization, spread by a vocal group of crit-
> ics, of the chain bookstores as a sort of intellectual McDonald's, a symbol
> of the dumbing-down and standardization of American life? (148)

Allen's celebration of this increased access to books makes a key point regarding the appearance of bookstores in towns where none had been before. Good bookstores are now in towns and suburbs, not just the big cities
and university towns where culture normally resided. To adapt the old
Hollywood adage that a movie would be successful only if it could "play in
Peoria," bookstores are now playing in Peoria and hundreds of other fly-
over cities that have never been on anyone's cultural map, let alone *The New
Yorker*'s.

While critics of the superstores deplore the standardization that comes
with the chains, this threat of decentralization is in fact the more disrup-
tive one to traditional literary culture. Janice Radway, in *A Feeling for Books*
(1997), traces a comparable attack on standardization by established literary
authorities in response to the success of the Book-of-the-Month Club in the
1950s, but since the delivery system was still direct mail, it didn't threaten
the sanctity of the *real* bookstore as outpost of literary culture. The appear-

ance of massive bookstores, located not just in mid-sized towns and suburbs but in strip malls surrounded by nothing but the worst excesses of consumer culture is a complicated development, because it confounds virtually all of the traditional distinctions between cultural and commercial space.

At this point I want to make my own prejudices regarding real and unreal bookstores abundantly clear, because I think it will shed a great deal of light on the argument to come. As a graduate student at the University of Iowa, I learned more about what it meant to live a vibrantly intellectual life from hanging out at Prairie Lights bookstore than I did in any of my courses. What I read for pleasure (and what I read for much of my dissertation) was shaped as much by conversations with its owner, Jim Harris, as it was by any of my professors. Had Barnes & Noble attempted to open a store down the block I would have helped form a human chain to try to stop construction or built barricades in the middle of the street and set them afire. When I left Iowa City for South Bend, Indiana, in the mid-eighties, I lived in a city without anything worthy of the name bookstore, long before Amazon appeared on the scene. When a Barnes & Noble, and then a Borders superstore eventually opened on the strip in nearby Mishawaka, they were greeted by the local community as momentous cultural events that suddenly changed everything. In the decade or so that I've been a regular customer at both superstores, I have never talked with a member of their staffs about a book, except to inquire about what's in stock. That being said, if they closed their doors tomorrow I would probably consider taking my own life, even though I buy as many books at Amazon and go there practically every night, sometimes several times a day. For me, Prairie Lights, Barnes & Noble, and Amazon are all real bookstores, because each performs a real function in my life as a reader, teacher, and father.

What has gone largely unexamined in the debates about the superstores is how these stores function as complex cultural sites within the popular landscape, commercial enterprises that become the location for a variety of literary scenes. Mixed-use sites, they evoke an ambience that's part Café Deux Magots, part Reading Room of the British Museum, where habitués can converse, with equal sense of appropriateness, about Gertrude Stein or Martha Stewart, right next door to, or across the parking lot from, literary hangouts like Outback Steakhouse, Old Navy, or Bed Bath & Beyond. What does indeed happen to literary culture when it goes to the mall, or shows up on the strip, especially in locations where no literary scene of any sort has ever existed before? Why do these stores generate such friction in terms of how we evaluate them?

While I'll be examining the superstore as a nation-wide phenomenon, I'm using my local Barnes & Noble and Borders bookstores as my base of operations. Laura J. Miller provides a detailed study of the evolution of the bookstore controversy in *Reluctant Capitalists: Bookselling and the Culture of Consumption* (2006), which goes far beyond the scope of this study, but I want to look closely at my local superstores to gain a better picture of what sort of stage set is required for self-cultivation. I was first struck by the singularity of these environments while sitting in the Starbucks café located in that Barnes & Noble, gazing up at the mural that wraps around the seating area. I began this book with an account of that scene because it reveals so much about the way the popular literary envisions itself as a kind of cultural experience which requires mise-en-scène of its own. There, in an imaginary literary café, a host of great authors sit at their tables: George Eliot cozied up to Henry James, who appears to be avoiding eye contact with Oscar Wilde, who stares languidly at the *litterateurs* below, while Raymond Chandler and Virginia Woolf sit at another table looking fiercely creative. This is not the sort of Great Authors murals where the literary gods loom above the public—here the great writers form a "scene" and the literary experience is envisioned as profoundly social. But what does the mural suggest about the sort of literary scenes that might be enacted below?

In his book *You Have to Pay for the Public Life*, the architect Charles Moore argued that public spaces that become significant sites in the cultural life of a community take on a monumental quality. Their monumentality depends on a process of *marking* a place:

> The act of marking is . . . a public act, and the act of recognition an expectable public act among members of the society which possesses the place. Monumentality, considered in this way, is not a product of compositional techniques (such as symmetry about several axes) or flamboyance of form, or even of conspicuous consumption of space, time, or money. It is rather, a function of society's taking possession of, or agreeing upon, extraordinarily important places on the earth's surface, and of the society's celebration of their pre-eminence. (25)

What I find so intriguing about the superstore phenomenon is that it depends on both kinds of monumentality—the public's taking possession

3. Borders store, viewed from parking lot, Mishawaka, Indiana, 2008

4. Barnes & Noble store, viewed from parking lot, Mishawaka, Indiana, 2008

of the site *and* compositional techniques that are decidedly flamboyant, at least by the standards of contemporary commercial architecture. How these stores are marked within the morphology of form vocabularies that constitute contemporary consumer design reveals even more about how "culture," specifically literary culture, is given a recognizable shape within landscapes dominated by malls and multiplexes by both the designers and users of these stores.

The relationship between independent and superstore bookstores is not the simple dichotomy between genuine culture and mere commerce that it is often alleged to be, nor is it simply a matter of chainstore bookshops differentiating themselves from the rest of mall/strip culture by appropriating so many of the functions and rituals associated with real bookstores (public readings, coffee bars, etc.). The monumentality of the superstore involves a library effect, which leads shopper-patrons to use them as substitutes for lending libraries, one of the original bastions of not-for-profit culture intended for the general public. The emergence of this library effect within the superstore environment represents an unprecedented hybrid of culture and commerce as a site designed for commerce at its most corporate but used as though it were a gift from a philanthropist. Just how consumer-dominated the superstore environment actually has itself become is a matter of debate. When the legendary independent bookstore Shakespeare & Co. closed its doors on the Upper West Side of Manhattan in 1999 due to competition from the Barnes & Noble store that had opened just a block down Broadway (a closing that was the inspiration for the film *You've Got Mail*), it issued a statement that defined the struggle between community and corporate might in no uncertain terms: "Our store has been a home for great literature and a sense of community that is getting harder and harder to find in New York City"; it lamented "the change in the retail environment on this particular stretch of Broadway, where generic corporately-owned stores dominate what was once an urban wonderland" (quoted by Karen Angel in *Publisher's Weekly* [1999]).

Yet this same Barnes & Noble superstore that is alleged to be a hothouse of corporate consumerism is invoked by Doreen Carvajal in the *New York Times* as an example of exactly the opposite: "The Barnes & Noble superstore is to this generation's avid readers what an Andrew Carnegie library was to those of an earlier era: community center, reading room and of course repository of thousands of books. The carefully calculated lounge-and-browse ambiance is so relaxing — so free from petty distractions of commerce that a

Manhattan customer died at the Broadway and 82nd street branch, nestled in an overstuffed chair and left to slumber undisturbed until closing." This ambiance, which produces what Carvajal refers to as "literary lounge lizards," bespeaks a redefinition of the bookstore as public space, privately owned but treated as quasi-public, a site where reading and consumption are somehow complementary but decidedly not coterminous. Ironically, the ambiance cultivated by the superstore has made reading something that one goes to *do* in a bookstore. Terry McCoy, coowner of another legendary independent bookstore, St. Marks Bookshop in Greenwich Village, has said of this new way of treating bookstores as reading rooms: "People think they can just sit down and read. They didn't used to do that a couple of years ago. We had to put out stools" (quoted by Carvajal).

His point is amplified by Renee Feinberg, a professor and reference librarian at Brooklyn College, who sees the superstore as a model for what libraries once were and might become again—places where people come to actually read books, to engage in reading as a social activity, rather than information depots where one does focused research and from which one departs as soon as possible. Feinberg interviewed students at Barnes & Noble stores throughout Manhattan in order to ascertain how they were using these stores campared with their college libraries. She discovered that most of the students did much of their studying, as well as much of their research, at the store, treating the "merchandise" as an open-stack library. At the Astor Place Barnes & Noble in Greenwich Village as she reports in a 1998 article in *Library Journal*, she found a store that "looked like an undergraduate library during final exam week, as students crammed and finished papers. (On weekends, however, Astor Place reminds me of a Left Bank café, as everyone reads newspapers and drinks coffee.)" While philanthropists like Carnegie and Henry Higginson were cultural gatekeepers eager to encourage social uplift, who, or what, is minding the cultural store at Barnes & Noble, a bookstore that seems to conceive of customer service in terms of leaving customers as alone as possible to follow their own agendas? As Feinberg argues, "Borders has been noted for testing its job applicants, while B & N has claimed it seeks a staff that won't intimidate customers." One of the staffers she interviewed summed up the differences quite succinctly: "The library is still involved with good reading to make good people, while B & N is willing to suspend 'good' and to stretch the limits" (50).

While the superstore appears to be far more egalitarian than the library Brahmins, who were nothing if not prescriptive, the relationship between

Brahmin and superstore culture is further complicated by the fact that the architecture and design one encounters at the superstore are far closer to the nineteenth-century Boston Brahmin vision of culture than anything in the surrounding vicinity. Charles Moore, in an essay on public architecture, declares the architecture found on the Stanford University campus to be outmoded: "The Boston architects of the nineteenth-century railroad tycoon Leland Stanford had their own clear notions, social and architectural, of the nature of hierarchy, and they manifested them with great success in the old Stanford campus. As its population grows phenomenally, the people who comprise it, rich and poor, come from all sorts of places and owe no allegiance to any establishment of the sort that exercises at least some control of money and taste in areas less burgeoning" (*You Have to Pay for the Public Life*, 122). Moore's argument may be compelling in reference to the different imperatives that have shaped architectural style in California, but I think it may be very productively reconceived in reference to contemporary commercial architecture on a far broader scale. The suburban strip mall is itself a product of postwar California style, yet marking what is a "cultural" location within that landscape has necessitated the incorporation of styles that are immediately recognizable as belonging to other, far earlier visions of culture as built environment. While the prescriptive cultural agenda that originally accompanied the styles favored by Stanford, Higginson, and their like may have been jettisoned, vestiges of those designs are now a vital component in the struggle to give visual form to the new hypercommercialized cultural landscape that has emerged at the start of the twenty-first century. The class distinctions of the late nineteenth century are then simultaneously leveled in terms of the very accessibility of this culture within the marketplace and also reiterated as a way of marking these stores as sites of cultural commerce.

The flourishing popular literary culture, in the form of both literary adaptations and superstore bookshops, has been a matter of developing a proper mise-en-scène. Lush Miramax adaptations such as *The English Patient*, *The Wings of a Dove*, and *Shakespeare in Love* have substantially redefined the look of the literary, and in a broader sense, they have been instrumental in changing the public's expectations concerning just what a literary experience should look like. In much the same way, the superstore fashions its own mise-en-scène for a literary experience—art direction is as important to the superstore as it is to Merchant and Ivory adaptation film. The exterior façades of both the Borders and Barnes & Noble superstores in my community stand out in drastic contrast to the rest of the strip mall that surrounds them in their historical other-worldliness. The Borders store sits in the middle of a vast parking lot it shares with Kohls, Old Navy, Dick's Sporting Goods, and Bed Bath & Beyond, all located at some distance away within the same mini-mall enclosure. The front of the store (see figure 3) suggests a civic building done in a neoclassical mode, its monumentality foregrounded by the red brick cladding, the massive columns and cornices that frame the entrance, and the grand peaked roof attached to the flat roof so common on the rest of the strip buildings, a kind of architectural top hat to import the proper degree of cost-effective *luxe*. The building seems to have learned from both Robert Venturi and Leland Stanford an extremely effective design that can be read, from passing cars, as Culture, but according to nineteenth-century design codes that clearly retain a significant residual force within the popular imagination.

The Barnes & Noble store located a few hundred yards further down the same strip sits alone within a similar mini-mall compound with a shared parking lot, its most prominent neighbor being the Outback Steakhouse. Here again the historical otherness of the façade stands out at a distance. Instead of the neoclassicism of the Borders store, this historicity is of more recent vintage: the brick, ornamentation, awnings, and rooftop lamps all suggesting an Arts and Crafts effect, an evocation of not just another, more literary period but also an earlier form of urbanity that now seems so *other* within this particular commercial landscape. The historicist nature of this façade may be as ersatz as the evocation of the wilds of Australia next door, or the quaintness of Old Mexico in Chili's Grill across the road, but the book-shopping experience depends on historical rather than geographic exoticism to mark it as a "destination" experience along the strip. In the summer of 2009 my local Barnes & Noble superstore moved to a new location within a shopping mall but the emphasis on a nineteenth-century façade became, if anything, even more pronounced (see figure 5). "Literariness," within high-tech information culture, is signified by an amalgamation of neo-aestheticist styles prominent when print was still the only medium of cultured exchange, a time when distinctions between high-brow and middle-brow were first being hardwired into the system of American culture.

The interiors of both the Borders and Barnes & Noble superstores feature the same combination of styles, invoking both the neoclassicism associated with the not-for-profit cultural establishments of the Gilded Age and the more streamlined, but nonetheless, vividly antique look of a transatlantic

5. New Barnes & Noble store, Mishawaka, Indiana, 2009

Arts and Crafts style. Once shoppers pass through the imposing columns of the front entrance, they encounter, immediately to their right, the café area. Here, the leather club chairs and couches are matched with Mission-style lamps. At Barnes & Noble, the Great Writers mural looms above a café area enclosed by metal railings featuring small colored squares, echoing the predominant ornamentation used throughout the store—Frank Lloyd Wright crossed with Charles Rennie Mackintosh, a sort of all-purpose Glasgow Prairie style.

The basic floor plan employed here is the stuff of nineteenth-century philanthropic culture. All aisles lead to a central rotunda with modified tunnel vaults leading off to the various corners of the store. The "public library" associations that come with such a design are immediately apparent. According to Nicholas Pevsner, the first library to feature a wall system arrangement of stacks (the Escorial) had exactly such a tunnel-vaulted structure, and this design quickly became the standard model for the modern library, first at the Vatican Library, then throughout Europe, and eventually across America as an ideal model of cultural architecture for the important civic establishments constructed during the golden age of philanthropic building (*A History of Building Types*, 134). The Gilded Age aspect of this design in all its civic-seeming monumentality is further emphasized within the rotunda at Barnes & Noble by a massive, ornate, gilded chandelier that looks like it would be more at home in the film version of *The Age of Innocence* than in a strip mall in Mishawaka, Indiana. The recent addition of an officially designated study area apart from the stacks (and café) only further amplifies the library atmosphere—this is where people come to *read*.

The monumentality of the superstore represents an attempt to mass-produce the aura of a "real" bookstore combined with a grand old public library. As such, the historical exoticism of the design reflects a residual desire to enjoy a cultural experience that is distinct from the surrounding strip mall, even as the superstore embodies the increasingly merchandized nature of literary pleasures. This aura may be considered ersatz by many critics, but these sites are marked two times over—by corporate architects in search of the proper stage set, and by patrons who mark these places as somehow their own, regardless of who actually owns them. The library effect is further amplified by the in-house publications produced by both Barnes & Noble and Borders. While the staff at the former may not be counted upon for its extensive knowledge of quality literature, its monthly *Discover Young Writers* booklet evidences how determined the superstores are to take on a curatorial function. The booklet is offered free as a critical selection of the best new literary fiction, apparently without profit motive as a public service—the sort of informed "advice" we would expect to get from a friendly librarian or an eager salesperson at an independent bookstore and that springs from the sheer love of books. As a publication that promotes the sale of these books, *Discover Young Writers* could be considered a print-based, high-toned version of an infomercial, since it provides information about books that will lead to their increased sales. But the nonprofit aspect of this selection process (this is all about the *quality* of this fiction) and the validity of that process (this is literary criticism, not mere bookselling) are given legitimacy by the award system that accompanies it, the annual Discover Young Writers Award (Borders has its own version of this, their annual Original Voices Award). The winners are featured within their respective store publications, and advertisements announcing the winners appear prominently soon after in the *New York Times Book Review* and *Entertainment Weekly*. This promotion benefits both the book in question and the award itself by making it appear to be a significant achievement, a pedigree like the Whitbread Prize or the PEN Faulkner. The Discover Young Writers and Original Voices Awards bestow cultural status on the books but also on the superstores themselves by insisting that they are serving a curatorial function—they are not just selling books, they are identifying the really great books for us the way a book reviewer or a librarian would, without vested interests. As such, they address not potential buyers as much as a community of book lovers.

Collecting Affinities in Amazonia, or Two Clicks of Separation

There is no better example of how tightly interconnected bookselling and book loving have become than the screen full of information that is presented to customer/avid reader at Amazon.com. Consumer information is supplied in profusion, but comes thoroughly interlaced with a discourse of passionate reading apparently unsullied by all those commercial appeals. Potential customers are not just addressed; they are interpellated into reading formations in which they are constituted as readers of a very particular sort, intended for books that are simultaneously defined in very particular ways as commodities to be purchased and objects to be read. The architecture of the Web site that is Amazon, like the architecture of the Barnes & Noble superstore, is built on the interdependency of culture and commerce. Both labor to create the impression that the "store" is really just a community of book lovers in retail disguise—they provides books, advice about which books to buy, and, just as important, the ideal site for the common conversation about the joys of reading. In his memoir of his experience as fiction editor at Amazon, *Amazonia: Five Years at the Epicenter of the Dot.com Juggernaut* (2004), James Marcus details how this intermingling of art and commerce was, in effect, built right into the system from the virtual ground up. When he started at Amazon in 1996, he was struck by the fact that

> even as Jeff (Bezos) hired an editorial staff larger than that of most magazines, and gambled his SWAT team of egg heads would be good for something—it was clear that art and commerce weren't necessarily the comfiest of bedfellows. You could, like me, ignore the potential friction. You could aim your work at some ideal, book-besotted reader and let retail take care of itself. But when you were writing something for Amazon—where, incidentally, nobody ever told me to make nice to a single title—you couldn't help but have the suspicion that your opinions were succumbing to the gravitational tug of the marketplace. This didn't mean you were corrupt: indeed, it sometimes led to a strange, neurotic vigilance about the purity of your enthusiasms. (23)

At this stage in its development, according to Marcus, the editors at Amazon imagined themselves as a kind of upstart independent bookstore, referring to Barnes & Noble as the "Evil Empire" because they embodied pure unadulterated commerce, pushing books as mere commodities in chain stores. Bezos encouraged the promotion of a certain number of noncommercial titles, because, according to Marcus, "they telegraphed certain qualities that Jeff wanted to see associated with the site. They made us seem eclectic, funny, smart and discriminating, minus any hint of snobbish superiority. And, in the early days, when the company was first locking horns with the deep-pocketed proprietors of B&N, this cachet was a real (if unquantifiable) asset" (115). Notice here that the positioning of Amazon vis-à-vis Barnes & Noble involves an implicit third element in this triangulation—"We're not mere hucksters for books like those guys, but, on the other hand, we're anything but snobs"—and on that middle ground, cachet can become a marketing strategy unto itself. Marcus's characterization of the editorial team as eggheads and bohemians raises an important point often lost in the demonization of mass market bookselling—just *who* worked there? Rather than confirming the widespread impression that chains and Web sites are run by corporate monsters with robotic minions trained to do their bidding, he presents a much more complicated picture, one that exposes the profound tensions within not just Amazon but the very infrastructure of popular literary culture.

Marcus details the increasingly conflicted relationship between Editorial and Marketing departments that developed as Bezos brought in his army of MBAs and their "culture of metrics" designed to measure customer enjoyment and cater to it more efficiently. The tensions between literary criticism and the selling of books were initially handled by a neat subdivision between editorial and marketing departments, the former providing the all-important *content*. According to Marcus,

> We were betting big on content. By setting up the equivalent of twenty on-line magazines and a budget close to a million dollars for reviews, articles, and interviews, Amazon was creating a true hybrid. It was neither a traditional store nor a traditional publication, but a back-scratching fusion of the two. Ideally, readers would flock to see what Toni Morrison thought about racial separatism, then exit with a copy of *The Bluest Eye* in their shopping carts. Editorial would thrive on its own and render unto Caesar (or Jeff) what was his. The reality, of course, was

more complicated. But in the early, iconoclastic heyday of the Web, it felt like a marvelous experiment. (106)

Marcus admits to being overwhelmed when he learns that *The New Yorker*, bastion of the traditional New York literary world, had expressed interest in interviewing the Amazon editorial staff. "The proposal was enormously flattering. Since when did a retailer's editorial staff end up in the *New Yorker*? (Since when did a retailer *have* an editorial staff?)" (150).

What complicated this equilibrium was the loss of confidence in *content* in 1997, which resulted in the merging of editorial and marketing departments at Amazon. The "Golden Age of Content" is brought to a close by these marketing types, who now encourage editorial to "*monetize those eyeballs*" (130). That monetizing required a new master strategy: personalization, in which the site would be rehung for each customer according to previous buying history. This move to personalization was the end of the equilibrium between the editors and the MBAS, because it introduced a new set of voices, namely customers, who were encouraged to provide their own reviews. Marcus's intense resentment of what he calls these amateur reviews exposes some of the most interesting tensions within his account of Amazon's history. On the one hand, the incorporation of customer reviews "seemed to validate all the rhetoric of Internet democracy. Here was an intelligent conversation about books conducted by a group of disinterested, disembodied spirits. . . . These were amateurs, in the most honorable sense of the word" (224). As such, they represented the natural extension of the site's ability to develop community and/or a target audience simultaneously. Marcus describes Bezos's dream of the Internet as a world in which "affinity would call out to affinity: your likes and dislikes—from Beethoven to barbeque sauce to shampoo to shoe polish to Laverne and Shirley—were as distinctive as your DNA, and would make it a snap to match you up with your 9,999 cousins. His was either utopian daydream or targeted marketing nightmare" (89). Marcus details his own reading of Emerson and other Transcendentalists during this period, fascinated by the possible connections: "Emerson had earlier kicked around the idea of a university without walls—a free-wheeling establishment where he could teach literature to a class of kindred souls. That never took off" (158).

The parallel never takes off within Marcus's book either, because it would seem to involve a kind of populist dimension that, by his own admission, he is "a bit tetchy about." He dismisses the use of customer reviews, which were themselves rated for their usefulness by other customers and then quantified accordingly as merely "the Culture of Metrics at its worst, with a dose of managerial quackery. . . . A reminder: art is not a popularity contest. Taste, talent and discrimination have nothing to do with numbers, case closed" (226). Discrimination and taste may have nothing to do with numbers, but they have a lot to do with who presumes to be able to have an opinion about books, a sticking point for Marcus, which becomes especially clear when he dismisses Amazon's decision to "throw in its lot with the vox pop" and begins submitting his own "customer reviews" under a pseudonym, "Jim Kibble"—and which eventually win him the Amazon.com Book Review Writing Contest.

In order to explore the vestiges of these battles between culture and commerce within the architecture of the Amazon site, and at the same time take a very close look at those customer reviews, I decided in the summer of 2004 to engage in an ethnographic exercise. In honor of Michael Cunningham's character Laura Brown, I went first to his book *The Hours: A Novel*. Once there, I saw the cover of the book, featuring the poster for the film, with prices for all nine editions of the novel: hardback, paperback, audio cassette (unabridged), audio CD (unabridged), audio CD (abridged), e-book (Adobe Reader), e-book (Microsoft Reader), and audio download. Two more overt consumer appeals came next: "Visit the DVD Store," where I could buy the novel in the form of adaptation film (*The Hours*, directed by Stephen Daldry), and "Better Together," *The Hours* and *Mrs. Dalloway* "Buy Both Now! for a special price." In addition to the price information, I was also being interpellated into a specific reading community, first by "Customers who bought this book also bought . . ." (featuring other titles by Woolf and Cunningham) and then by "Popular in . . . ," where, upon going to see where *The Hours* was especially popular, I learned that I could join a Purchase Circle: "Amazon.com is calculating thousands of bestseller lists. No matter where you *work, live*, or *go to school*, we'll probably have a Purchase Circle for you." Here the consumerism could hardly be more overt, since the connections that link readers sharing similar tastes are defined entirely in terms of buying patterns—not a reading circle, or even a fan circle, but a purchase circle.

Yet that screen also includes links to an even greater profusion of avid readers, whose discourse is made up of languages of aesthetic evaluation that make no mention whatsoever that these books are consumer items. "Customer Reviews" follow the price and edition information, which is bordered by lists of two sorts: "Listmania" and "So You'd Like to . . ." guides." I wanted to see what Laura Brown (who was reading all the Woolf novels, one at a time) would have encountered had she gone to Amazon .com, rather than her local library, so I clicked on "Buy Together" and went to the *Mrs. Dalloway* page, to get a sense of what she could have learned from the customers instead of asking her local librarian. The first entry in the "So You'd Like to" guide was "So You'd Like to . . . read the best books without having to endure the bad ones? A guide written by bel-78." This guide expressed the same sentiments as the letter writer to *Ladies Home Journal* in 1906—here was someone in search of good books who had come to Amazon, rather than *Ladies Home Journal* or her local librarian, and now offered to return the favor, as it were, for other avid readers like herself,

> I love to read, and I have read quite a lot of books. Many are great, but others are really not worth it. So, given that some Amazon lists have helped me a lot when deciding which book to buy, I concluded that trying to do the same for others was only fair. The order in which I put the books doesn't mean anything: I liked them all. If a phrase is between inverted commas, it means that I've copied it from an editorial review I consider specially good but I must warn you, however, that you might hate the books I loved, or think books I deem boring are interesting. The reason for that is that tastes vary. Anyway, even taking that into account, you might find some of these tips helpful. And that is my purpose. After all, so many good books, so little time. (Read 23,217 times, May 3, 2004)

I've quoted this statement in its entirety, because it articulates so many of the taken-for-granted assumptions that form this imagined community of readers. Unlike the woman who asked the resident authority at the *Ladies Home Journal* for advice, bel-78 has obtained culture and feels empowered to offer a list of her own, her authority resting on her love of books and her range of reading experiences rather than a formal education in the professional reading practice. She clearly feels she owes something to her community of fellow avid readers, whom she considers to be anything but a Purchase Circle. There is no mention of the marketplace, but neither is there any suggestion of an elitist alternative to it. She takes great delight in offering her opinions about quality reading, but her list comes with a disclaimer—tastes vary. She incorporates editorial reviews, but only if they confirm her perspectives.

Literary authority here resides within the imagined community, rather than coming down from above, even while it celebrates the transcendent nature of a literary text as something far beyond the realm of mere best-sellers. The notion that this community of readers has a special status, that they are somehow all kindred spirits serving in effect as each other's experts because they are so passionately committed to books is crystallized by the title she puts at the top of her list—*Fahrenheit 451*. Even though Ray Bradbury's novel, as a science-fiction novel, would normally fall into the category of genre fiction rather than literary classic, it is a favorite for this community because it imagines readers as imperiled counterculture, possessing a secret knowledge of the wonders of reading unavailable to the rest of the population. Within the past decade there has been an increasing amount of research into the diversity of Internet communities, from David Porter's *Internet Culture* (1997) to Sherry Turkle's *Life on the Screen: Identity in the Age of the Internet* (1997) to Julian Dibbel's *Play Money: Or How I Quit My Day Job and Made Millions Trading Virtual Loot* (2006) to Henry Jenkins's *Convergence Culture: How Old and New Media Collide* (2006). Jenkins explores the participatory nature of Internet fan communities that revolve around *The Matrix*, *Star Wars*, and *Harry Potter* franchises, detailing the frenetic creative activity of fans as they invent elaborate extended universes for their favorite characters. What I find particularly fascinating about the participatory culture formed by the listmaniacs and guide writers at Amazon is that it revolves around another sort of project not addressed by these other studies, yet it's one that is pursued with equal fervor. These fans exist to make taste distinctions, to demonstrate their expertise not about what is perceived to be a cult phenomenon such as playing a particular video game but to take possession of canonical literary masterpieces in the most public domain. They articulate their own identities not through role playing but by insisting on their singularity as reader-connoisseurs. They don't imagine the further adventures of Kirk and Spock or Harry and Ron—their lists and guides become adventures unto themselves.

Taken together, the "So You'd Like to Be" guides and "Listmania" entries on the *Mrs. Dalloway* page that the contemporary Laura Brown may choose to explore at Amazon provide a neat composite picture of the differing reading formations that intersect here. The "My Virginia Woolf Reading List" and "Who's the Fairest of Them All" are dutiful homages to Woolf, thoroughly respectful of literary excellence. Each of these lists is bordered by still more lists, some of which continue along the same lines, obviously driven by a kind of missionary zeal to be informative about great literature, as evidenced by their very titles: "So You'd Like to . . . immerse yourself in British Classics: a guide by irmita, English Graduate Student and Teacher," "So You'd Like to . . . know Who's Who of British literature: A guide by writetothebone, a creative writing teacher," and "So You'd Like to . . . have a firm base of Western literature: a guide by redsox989, employee of Borders, reader." This last guide is particularly interesting because redsox989, an employee of the superstore, appears to be as driven by a pedagogical mission as the actual teachers of literature and ironically enough, it is this guide that is most elitist in its trumpeting of the Great Books against "the modern stuff and pop lit."

Another of the guides at the *Mrs. Dalloway* page, "Books I've Read This School Year: a list by rachelharin, wants to read more," leads to a host of interrelated lists, composed primarily by high school students. These lists reflect another reading formation situated neatly at the intersection of an Amazon Purchase Circle and high school Advanced Placement English classes. The repetition of a number of the same titles throughout these lists (*The Great Gatsby, Brave New World, 1984, Great Expectations, The Grapes of Wrath*, etc.) bears witness to the force of a standardized curriculum for so many American high school students; but their attitudes, and the languages of evaluation that they use to express those intensely held opinions, reveal a complicated, often ambivalent set of values, an ambivalence so ubiquitous that it appears to be a distinguishing feature of this community. Some of these lists and guides take an explicitly pedagogical position, offering information in semiprofessional tones to budding connoisseurs: "So You'd Like to . . . take an English AP Class with me as your instructor: a list by Kauskih, high school student and writer," or "Read the Top 50 Books Which Changed My Life: a guide by j2d2, a voracious reader," and "Outstanding Literature (no particular order): a list by faulkner600, connoisseur." But other guides offer a more conflicted account of the quality reading experience, suggesting a less than perfect conversion to professionalized reading among these avid readers. A few guide writers add favorite titles to their list of the canonical novels, but they obviously feel the need to justify their choices, and thereby give themselves a certain authority by using the languages of appreciation they are in the process of acquiring in their high school English classes. "The Twenty Best Books I've Read: a list by Connor Dirks, literary analyst," for example, includes the usual classics found on so many other lists, but starts with *The Gunslinger* by Stephen King at the number 1 spot: "Not recognized as a classic, but a masterpiece of allegory told by one of the best storytellers ever." Dirks's list also anticipates his peers' suspicions about this choice, so he sometimes acts as middleman between teacher and classmate: number 2, "*The Sound and the Fury*—Cryptic, but Faulkner has something to say. Wow"; and number 8 "*The Stranger*—It's not just for the French. The story is amazing." Other list makers take a more defiant relationship to that imaginary English teacher, so one encounters lists made by perfectly interpellated reading subjects, "Books I've Recently Read (and all students should)" alongside lists that try to locate valuable reading experiences despite that instruction: "Books That I Didn't Mind Reading (and You Won't either)." A few of the lists take an overtly ironic tone that allows the list maker to be both inside and outside at the same time, clearly bent on demonstrating that they have, *of course*, read all the canonical text that they are supposed to read, but just as determined to promote their *own* singularity. In the introduction to "So You'd Like to . . . inadvertently become known as a wry intellectual: a guide by Bobnothingelse," for example, the author says: "So far I sound like a snob. My name is Bob and the general consensus seems to be that I am indeed an allusive and wry teenage intellectual, though my previous conception of myself remains. I think I am a simple and nitwitted girl. In any event, somebody suggested that I make a guide of how to become an unappreciated geek freak who listens to classical music." This leads to an even more ironical list, "See What Bob Has Read in High School Part I."

After perusing these AP lists, I returned to the *Mrs. Dalloway* homepage, where I clicked on the last guide listed there, "So You'd Like to . . wow your Sweet Baboo," only to discover another interconnected constellation of lists and guides uniting another parallel community of avid readers who were far more emancipated from academic reading protocols in their pursuit of reading pleasure. Within this group of guide and list makers, reading literary fiction was given a different use value, exemplifying perfectly Tony Bennett's notion of a reading formation: "Different reading formations produce their own texts, their own readers, their own contexts" ("Texts in History," 10). Instead of reading *Mrs. Dalloway* in order to gain a greater understanding of Woolf's genius or in order to become a "know-it-all" about modern classics, these readers situated the same novel in a different context: in women's fiction—but of a very particular variety. The fact that these lists were far more heavily gender-based, and also far more ironical about how one was supposed to talk about literary fiction, is exemplified neatly by Sweet Baboo's guide, which was broken down into two lists. The first is "for the Lady in Your Life" and included these suggestions: "*The Hours*, Get her this and she won't drag you to the movie (I love the movie, but then I'm a chick . . .)," and "*Mrs. Dalloway, The Hours* is based on this novel by Virginia Woolf. You will look WAY intellectual with this one." In addition to Cunningham and Woolf's novels, Sweet Baboo included a second list, with Cathi Hanauer's *The Bitch in the House: 26 Women Tell the Truth about Sex, Solitude, Work, Motherhood and Marriage*; Janis Jaquith's *Birdseed Cookies: A Fractured Memoir*; Allison Pearson's *I Don't Know How She Does It: The Life of Kate Reddy, Working Mother*; and Jill Connor Browne's *The Sweet Potato Queen's Big Ass Cookbook (and Event Planner)*. The common denominator here, unlike in the high school students' lists, is situational, the main distinguisher being not the stylistic achievement of Great British Literature or Great Novels of the twentieth century, but rather Stories of "Alienated Women," or more precisely, "Stories about Smart-Mouth, Discontented Women—English, American Southern, and otherwise." Here there is no evidence of any need to justify or defend the inclusion of noncanonical alongside the canonical choices; Woolf becomes an honorary member of the Ya-Ya sisterhood and apparently, she's the better for it. If only Clarissa had had that *Big Ass* event planner, how differently things might have gone for both character and author. Or if Woolf and Sylvia Plath, also ubiquitous on these lists, had read *Prozac Nation*—required reading on virtually all of the related lists on this page (*Phenomenal Women, Women on the Verge of a Nervous Breakdown*, etc.)— what a different course literary history may have taken.

Another sort of evaluative criterion is used by these list makers, which allows them to situate the canonical novel alongside the memoir and cookbook, and privilege all three according to another rubric of value. Elizabeth Long's work on reading groups in and around Houston (published 1987, in the journal *Cultural Studies*) is relevant in this regard, because she discovered that the readers she encountered read classics but define that category in *experiential* terms: "A classic is great because it *does* something for someone: it provides a reading experience that can transcend the ephemerality and flux of daily living and so enrich or move the reader that it finds a permanent niche in her memory. This stands in direct opposition to the intellectualist tendency to produce formal aesthetic analyses" (315). I think this important distinction can be made even more precise in these lists. The tension is not between experiential and aesthetic reading as such, or between intellectual and ordinary readers as such, because the list makers at Amazon are intellectual (no matter how ironic they may be about it, they're college-educated, informed, avid readers) and they are clearly in search of aesthetic experience. But what makes a book so transcendent that it removes the reader from the flux of day-to-day life into some other realm of experience depends on its experiential use value. Another one of these Smart-Mouth Women lists is provided by Janis Jaquith herself, an author (*Birdseed Cookies: A Fractured Memoir*) featured on Sweet Baboo's list. Her list, "In the Footsteps of Oprah," includes *The Divine Secrets of the Ya-Ya Sisterhood*, assorted contemporary popular literary novels such as *Bel Canto* and *The Secret Life of Bees*, and self-help books such as *Psychic Secrets: Your Guide to Dreams, Hunches, and Spirit Contact* ("This is a funny smart book about growing up in a psychic family. Read it and you'll learn to foster your own psychic abilities"), along with her own book, *Birdseed Cookies* ("Okay, I wrote this one. But trust me, you'll love it. It's a collection of my public radio essays. You'll laugh, you'll cry, yadda, yadda, yadda").

The fact that Jaquith's authority rests on her status as a National Public Radio celebrity like Nancy Pearl, suggests a great deal about this group of readers (it's taken for granted that they are NPR-listening women, and two of the books on her list are by other NPR figures) and the librarian function she claims for that group. AP high school students reading Woolf as a literary classic or NPR-listening women reading her as a self-help book are only two clicks of separation away from each other at Amazon.com. When I used to explain to my students how an interpretive community can make an enormous difference in determining how a given novel is to be read and evaluated (how the same novel can be a radically different text depending on how it comes to us as already mediated, already humming with particular types of meanings), I would cite Anne Rice's *Vampire Lestat* (1987), arguing that they would read the novel one way if they were directed to it by a friend as a great beach read, and very differently if they were asked to read it for a college course in feminist Gothic fiction. They would see the point immediately, and build on it themselves with only the slightest encouragement from me, locating the very significant differences in the respective reading formations that made that book the perfectly appropriate reading material in each case, recognizing that word of mouth and the academy depended on different delivery systems, intertextual frameworks, and interpretive protocols, all of which would constitute them as reading subjects of a particular type in each formation, since the novel would be a fundamentally different book-to-be-read in each case. But the distance between those two ways of reading is virtually eliminated by Amazon, where one and the same delivery system directs readers to *Mrs. Dalloway* as canonical novel or as arch-literary self-help book. Whether we prefer to label that experience as a purchase circle, reading community, interpretive community, reading formation, or taste community, the difference between them is a matter of clicks, which can either maintain distinct borders or overcome them almost instantly, since the links to each set of lists and guides appear on the same page as co-equal options. Click in the direction of precollegiate, AP English students, and you find "So You Want to . . . be a Left Bank intellectual"; click toward the postcollegiate, NPR-listening Women, and you find "So You Want to . . . sprawl on the beach with a great book."

I have introduced pre- and postcollegiate here in order to further delineate the differences between these two groups, but also to suggest a temporal dimension to our understanding of the reading communities—that these are the same readers, not just at different stages in their lives, but at two different moments in regard to the professionalized reading lessons that they receive within the academy. In other words, the differences here are not a matter of rigid either/or dichotomies founded on inherent differences between high- and middle-brow cultures; they are, rather, shifting, overlapping distinctions that make the traditional hierarchy of taste cultures seem far too monolithic.

The NPR-listening Women may be interested in beach reading (and those lists may include *The South Beach Diet*), but they also include quality literary fiction. In the summer of 2004, the May 14 issue of the *Wall Street Journal* published its annual guide to "Summer Reading," formulated by a resident critic, Robert J. Hughes, who interviewed "everyone from editors to agents to independent book-store owners and big retailers." According to Hughes, the most significant development was what he called "the beach-blanket brainy trend," and he quoted Elaine Petrocelli, owner of the bookstore Book Passage, to confirm this development: "Traditionally we thought people wanted to do light reading in summer. We were probably wrong" (W14). He goes on to stress the way in which publishers are trying to sell these beach-blanket brainy books to the forty-and-older audience. While the reading habits of this audience may not be animated by the same factors that lead AP English students to read just as avidly, both are still driven by a need for self-cultivation, even at the beach, perhaps the most notoriously nonintellectual location within American culture.

The lists and guides made by members of both reading communities reveal how thoroughly ingrained the need to self-cultivate is, because it can't be eluded, even in locations where it's not supposed to be pursued. The act of evaluating books outside the academy, according to what they take to be their own criteria, is done with enormous gusto and confidence. Just reading is not enough. One could argue that reading and evaluating have obviously always been interdependent pleasures, but the desire to make those evaluations public in actual reading groups or via Amazon's virtual reading communities makes it abundantly clear that the need to demonstrate one's personal taste in terms of the books one chooses forms an essential part of the pleasures of reading. That books can now function just as effectively as "mere" consumer items such as clothing or furniture as a public manifestation of one's taste—and that this is a conviction held by "mass" audiences and not just intellectuals of the traditional variety—is a major factor in transforming literary culture into popular culture.

These tensions between commerce and culture, between bookselling and self-cultivation at Amazon, where both are undertaken so feverishly, cannot be adequately accounted for by a traditional taste hierarchy. While the terms "high-brow" and "middle-brow" still circulate throughout American popular discourse, they seem at best vestigial expressions of an earlier time, used most often from above and in a negative, disdainful way to reject a particular book or film. While the taste cultures that intersect at Amazon may indeed delight in rating books according to their own evaluative criteria, they appear to have no interest whatsoever in positioning themselves in regard to any commonly agreed-upon hierarchy. Comparing the lists of AP high school students and the NPR-listening women suggests that the traditional relationship between taste and education doesn't develop in the way we have been led to believe, that is, that the more educated people become, the more they adopt the protocols of artistic appreciation that they acquire through a university education. But it is not a matter of sliding back down a hierarchy either, seeking only light entertainment from further down the brow scale once they enter the "real world."

To account for both the simultaneity and diversity of these communities, each evaluating books so exuberantly with such a high degree of self-satisfied confidence, and each investing the very act of reading itself with such different goals, we need to turn the hierarchy of taste cultures envisioned by Herbert Gans (1974) not upside down, but on its side, as it were, because the best way to envision the parallel nature of these reading communities is along a vertical rather than horizontal axis. Amazon institutionalizes that verticality by offering different reading communities as coequal options. The message that the architecture of Amazon drives home is not populist in the traditional sense of disavowing taste distinctions (i.e., since there's no accounting for taste, don't worry about yours, dear customer, just go ahead and buy something). The homepage for literary novels is an intersection of conflicting taste cultures, each endlessly reinforcing its own notions of pleasure (so go ahead and account for tastes to your heart's content, dear passionately committed reader, you'll find validation here).

If any figure is going to emerge as a taste maker on an international scale within this world of frenetic popular connoisseurship, that person would have to have massive reach in terms of media exposure, and would also have to be able to talk the talk of reading pleasure in a way that would establish him or her as an authority, and at the same time, still be completely of that community of amateur readers. And that person could have no vested interest in the selling of books whatsoever in order to function like a national librarian. They are the subjects of chapter 2.

2

BOOK CLUBS, BOOK LUST, AND NATIONAL LIBRARIANS

*Literary Connoisseurship
as Popular Entertainment*

New York may publish the books but Seattle significantly
defines America's reading list.
—Nancy Pearl, interview in *New York Times*, 2008

It's not too much of an exaggeration—if it's one at all—
to say that reading saved my life.
—Nancy Pearl, *Book Lust*

"I wasn't scared!"
—Message printed on Oprah Book Club T-shirts during
the *Anna Karenina* 2004 Challenge

Given the seemingly endless number of titles, all made increasingly accessible through superstores and Web site booksellers, title selection has become one of the most pressing concerns within the popular literary culture. The exhilaration of infinite access generates a concomitant anxiety
regarding individually meaningful selection. The listmania at Amazon is
response to this excess of access, but it also suggests that the selection process is complicated by more than sheer volume. The search of the right title
is not just a matter of finding good books in the abstract sense of the term,
as one might make key acquisitions for a permanent home library. As the
pleasures of reading have become increasingly social, title selections must
be a visible demonstration of personal taste, at that moment. The desire

for the right title, driven by a persistent need to self-cultivate, but without a reliable authority that could be trusted to make the essential fine distinctions, has resulted in a taste vacuum that has been filled by the literary taste maven as media celebrity. That taste vacuum was produced by an increase in the number of available choices and also in the number of readers for whom selection had become a dilemma, without any existing mechanism for delivering the necessary expertise on a scale that could effectively satisfy that audience. New reading authorities had to emerge from within the mass media in order to reach a mass audience of readers in hot pursuit of the right book, just as a wine connoisseur like Robert Parker or a home-keeping diva like Martha Stewart exploded on the scene as national experts when they developed delivery systems for dispensing information that was suddenly considered vital on a very grand scale.

Those literary taste mavens are responsible for creating what Nancy Pearl refers to as "America's reading list." Despite the ever-expanding number of titles and target audiences, there is still a fair amount of common reading going on, directly inspired by authorities that function as national librarians. New York may still publish the books, but more of the power brokers who actually shape America's reading list are concentrated in Seattle in the form of editors at Amazon, Starbucks, and Costco (as well as by Pearl herself, who is based in Seattle and reaches the nation via her role as book critic for National Public Radio), since it is their recommendations that identify the most prominent titles on that national list. And once we factor in Chicago-based Oprah Winfrey, the decentralization of literary culture becomes even more dramatic. But charting the new locations of literary authority in the United States involves more than just moving the pins on the map from one coast to the other. The most striking change in this new cartography of literary taste making is where that expertise is now located and readily accessed—deep in the heart of electronic culture.

In her study of British reading groups Jenny Hartley argues that title selection is the most complicated problem: "How do groups choose what to read? The answer in most cases is 'with difficulty.' On some of our visits to groups we have been struck by the way they can take almost as long choosing what to read next as they do discussing this month's book." The crux of the matter is knowing which authority to trust—Hartley quotes one book group member to this effect: "We often used to choose from the Booker list, but we have so often been disappointed in recent years that we don't bother as much now, but go more on reviews and for personal recommendations"

(45). For the British readers Hartley interviewed, the choice of authorities was limited to a neat dichotomy—either by official literary culture (awards and reviews) or word of mouth. The emergence of a third alternative between these two options has become one of the defining features of popular literary culture in North America—literary authority in the form of thriving, mass-mediated connoisseurship.

This need for advice about choosing the right title by first choosing the right reading expert who shares your sensibility has given rise to a mini-industry in guidebooks about the pleasures of reading. They have come to dominate the Literary Criticism sections at both Barnes & Noble and Borders, and one also encounters them regularly within superstores on end-cap displays—Michael Dorris, *The Most Wonderful Books: Writers on Discovering the Pleasures of Reading* (1997); Anne Fadiman, *Ex Libris: Confessions of Common Reader* (1998); Steven Gilbar, *Reading in Bed: Personal Essays on the Glories of Reading* (1999); Kevin Graffagnino, *Only in Books: Writers, Readers and Bibliophiles on Their Passion* (1996); Rob Kaplan, *Speaking of Books: The Best Things Ever Said about Books and Book Collecting* (2001); Sara Nelson, *So Many Books, So Little Time* (2003); Anna Quindlen, *How Reading Changed My Life* (1998); Lynne Sharon Schwartz, *Ruined by Reading: A Life in Books* (1997); Ronald B. Schwartz, *For the Love of Books: 115 Celebrated Writers on the Books They Love Most* (2000); and the list continues. My main focus in this chapter will be the reading experts who have taken this "Passion-for-the-Glories-Available-Only-While-Reading-These-Wonderful-Books-that-Have-Changed-My-Life-and-Will-Certainly-Change-Yours-Too" message to the widest possible audience. In other words, I want to concentrate on the reading authorities that have their own calendars, Web sites, and radio and television programs—the authorities that have taken "book talk" far beyond the realm of books. As cross-media phenomena they exemplify perfectly the way authority functions in what has come to be called convergence culture. At the same time, paradoxically, they represent a countervailing trend within the heart of that convergence—the celebration of the absolute singularity of reading as a transformative cultural activity that can occur only in books and nowhere else in the hypermediated cultures where that reading takes place.

Anyone hoping to gain recognition as a preeminent authority about which books to read for divergent reading communities would have to convince a mass audience that she or he could be trusted as the curator who *knows what you'll like* even better than the list-making customers at Amazon. They would have to possess some kind of specialized knowledge about books beyond that of most amateur readers, an ability to convey a *passion* for books without profit motive or vested interest of any kind, a delivery system at their disposal to get their advice to a national audience, and most important, a talent for making thousands of amateur readers believe that their recommendations can be expressions of *their own* personal taste. I want to look closely at two media celebrities who, in very different venues, have managed to combine those characteristics so successfully that they have come to function as national librarians—Nancy Pearl, reading adviser for National Public Radio, and Oprah Winfrey and her famous Book Club that appears regularly on her Web site and syndicated television program.

Pearl's overwhelming passion for reading is the heart and soul of her extremely successful guide, *Book Lust: Recommended Reading for Every Mood, Moment, and Reason* (2003), and her follow-ups *More Book Lust: Recommended Reading for Every Mood, Moment, and Reason* (2005), *Book Lust: The Journal* (2005), *Book Lust 2005: A Reader's Calendar*, and *Book Lust 2006: A Reader's Calendar*. That's an awful lot of lust, but hers is a credentialed lust. Her standing as disinterested book maven rests solidly on her status as a professional librarian and her role as a book critic for National Public Radio and director of the Washington Center for the Book. The only retail operation she mentions is a "wonderful independent bookstore, Yorktown Alley, Tulsa, Oklahoma," which, along with her experience at public libraries, has allowed her "to grow as a reader and to share [her] knowledge and love with other readers" (*Book Lust*, x). Knowledge and love are completely interdependent, and the appeal to a community of book lovers gives her reading a transcendent purpose. She establishes her bona fides, though, with a simple declaration in the first sentence of *Book Lust*—"I love to read." She then elaborates on its rewards:

> Reading has always brought me pure joy. I read to encounter new worlds and new ways of looking at our own world. I read to enlarge my horizons, to gain wisdom, to experience beauty, to understand myself better and for the pure wonderment of it all. I read and marvel over how writers use language in ways I never thought of. I read for company and escape. Because I am incurably interested in the lives of other people, both friends and strangers, I read to meet myriad folks and enter into their lives—for me a way of vanquishing the "otherness" we all experience. (ix)

The sort of reading she advocates is anything but the professionalized close reading of the academic variety—no apprenticeship is required, and, judging by the conversational tenor of her prose, anyone can talk the talk of loving books the way she does. This is the kind of authority that the woman who wrote to the *Ladies Home Journal* in 1906 was looking for—an expert advice giver who believes the cultivation of self is there for the taking; it's just a matter of wanting to improve yourself and asking the right person. The therapeutic benefits of reading could hardly be more explicitly articulated. After detailing the pains of her dysfunctional family life as a child, Pearl states: "I spent most of my childhood and early adolescence at the public library. . . . It's not too much of an exaggeration—if it's one at all—to say that reading saved my life" (x).

As Pearl describes the therapeutic benefits of this reading experience, she names the people and institutions who helped her realize these pleasures, citing public radio stations, public libraries systems, and even favorite childhood librarians (Miss Long and Miss Whitehead), but not one professor or even so much as an inspiring junior high English teacher. Her formation as a reader apparently had nothing to do with reading in school of any sort. No special apprenticeship was required, just a community of like-minded book lovers all anxious to turn each other on to books. Interestingly, the only mention made of book learning of the traditional sort comes in the second entry in *Book Lust*: after "A . . . My Name is Alice" (books written by women named Alice) comes "Academia: the Joke" (books that satirize the academy). The single acknowledgment of some kind of authority on all this passionate reading comes in the chapter entitled "Books about Books." There she begins by saying, "Bibliophiles love nothing better than making the acquaintance of other book lovers—especially between the pages of a book. Here are some people whose books about books I've especially enjoyed." She lists Clifton Fadiman, Anne Fadiman, Francis Spufford, and a host of other popular journalists and novelists. Literary criticism and bibliophilia are apparently on separate planets, because for Pearl, reading is all about pleasure, a point made abundantly clear when she introduces her "rule of fifty"—one should read at least fifty pages of a book before setting it aside, but no more than that, should it prove tedious, because, "no one is going to get in heaven by slogging their way through a book they aren't enjoying but think they *ought* to read" (xiii, emphasis mine). The world of "ought to read" is clearly the domain of English professors, but bibliophiles, to use

Pearl's own phrase, read "to be transported" and boring books won't get you anywhere.

This characterization of book lovers as a congregation united by their transcendent faith in reading pleasurable books culminates at the end of Pearl's introduction, where she quotes Virginia Woolf (shorn of any class snobbery or modernist prejudices) in order to convey the spirituality of the experience: "I have sometimes dreamt that when the Day of Judgment dawns and the great conquerors and lawyers and statesmen come to receive their rewards . . . the Almighty will turn to Peter and will say, not without a certain envy when he sees us coming with our books under our arms, 'Look, these need no reward, we have nothing to give them here. They have loved reading.'" Now this is the Woolf that Laura Brown wants to become one with, the patron saint of common readers who is a *reader* first, and great novelist only as a result of that experience. The popular, middle-class fiction abhorred by Woolf is recommended just as enthusiastically by Pearl as more recent versions of the modernist alternative. She includes a number of "Too Good to Miss" entries devoted to her favorite authors, including both Ross Thomas and Richard Powers. Within this spiritualization of reading, populist readers and modernist readers can apparently lie down together in the bosom of bibliophilia. As a librarian extraordinaire who brings knowledge to a world outside the walls of the academy, Pearl is an early-twenty-first-century incarnation of the late-nineteenth-century public lecturer; and as a someone who celebrates the spiritual dimensions of reading pleasure, she is the bibliophile incarnation of Sister Wendy, a celebrity member of the secularized priesthood that ministers to the common art lovers in search of uplifting aesthetic experience. By performing the all-important selection process, and then relaying that information in conversational speech, she offers common readers a form of popular connoisseurship, a taste for books that is decidedly informed, and just as decidedly accessible to all.

Unlike the connoisseurship of the popular found in fanzines or chat rooms devoted to the glories of a particular television program or graphic novel, this popular connoisseurship dismantles the traditional links among discernment, specialized discourse, and rarefied audience. The foundation for this countersystem is an informed reading in pursuit of pleasure, devoid of guilt pangs or ought-to-have-reads—a *cultural* activity given license to be enjoyed as popular culture. And that reading produces such transformative, out-of-the-body experiences that it can only be described in sexual or spiri-

6. Front cover of *Book Lust: Recommended Reading for Every Mood, Moment, and Reason* (2003), by Nancy Pearl

tual terms. It's either lust, or meeting Sister Virginia at the Pearly Gates—this sort of reading is never merely an intellectual transformation. The cover of *Book Lust* captures this perfectly—"LUST" in bold, block letters laid over a photo of the headless author, holding what appears to be a hymnal against her chest.

As popular as Pearl has become through her books and calendars in her role as NPR's house librarian, her national impact pales next to that of Oprah Winfrey, who has managed to achieve the role of national librarian without any such professional credentials, within the heart of commercial television. Amazon, Barnes & Noble, and Borders provide the sites, and to a certain extent, the infrastructures for like-minded readers to connect and then become a mutually reinforcing taste community in which they serve as each other's guides about what to read next; but the remarkable commonality of the lists suggests a larger force, a higher authority with the ability to reach very broad audiences nationwide. For the precollegiate avid readers (the AP English students discussed in the previous chapter) the answer is relatively simple—standardized curricula and pedagogy, the persistent downloading of the same masterpieces, and the same ways of talking about literary texts inevitably produce a high degree of consistency on the lists—only the level of student irony varies. But in the lists and guides made by the postcollegiate readers at Amazon, especially those assembled by the female readers who conceive of reading as a sanctified form of escape from their daily lives (*Books for a Peaceful Time Alone*, *Books for Solitude and Quiet*, etc.), one finds an even greater commonality in terms of titles and the way one talks the talk of book loving. Amazon may provide the infrastructure, but this consistency of titles, chosen by an extremely cohesive taste community, is due directly to the Book Club.

Oprah Winfrey, more than any other figure or factor, represents the complicated interplay among commerce, culture, and self-cultivation within the popular literary. Her power to turn novels into bestsellers of a magnitude comparable only to blockbuster franchise films has been extensively reported in virtually every form of American mass media. The announcement of a new title has automatically led to bestseller status at Amazon within twenty-four hours and immediate placement on the tables inside the front door at superstores. My chief concern in this chapter will not be the sales figures but the way Oprah functions as the preeminent national librarian, seemingly outside the realm of commerce. Two book-length studies of her Book Club, Kathleen Rooney's *Reading with Oprah: The Book Club That Changed America* (2005) and Cecilia Konchar Farr's *Reading Oprah: How Oprah's Book Club Changed the Way America Reads* (2005) have covered a broad range of issues, but I want to look closely at the way Oprah functions as an authority on reading for an imagined community of self-cultivators that numbers in the hundreds of thousands and who come to her expertise within the heart of consumer culture. Like the local librarian, she recommends books as choices, not products, as expressions of taste, not mere commerce, and therefore she can be trusted implicitly. She chooses these books because she loves them and knows you will too. As Laura Miller has said in her assessment of the Book Club: "Winfrey may be a performer, but her job is to perform herself, and in selecting titles for her book club, she has always seemed to be choosing on the basis of personal taste" (2001). Talk about bookselling rarely enters the conversation, even though the program is aired on advertiser-driven television as a product of her Harpo Productions, Inc., an entertainment conglomerate unto itself. Winfrey chooses only books sold by *other* publishers and thereby remains somehow apart from the commercialism of bookselling, even as her "picks" generate more book sales than any other figure or force in publishing.

The success of Oprah as the consummate reliable authority, however, depends on more than her ability to pick appropriate titles. She also provides a way of talking about literary titles that is nonacademic but thoroughly self-confident, thereby empowering readers to read and talk about her selections without performance anxiety. Her choice of titles can be trusted so implicitly because they are appropriate to that manner of reading. But what distinguishes that manner of reading? She is the featured oral performer for a textual community. In their ethnographic studies of how the activity of reading began to take particular shape in medieval societies, Brian Stock (*Implications of Literacy*, 1987) and Nicholas Howe ("Cultural Construction," 1999) detail the ways in which reading is decidedly not the free-floating, solitary pleasure that it is too often imagined to be, but instead a historically specific activity requiring certain rituals and protocols that bestow it with particular values in different contexts. Howe's account of how such textual communities form the basis of the "cultural construction of reading" provides a useful corollary for understanding the ways in which reading *literary* fiction is made accessible to contemporary television audiences:

> In a culture unaccustomed to the written text, the act of reading would have seemed remarkably like solving a riddle, for it meant translating meaningless but somehow magical squiggles on a leaf of vellum into significant discourse, even and most remarkably into sacred scripture. What was alien, opaque, seemingly without meaning becomes familiar, transparent, and meaningful when read aloud by those initiated in the solution of such enigmas. Without the dimension of oral performance, reading of this sort could not be made into the solving of a mystery. The squiggles must be made to speak. . . . Both readers and listeners belong in a community at once textual and spiritual, written and oral, in which intellectual and spiritual life is created through the communal interchange of reading. ("Cultural Construction," 6, 7)

In much the same way, the avid, nonprofessional readers of the early twenty-first century come to literary fiction in an arena of popular culture formerly unaccustomed to literary language—a culture that is both written and exuberantly oral, in the form of television chat show book clubs and reading group discussions that make the reading activity into an explicitly communal interchange, dependent upon someone properly initiated to solve the mysteries hidden in the literary text. The fact that the most reliable authorities for this audience now come from the realm of popular culture rather than the academy makes this a very particular kind of interpretive community animated by its own "spirituality," if we conceive of the spiritual here as that factor which makes reading an uplifting and transformative experience. Oprah performs a very similar function for her viewers within a televisual context as a skilled public explicator who translates the opaque into something familiar, transparent, and meaningful for people unaccustomed to the intricacies of reading in oral cultures. She makes her selections but, just as important, provides a way of experiencing those selections that invests reading with entertainment value for television watchers, who are encouraged to become, or continue to be, avid readers. The now legendary exchange between Winfrey and Toni Morrison is particularly indicative of this power. According to Oprah, she was fascinated, but also baffled as she first read *Beloved*. When she called Morrison and asked, "What is *that*?" The author replied, "That, dear, is called *reading*" (quoted in Lisa Schwarzbaum's 1997 article in *Entertainment Weekly*). Having been initiated into the mysteries of the Word, Winfrey takes the message to her viewers and provides a way of talking the talk of reading that renders the formerly opaque into the transparently meaningful, and the mysterious becomes transparent. Winfrey "makes the squiggles speak" in ways that make them suddenly seem directly addressed to her viewers/readers, at which point her personal taste and the taste of her viewers/readers can become so tightly interwoven that the boundaries between them fade away into a common way of talking about the same type of fiction.

Oprah and "An-na, An-na Karenininina"

In order to discuss the way this particular textual community operates, I want to look closely at a specific Book Club segment on the *Oprah Winfrey Show*—the one devoted to Tolstoy's *Anna Karenina*, which aired September 15, 2004. I have chosen this particular program because I think it is the most revealing in terms of how Oprah's authority as oral performer works for her "Book Clubbers," and also because it is extremely self-conscious about the Book Club's cultural impact. This analysis goes into considerable detail in order to capture the combination of different evaluative criteria that are used by this community as they talk the talk of reading.

When Oprah announced that Tolstoy's novel was going to be the Summer Selection for the club, she admitted in her introduction to the novel at her Web site: "I've never, ever chosen a novel that I had not personally read. It's been on my list for years but I didn't do it because I was scared. Now I'm going to team up with all of you and read it together." Here, authority rests on this admission, because her fascination, coupled with a lack of expertise in Russian literature, makes her eminently trustable as the explicator of the squiggles—they're squiggles for her too at this point, but by reading and talking about it together, the squiggles will become transparent. This segment, then, was welcoming back the Clubbers after their summer with Tolstoy, at 817 pages the longest book ever chosen for the Book Club and the only one that Oprah was reading for the first time right along with them.

That the Oprah Book Club is intended to be a genuinely popular experience designed to appeal to amateur, nonprofessional readers was never more vividly clear than on this particular program. The *Anna Karenina* segment was the second half of the program; the first half was devoted to Oprah's guest Barry Manilow, who performed a mini-concert of songs requested by audience members. In addition to the performances and the repeated plugs for his new album, *Barry Manilow Scores*, the viewers were introduced to a number of audience members who told their personal "Barry" stories. They were invited by Oprah in response to their letters urging her to invite Manilow, and she even says during this segment, "You all can stop writing me letters about this now," because she has made their wishes come true. Manilow finishes this half of the show with a stirring rendition of one of his biggest hits, "Copacabana," and then, after being thanked by Oprah, he adds a new verse of "Copacabana" as a kind of encore and segue into the Book Club segment: "Her name was An-na, An-na Karenininina." The crowd roars appreciatively (fade to commercial).

Book Club Segment

Coming back from the commercial break, Oprah now talks directly to *us* (viewers at home and studio audience, as one expanded club):

Oprah: Last June I could not wait to reveal my Summer Book Club choice. *An-na, An-na Karen-nee-na* [sung to the tune of "Copacabana"] was our Book Club's first Russian masterpiece, and I was thrilled — but would you be as thrilled as I was? I couldn't be sure, so while I was on vacation reading *Anna*, our Book Club producers followed the story.

[Cut to: *Harpotone News*: Parody newsreel, made in the style of Welles's "News on the March" in *Citizen Kane*, complete with archival black-and-white footage and booming voice-over narration.]

Voice-over: Headline, June 1st, 2000 and 4. While thousands wait in eager anticipation, Oprah announces her Summer Book Club Selection.

[Archival images of crowds in streets, followed by another archival interior shot of a 1950s American family, watching their television, where Oprah has been digitally inserted on the screen.]

Oprah: Don't be scared. It's *Anna Karenina*.

Voice-over: Millions cheer and celebrate; the classic novel makes headlines around the nation and around the world, making it *the* summer read.

[More archival crowd scenes, then traditional newspaper montage featuring actual news stories responding to the announcement with titles such as "Tolstoy Top Seller Thanks to Oprah," "Yo, Tolstoy, We're Reading Oprah's Choice," "Thumbs Up to Count Tolstoy," and so on.]

Voice-over: People travel from near and far to be the first in line to get their copies, pushing *Anna Karenina* to the top of the charts! The 126-year-old Russian romance finds new life as it becomes number 1 on the *New York Times*, *USA Today*, and *Publisher's Weekly* bestseller lists, winning the coveted triple crown of book publishing.

[Shots of each of these newspaper's bestseller lists, and then shot of a newspaper article detailing this "triple crown" achievement.]

Voice-over: As June becomes July, and July, August, seventy thousand brand-new readers join Oprah's Book Club. At Oprah.com they sign up for the summer training program, "Read Along with Oprah Each Week," and engage in fascinating book discussions with members as far away as Sydney, Australia.

[Montage of several Web site pages, old-fashioned globe with Sydney highlighted.]

Voice-over: And with half a million total members and growing, Oprah's Book Club is truly the biggest in the world.

What I find especially fascinating here, first in Oprah's introduction, and then again in the *Harpotone* newsreel, is the rapid alternation between earnest appreciation and ironic undercutting of the featured book and the Book Club itself. Oprah sings the title as if it were a Barry Manilow song, then immediately gets reverential. The "newsreel" at first appears to be a complete send-up, but then goes about detailing the impact of the Oprah choices, complete with correct figures and actual newspaper articles that, in effect prove how enormous that impact really is. The book talk here is alternately deeply sincere and blithely ironic, with the tone changing practically every other sentence, and often within the same sentence, as if the assertion of seriousness about reading must come with near instantaneous disclaimer, only to be reasserted again almost immediately. After the newsreel, we come back to Oprah in the studio, and she reiterates that this was the first book she had not previously read:

Oprah: I tried to keep the same schedule that was offered online. Anyway, I began to wonder, was everybody going to finish this gigantic novel. After all, we had moms who hadn't read a book since high school. So if you hadn't read a book since high school, this was a tough one to pick up. Book Clubbers who'd never read Tolstoy, *I* was one of them. So let's go to the videotape.

[Cut to: Another mock documentary, this one in color, but with the same booming voice-over. Group of Book Clubbers all in matching T-shirts ("I'm Not Scared" emblazoned on chest) warming up for a race, followed by marathon race footage with each runner carrying same copy of *Anna Karenina* as they push baby strollers, stumble over in street, and so on.]

Voice-over: They came from across the globe, Book Clubbers ready to take the 2004 Anna Karenina Challenge—eight long sections, 817 pages, twenty-three complicated Russian names. The only thing they had to fear was fear itself. They would battle elements. Summer heat. Busy family schedules. . . . Could they do it? Could they conquer Tolstoy?

[Cut to: Studio, where the "marathon" Book Clubbers rush onto the stage surrounding Oprah, chanting, "Anna! Anna! Anna!" as they hold their copies over their heads. Oprah urges them on.]

Oprah: You're beautiful. Thank you. OK. Oh, great, guys. Nice enthusiasm. OK. These are cute T-shirts, and the front says, "I wasn't scared!" That's because when I first announced the book, I said to everybody, "Like, don't be scared [pronounced *skerred*]. You did it! And on the back it says, "Anna Karenina Summer 2004." Fantastic. I know. Were there times, though when you thought you couldn't finish it? All the time? [Laughter] I have to say that this summer I was with my trainer Bob Green, and every time he'd say, "What are you doing for the rest of the afternoon?" I'd go, "Finish *Anna Karenina*." It's like a running joke in my house. Next our star-studded Book Club signs up a famous funny member. And later, where in the world are we going to go next? Our brand new book. We'll be right back.

Notice here the assertion that she's *just like* her Clubbers, slugging through the novel just like they did, the coach who does calisthenics with the team. Her affirmation of solidarity with the other Clubbers new to Tolstoy, especially the moms who hadn't read a novel since high school and pushed their babies in strollers as they trudged on through the novel, could hardly be more emphasized, at least until she tells us about her conversation with her personal trainer, which puts her on a somewhat different plane—the megacelebrity who is doing this because she just loves reading so much. The fear of the squiggles is acknowledged (especially since there are so many of them, 817 [!] pages' worth), but what is more strongly affirmed is that the fear was overcome together, with Oprah (a recovered fearful reader).

[Commercial Break]

[Plot synopsis feature: Montage of images from the *Exxon Masterpiece Theatre* production of *Anna Karenina*, accompanied by disembodied voice of Oprah telling the story of the novel, and speaking lines of significant dialogue related to the images onscreen. (Quoted lines are italicized.)]

Oprah's voice-over: From the famous first line, "*All happy families are alike; each unhappy family is unhappy in its own way*," Tolstoy captures us instantly in his web of lust, deceit, infidelity, and unbridled passions. Our tragic heroine, Anna Karenina betrays her husband and begins a fated romance with Count Vronsky, a handsome young soldier.
"*Your husband is an important man. There will be a scandal!*"
Their torrid love affair erupts when Anna's husband confronts her.
"*I'm his mistress. I hate you!*"
She then reveals her scandalous secret.
"*I'm pregnant.*"
"*We'll say the child is mine. Dear God!*"
Anna is faced with a decision no mother wants to make. It will haunt her for the rest of her days.
"*Things will go on as before, but you will lose your son!*"
[Child's voice] "*Please don't go!*"
Unable to live in the world she created . . .
"*I've given up everything for you!*"
And incapable of living without Vronsky . . .
"*You're destroying me!*"
Anna unravels, and Tolstoy leaves us with a searing glimpse of a tortured soul.

The incorporation of footage from the *Masterpiece Theatre* production, combined with this voice-over, sums up the Oprah Book Club like an epigram, because the reading experience is visualized two times over—we watch a television production of the novel within another television show dedicated to the successful reading of the novel. This is the world of Merchant-Ivory reimagined by Margaret Mitchell on daytime television. The decorative tastefulness of *Masterpiece Theatre* is retained, but also transformed. The plot points may come from Tolstoy, but the overheated, lustful language translates him into genre romance, with a difference. Yet this is lust for reading *mothers*, the Clubbers who, we've already been told, may not have read a book since high school and have been seen pushing baby carriages while reading their copies of *Anna Karenina*. Now we know why! This is a novel, but rather than reading passages aloud, Oprah narrates the television images, transforming the novel into a hybrid, teleliterary experience that is as much about watching as it is about reading.

[Cut to: Celebrity guest-reader interview.]

Oprah [talking directly to audience]: I'm looking at all the people who weren't scared. Our newest Book Club member is Megan Mullally, hilarious star of *Will and Grace*. Welcome Megaaaaan! Take a look.

[Cut to: Videotape interview with Megan Mullally. Montage of shots featuring her assuming various reading postures around her apartment. She holds up her copy, littered with Post-it notes marking key passages.]

Disembodied voice of Oprah: We can see that Megan is a girl who likes to be prepared.

Megan: I just want to point out the nerd factor happening here, the notes up the side of the page. I'm ready for my quiz.

Voice of Oprah: Hey, Megan, this is not a test, but we do want to know what you thought of our Book Club Pick?

Megan: I heartily recommend it to one and all because it's so rich. It's pretty great. There were times when I must admit, because it is 817 pages long, that I wasn't sure if I was going to make it. But you can't wait to get back to the story.

Voice of Oprah: And what does Megan think of Anna the tragic heroine?

Megan: The whole, like breakdown, Anna Karenina's entire like mental unraveling is really interesting. [Shot of Megan underlining passages in her copy as she reads.] Of course, now she'd just like take some Paxil and it would all be good, but they didn't have those mood stabilizers back then, apparently.

Voice of Oprah: And to those book lovers who have not finished?

Megan: It is a little intimidating, but it's worth it, and because of that it's rich and it really does give you a full sense of human nature that's universal.

Voice of Oprah: And for Book Club members who might want further study?

Megan: Well, you can just attend my college course that I'll be teaching at Yale if you have any further questions on the material. [Big laugh from studio audience.]

Oprah: That's Megan Mullally. Thank you, Megan. You can watch Megan on *Will and Grace*, one of our favorite shows, on Thursdays on NBC. Next, we're just minutes away from revealing our next book. And it's easy. It's easy. I thought you needed a break. It's fascinating. You'll be happy I picked it.

The celebrity guest-reader is introduced to the audience just as she would be on a talk show, complete with plugs for her television series at the beginning and end of her interview. The Book Club segment at this point familiarizes Tolstoy three times over — as a book that another celebrity reads just like you did, a familiar person from a popular television series you've seen before, interviewed as though she were a guest on a talk show like *Rosie O'Donnell* or *David Letterman* that you've seen throughout your entire life. Within that all-too-familiar world, the idea of reading in *school* becomes a source of humor; as Megan has exam anxiety, Oprah assures her this not that kind of book discussion (no evaluation of your reading will be done here), and then she jokes about teaching a course on Tolstoy at an elite university. Yet, between the ironic remarks about reading done in a school setting, there is another assertion of an almost reverential seriousness about the book as an experience that gives you a "full sense of human nature that's universal" and therefore needs annotations in the form of Post-it notes and underlining of key passages, just as one reads a classic novel for a class.

Oprah closes this segment by assuring her Clubbers that they will approve of her next selection, the supremely confident curator who "knows what you'll like."

[Cut to: Public service announcement for the Angel Network. Sudden introduction of another video segment featuring montage of Russian orphans, accompanied by Oprah's voice-over.]

Oprah: In honor of our Book Club selection *Anna Karenina*, we are proud to announce that our $50,000 Angel Network Award goes to a culture project in St. Petersburg, Russia. Thousands and thousands of storybooks written in Russian will be making their way to these children who have so very little. Together with your help, our Book Club and the Angel Network are bringing the joys of reading to boys and girls all over the world — one book at a time, and I thank you for it!

Here Oprah becomes not just the nation's, but the world's librarian, as she spreads the joys of reading in an overtly philanthropic manner, sounding like a contemporary, televisual version of Andrew Carnegie. She brings books to the people, for free. Here we could not be further from the world of commercial-driven television and the commodification of books. But then, suddenly, she thanks someone else.

> *Oprah* [back in studio, talking directly to us]: Thanks to all of you who have logged on to Oprah.com and shopped our boutique. I want to show you the newest addition to our line. These are cute. They're cute little pink pajamas, little pajamas that say Oprah's Book Club on the pocket. [Applause.] They're little pink checks [Close-ups of pocket with logo, then Web site catalogue picture] with a little lace trim. I designed these with Karen Neuburger. OK? So if you'd like some to get cozy you can wear these all day and not take your pajamas off and just curl up.

At this point, the philanthropist becomes saleswoman and the program changes from a Save the Children charitable appeal to the Shopping Channel, complete with close-ups of the product and voice-over descriptions of its selling points. The marketplace has invaded the library, but apparently there is no sense of a contradiction lurking anywhere on the premises. While Oprah may not actually have any financial interest in the books being read, she does sell the accoutrements for all that reading, a line of reading clothes at her own boutique. There's more than reading tips at this Web site. Oprah is a full-service oral performer, selecting the books, narrating the story, providing "handy-dandy reading strategies," acting as our good-will ambassador to the world in need of books, even designing the right clothes to wear while reading those selections. By this point, the fact that this reading community is also a target audience, and that both are being cultivated carefully, is explicitly acknowledged by the program.

> [Cut to: Announcement of the next Book Club Selection. Oprah on stage, surrounded by boxes of books with "Top Secret" printed on the side.]

> *Oprah*: OK. You know what these top secret boxes mean. The Pulitzer Prize–winning novel I'm about to reveal was written by a Nobel Peace Prize–winning American author. That's a big clue. You can

do anything now that you've read *Anna Karenina*. So really don't be scared. It's a sweeping saga that's been called a universal tale of the destiny of man. It's also juicy as all get out, so it has a concubine [breaks into comical "black" voice]—that always helps when you got a couple of concubines, got a couple of concubines, and you got me. It's got affairs, vicious family feuds, and this novel's going to keep you up at night and it will not take you a long time to read it. It's really, really good because it's *The Good Earth* by Pearl S. Buck. It's solid. You've read it before? Well, read it again! We'll be right back.

The announcement epitomizes all of the main features of this textual community's way of talking the talk of reading literary books. Here again we find the rocketing back and forth between reverence for the classic and ironic undercutting of any seriousness complete with concubine jokes in comical black voice. This is a book that has *two* pedigrees, so it must be worth reading, especially since it too can be made to sound like a lost Margaret Mitchell novel. And it's another one of those "universal tales about the destiny of man" that must be something like a novel that gives you "a full sense of human nature that's universal." Least anyone make light of this appeal to universality as a transcendent characteristic of literary greatness, remember how important universality and oneness were for Harold Bloom: "Read deeply, not to believe, not to accept, not to contradict, but to learn to share in that *one nature* that writes and reads." Bloom and Oprah know something about the connection between universal tales and appealing to mass audiences.

The program concludes with an announcement from the host that reiterates one last time the complicated, ambivalent relationship between the reading one does in the Book Club and the sort of reading one does in school. The latter may be deserving of ironic disdain, but it nevertheless provides a high degree of legitimacy in terms of title selections.

Oprah: So we just announced our new book, *The Good Earth*, by Pearl S. Buck. Head out to your bookstore today and get your copy. There are plenty in the libraries. And log on to Oprah.com—print out this handy-dandy character guide. There it is on your screen. You'll also have a map of China and a reading strategy. So we're going from Russia to China. We're now in China. OK? Now we have some special guests who are going to help me out. Our Book Club elves today are all honor students from Mrs. Fredney's Advanced English class at Marion High School on the South Side of Chicago. They'll be reading *The Good Earth* this fall in class. Come on out, elves. Bring on the books for everybody, all of you honor elves. 'Bye, everybody. Happy reading! Join us for OxyGen. Barry Manilow will be right back. Thank you.

Here Oprah brings on the books for everybody, the national librarian handing out books to audience members as if they were so many Russian orphans. She directs them to bookstores (go *today*) but also to libraries—her lack of financial gain in all this being reiterated one last time. Here too she brings together her Clubbers and AP English students, the reading community at Amazon that was definitely not reading the titles that Oprah and company read, at least until the return of her Book Club, and she began choosing exactly the sort of novels they read in high school AP English classes.

Bibliotherapy and Taste Therapy

Throughout this segment, Oprah's power as oral performer for this community of readers depends on more than her ability to function as kindly librarian. To return to Hartley's research on British reading groups, she does not comment specifically on the Oprah effect, but she argues that one of the chief differences between British and American reading groups is that the latter places far greater emphasis on the therapeutic dimensions of reading:

> Many of the groups contributing to Ellen Slezak's *Book Group Book* would agree—"While the books remain our reason for meeting we have become the story"—whereas I suspect most UK groups would disagree loudly. This is where British and US groups diverge most. The reading lists which Slezak has collected from US groups have books on psychology and personal growth which very rarely appear on British lists. And in America reading together and self-help have taken yet another logical step in a healing art which is relatively unknown in the UK. *Read Two Books and Let's Talk Next Week* is the title of a collection of essays by mental health practitioners devoted to bibliotherapy using reading as a tool to assist the therapeutic process. (114)

Hartley does not pursue this argument, but a comparison between the Oprah Book Club and bibliotherapy can be very productive in terms of specifying the hybrid nature of that talk and the role Oprah plays as within that reading culture as public explicator. This is not to suggest that Oprah is simply engaging in bibliotherapy on a grand, televisual scale because the points of divergence are as revealing as the points of convergence. In *Read Two Books*, for example, the authors Janice Maidman Joshua and Donna Di-Menna, organize their book in terms of clinical problems—domestic abuse, adult children of alcoholics, and so on—and offer summaries of relevant self-help books under each rubric without mentioning any fictional titles whatsoever. In *Bibliotherapy, the Interactive Process: A Handbook* (1986), Arleen Hynes (founder of the first hospital-based training program in bibliotherapy in 1974 at St. Elizabeths Hospital in Washington) and Mary Hynes-Berry advocate the use of fictional titles but stress the difference between bibliotherapy and book groups, insisting that the former is devoted to therapeutic development of the individual, while the latter is "more a literature class" and therefore is more concerned with aesthetic issues. According to the distinctions they draw between reading for bibliotherapeutic reasons and reading for a class, the Oprah Book Club appears to straddle those categories and complicate any hard-and-fast distinctions between them. They argue:

> In a class, the interaction takes place between the student–literature-teacher; the literature is usually considered to be the object of discussion rather than a tool. The teacher's goal is to help the student achieve some insight into the meaning and value of the work as written. Discussion might focus on historical context, nature of the genre, structure, use of imagery or language, or presentation of dominant values. In bibliotherapy, however, the value of the literature depends strictly on its capacity to encourage a therapeutic response from the participants. The individual's feeling-response is more important than an intellectual grasp of the work's meaning. Thus, in bibliotherapy even a misinterpretation of the text will be considered both legitimate and useful if it leads to the release of feelings or insights related to self-understanding. In other words, the use of literature in bibliotherapy reflects the goals of therapy rather than those of education. (43)

Even a quick visit to the Oprah Book Club Web site reveals a hybrid mixture of both ways of reading, a concerted effort to provide information about the meaning of the work as in a class (interviews with authors or experts, short analyses of different aspects of the novel, maps of reading strategies, etc.) and other material that moves in the direction of reading as self-realization. But the distinctions between bibliotherapy and the Oprah Book Club become even harder to draw in reference to the role of the *facilitator*, the figure who, for Hynes and Hynes-Berry, is both the linchpin for genuinely interactive bibliotherapy and what separates it from pleasure or academic reading. They acknowledge the traditional role of the librarian as provider of readers' advisory services but stress the differences between librarian and the facilitator:

> In the early 1920s, some librarians made a point of searching out and offering reading materials specifically for their therapeutic potential. . . . Since then, numerous librarians, counselors, English teachers, and social workers have compiled lists and made suggestions for reading they believe will help an individual's growth or offer insight into a personal crisis. . . . We do not mean to suggest that recommended readings cannot serve therapeutic ends. On the contrary, there are many cases in which a librarian, teacher, or counselor's thoughtful suggestion has provided a reader with just the right book—a work that triggered a significant and growth-producing feeling-response to some need. The point is that the interaction takes place between the reader and the work and does not directly involve the person who made the suggestion. . . . In other words, in this mode—which can be identified as interactive bibliotherapy— the process of growth and healing is centered not as much in the act of reading as in the *guided dialogue* about the material. In effect, the triad of *participant-literature-facilitator* means that there is a dual interaction: The participant's personal response to the story is important, but dialoguing with the facilitator about that response can lead to a whole new dimension of insight. (125, emphasis mine)

Given this account, Oprah is not just the well-intentioned librarian but a master facilitator, since a triadic relationship is the foundation of her Book Club—this is *guided* reading that takes place in a kind of imagined dialogue with the facilitator. She is not like the librarian who merely recommends a good read and then discreetly fades out of the picture. She narrates *Anna Karenina* during one key segment of the Book Club show, but throughout the program she remains the narrator of *their* story as Book Club readers of the novel. This is not to suggest that this kind of guided reading is as attuned to the needs of the individual participant as a formal therapeutic situation would be, but the emphasis is as much on soliciting feeling-responses and shaping them into narrative form as it is on knowledge of the work as such. Given the frequent discussion of self-help books and therapeutic experiences involving a wide variety of problems on her programs, the cultivation of feeling-responses of a nonliterary sort has been a distinguishing feature of the program since its inception. Oprah's Book Club is so successful because it facilitates reading as a form of self-cultivation that combines the formerly antagonistic, making knowledge of the work and knowledge of one's own feeling-responses equally legitimate and somehow mutually reinforcing.

It would be easy to argue that Oprah puts the "self" in the self-culture of reading, but the incorporation of information about the work reveals a need to provide the inside scoop, the information needed to read confidently, knowing that this is a genuine educational experience and therefore, a meaningful form of self-cultivation. The interplay between the two only intensified when Oprah restarted the Book Club in 2004, with literary classics such as *East of Eden*, *The Heart Is a Lonely Hunter*, *One Hundred Years of Solitude*, and *Anna Karenina*, exactly the sort of canonical books found on the lists of the AP English students at Amazon, the readers who were learning about the works and provided their own feeling-responses unfacilitated by their English teachers. The need to respect the literary work, even when it might mean a loss of authority about feeling-responses, became especially clear with the choice of *Anna Karenina*. Here the work is respected to the point of awe, but it is worthy of reading because "all of us" are reading it together—Oprah's authority as a facilitator is only intensified by her admission that, like you, she hasn't read it but she's heading the expedition into the wilds of nineteenth-century Russian fiction, and readers never doubt that they are in good hands because of that admission. Likewise, she tells her audience that even if they have read *The Good Earth* before, they should read it again, because reading it together with other Clubbers, facilitated by Oprah, will produce a profoundly different experience from any previous, unfacilitated reading.

In order to appreciate the nature of Oprah's authority as literary tastemaker who is both an authority and one of us, I think it's useful to compare her to two other taste mavens who have brought what were formerly thought to be elite tastes to a mass audience—Martha Stewart and Robert Parker Jr. All three have gained unprecedented influence by making refined taste into popular taste, whether it be for literary fiction, "home keeping," or wine appreciation, but the nature of the expertise, and its relationship to the marketplace, is quite different in each case. Like Oprah, Stewart provides lessons in connoisseurship that allow the uninitiated to gain confidence about formerly intimidating cultural pleasures at warp speed. And Stewart is also a facilitator of sorts, showing viewers how to transform their feeling-responses into room decorating, antique collecting, and gardening skills step by step, in implied dialogue form. But while Stewart is there *with* you, televisually speaking she's not one of *us*, for her superiority is never in doubt; she has deigned to share her secrets with viewers, but those power relations remain firmly in place. And unlike Oprah, Stewart's expertise is commodified two times over—first, as vital information delivered via her television program, magazine, and Web site, and then as consumer goods, which allow for the realization of that taste advice via purchases from her catalogue, her Web site, or K-Mart, where Martha Stewart's Everyday Collection is available nationwide. The Oprah Book Club, on the other hand, does not sell the books it selects via Harpo, Inc. It refers readers to books published by other commercial interests within the marketplace, thereby allowing Oprah's recommendations to be untainted by financial gain. Granted, it offers paraphernalia related to the Book Club at the Web site (T-shirts, those cozy pajamas, etc.), but the guided reading experience is "free."

In its ability to inspire the sale of millions of books yet retain a purely advisory/facilitator function apart from the filthy lucre of the publishing industry, the Oprah Book Club resembles Robert M. Parker Jr.'s wine newsletter, *The Wine Advocate*, which has had every bit as profound an impact on wine drinking in the United States as Oprah enjoys in the publishing world. Parker's newsletter is entirely subscriber-supported, taking no advertisements because they would jeopardize the consumer advocate nature of the publication, a point insisted upon in the mission statement printed on the cover of every issue: "*The Wine Advocate*, first published in 1978, relentlessly pursues the goal of providing valuable, uncensored, totally independent and reliable information on wine and issues affecting wine quality to those consumers in search of the finest wines and best wine values." Parker's expertise, like Oprah's, floats above commercial interests and introduces, at the same time, a new language of connoisseurship articulated in terms of hedonistic pleasures that the right wine provides to new mass audiences of quality wine drinkers. This language of connoisseurship combines knowledge of wine as *a work of art* (copious details about varietals, wine makers, vintages, residual sugar levels, etc.) with abundant descriptions about taste expressed in decidedly nonelitist terms (e.g., "mind-blowing," "a staggering fruit bomb of a wine," "gobs of fruit," and frequent incorporation of lyrics from Neil Young songs in the section titles). While wine connoisseurship was, for centuries, an elite taste restricted to the upper classes, in which the knowledge of wine was handed down just like a wine cellar, Parker's readers can acquire that cultural expertise, but only if they are driven by *wine lust* rather than snobbery. Yet within that realm there is no question about who has the master palate. He evaluates for us, and as in the case of Stewart, a loyal audience pays for that expertise, even if Parker sells no wine himself. (When he did acquire a one-third interest in an Oregon vineyard in 1992, a disclaimer was added to the mission statement: "Because of an obvious conflict of interest, the wine produced from this vineyard will never be mentioned or reviewed in anything written by Robert M. Parker Jr.") While Parker may stand apart from the industry as the champion for the readers he initiates into the delights of wine appreciation through his own nationwide, taste delivery system, Parker's expertise is not offered free to all who might listen; a subscription to *The Wine Advocate* is currently two to three times more expensive than that of any American food magazines such as *Bon Appetit* and *Food and Wine*. Knowledge about taste may be acquired rather than inherited, but it's still a commodity for sale.

The Corrections *Controversy: A National Referendum on Literary Authority*

Oprah's status as America's librarian/facilitator depends on a form of cultural authority that is both nonelitist (she's one of us, she hasn't read *Anna Karenina* either) and noncommercial (she's not selling any books, just encouraging people to take delight in reading as a way of learning about themselves). Because of that status, her conflict with Jonathan Franzen became a kind of national referendum on the legitimacy of popular literary culture in the United States. Once it was selected by the Oprah Book Club, Franzen's novel *The Corrections* (2002), became a bestseller within hours and remained the bestselling book in America for weeks thereafter. On the face of it, this would have seemed like the perfect realization of the author's dream of bringing the "social novel" back to a broad general readership, that audience beyond the priesthood that John Barth argued literary fiction would have to connect with if it were to have a future. But when Franzen expressed misgivings about the impact that the Club Selection would have on his book he was disinvited from the television program, at which point the story became front-page news in the *New York Times* and the subject of dozens of articles and opinion pieces on television, radio, and print publications. In the surprisingly vociferous controversy that ensued, Oprah and Franzen were very quickly made into exemplars of the two figures that have loomed over self-cultivation for over a century—the librarian, who brings knowledge to the people, and the modernist artist, who creates genuine art and therefore must avoid the taint of anything that smacks of mass culture. What was at stake in the controversy, at the most fundamental level, was just who literary culture belonged to, who could function as its experts, and who got to be a player in the game of serious reading.

That Franzen was insistent upon maintaining his status as latter-day modernist novelist could hardly have been more explicit, given his explanation of why he felt uncomfortable as an author in Oprah's Book Club: "I feel like I'm solidly in the high-art literary tradition. She's picked some good books, but she's picked enough schmaltzy, one-dimensional [ones] that I cringe, myself, even though I think she's really smart and she's really fighting the good fight" (Franzen here sounding uncannily like the Virginia Woolf who said, "If anyone calls me middle-brow, I shall stab them with my pen"). The interview where Franzen offered these remarks, in 2004, was published, not coincidentally, within the realm of official literary culture—the Web site for Powell's Bookstore, one of the best known independent bookstores in America. He was also bothered by the Oprah sticker on the cover of *The Corrections*: "I'm an independent writer and I didn't want that corporate logo on my book" (quoted in *Oregonian* 12 [2002]). Franzen had already articulated his contempt for what he called "technological consumerism" in his manifesto "Why Bother?," an essay that originally appeared in *Harper's* magazine in 1996, well before the publication of *The Corrections*. There he marshaled most of the time-honored charges leveled against mass culture, inveighing against the "cultural totalitarianism" at work in a country that "grows ever more distracted and mesmerized by mass culture," where culture is overrun by the marketplace. Television, of course, is one of his chief targets; in his essay he refers to "the banal ascendancy of television, the electronic fragmentation of public discourse" (58). This fragmentation is inevitable because television is driven solely by consumerism: "In the world of consumer advertising and consumer purchasing, no evil is moral. . . . [T]he only problems worth advertising solutions for are problems treatable through the spending of money" (69, in *How to Be Alone*). Most horrifying of all, this is a world in which "publishing is now a subsidiary of Hollywood, and the blockbuster novel is a mass-marketable commodity, a portable substitute for TV" (85). This diatribe on the evils of mass culture as nothing more than commodity fetishism (at which point, anything on television is, ipso facto, part of a corporate conspiracy and, therefore, the antithesis of genuine culture) obviously plays well with Powell's shoppers, since it has functioned as the old-time religion of official literary culture for decades ("It was good for Adorno's children and it's good enough for me! Sing it with me now! Gimme that old time . . ."). This mass culture bashing reaches its zenith in Franzen's particular rendition of the old hymn: "The feeling of oppositionality is compounded in an age when simply picking up a novel after dinner represents a kind of cultural *je refuse!*" (90).

But just how does that *je refuse* business actually work? Does it depend on the type of fiction being read? Or the intellectual class formation of the reader? When Oprah's viewers pick up *One Hundred Years of Solitude* after dinner, do they refuse the evils of mass culture even if they are reading that novel because it was recommended to them by a mass culture celebrity who has made literary novels into instant blockbusters, reading a copy they've bought at superstore bookstores out at the mall or down on the strip, reading a story they may see eventually as a Hollywood adaptation at the multiplex across the parking lot from that superstore? And if it doesn't constitute the proper *je refuse*, why doesn't it? Is it due to the quality of the novel, or the quality of the readers? Or is it because they are common readers rather than the uncommon readers who share that certain "oppositionality"?

One of the most insightful opinion pieces offered during the controversy, one that was predicated on a quite different conception of reading, appeared in *Library Journal* in 2002. The journal's editor, Francine Fialkoff, saw Franzen's discomfort as a missed opportunity. She begins by introducing the term "book bait," what librarians once called books they gathered to entice young readers, "built on the wisdom of public librarians who understood that it doesn't matter what young adults read as long as they do read." She quotes Frances Perkins's *Special Report on Public Libraries in the United States*, written in 1876: "The *habit of reading* is indispensable. That habit once established it is a recognized fact that readers go from poor to better sorts of reading." Those who intend to organize a public library for popular reading, and who intend to exclude trash, may as well stop before they begin. Fialkoff argues:

If only Franzen were familiar with library history and philosophy. . . . In the frenzy of his misgivings Franzen blew the opportunity to bring the gap between popular, or middle-brow fiction, and his own "high-art literary tradition." . . . Given the concerns he expressed in his *Harper's* essay about the demise of the social novel, the novel of manners, how wonderful it would have been had Franzen appeared on Oprah's show to talk about just such a novel. Librarians have shown us that one way to create high-brows out of middle-brows is to give readers avenues they can be comfortable with and that's what Oprah's Book Club does. The Oprah appearance would have given Franzen access to an even broader readership than he already has, and it may have helped elevate the reading tastes of some of those viewers. (52)

Within Fialkoff's conception of this habit of reading, the excesses of consumerism are irrelevant; elevating tasting and the increased access it requires apparently neutralizes the harmful effects of consumerism just as certainly as they contaminated all they touched within the discourse of the high-art literary tradition. For Franzen, as was the case with Woolf, Leavis, and company, the habit of reading is not enough—there's reading, but then there's *reading*. In the concluding section of "Why Bother?" Franzen recounts his conversations with Shirley Brice Heath concerning who reads, and why they acquire that habit. In her research on the readers of "substantive works of fiction," Heath found that two things have to be in place: first, the habit of reading such books had to be heavily modeled when they were very young by parents who read serious books and encouraged them to do the same; and second, young readers had to find a person with whom they could share their interest. As for the former, class was an important determinant in inculcating this habit of reading, but according to Franzen's account of Heath's work,

Class matters less in other parts of the country, especially in the Protestant Midwest, where literature is seen as a way to exercise the mind. As Heath put it, "Part of the exercise of being a good person is not using your time frivolously. You have to be able to account for yourself through the work ethic and through the wise use of your leisure time." For a century after the Civil War, the Midwest was home to thousands of small-town literary societies in which, Heath found, the wife of a janitor was as likely to be active as the wife of a doctor. (78)

While Franzen obviously offers this as evidence of the halcyon days of a once-vital reading culture in America that now no longer exists (or at least, that he didn't seem to think existed in 1996), it does not lead him to appreciate comparable reading societies—namely, book clubs—in the contemporary period. What fascinates Franzen in his conversation with Heath is her characterization of *another* type of reader. He tells Heath that reading was never modeled for him, that he couldn't remember either of his parents ever reading a book, except aloud, and to him. "Without missing a beat Heath replied: 'Yes, but there's a second kind of reader. There's the social isolate—the child who from an early age felt very different from everyone around him. . . . What happens is you take that sense of being different into an imaginary world. But in that world, then, is a world you can't share with the people around you—because it's imaginary. And so the important dialogue in your life is with the *authors* of the books you read. Though they aren't present, they become your community" (77). Franzen sees himself as this second kind of reader, especially when Heath tells him that readers of the social-isolate variety are much more likely to become writers than those of the modeled habit variety.

Heath's categories are extremely useful in delineating not just different types of readers but the radically different kinds of reading communities that the librarian and modernist writer envision. For Oprah and her viewer-readers, reading is a *social* act in which the talking about a book together is one of the preconditions for pleasurable reading. Even though the discussion may take place on television or at the Web site, the actuality of that community is repeatedly reiterated and celebrated as one of its most appealing features. As a social-isolate reader, Franzen had no need for such a community, because such interaction is at best superfluous, and at worst, destructive of his oppositionality. The title of the collection of essays that includes "Why Bother?" is, after all *How to Be Alone*. Franzen could have functioned in Oprah's reading community only as an author, and not as a fellow reader of good books, a point made quite clear in an interview on National Public Radio by his dismissal of some of her "schmaltzy" selections, which made him "cringe" and, even more tellingly, by his characterization of her program as a "coffee klatch." The inherent misogyny in such a term echoes the modernist rejection of women's culture as mass culture at its most vapid, a point explored compellingly by Kathleen Fitzpatrick (in *The Anxiety of Obsolescence*, 2006) in her assessment of the controversy: "This battle between the literary and the televisual pits the white male literary humanist against the black female producer of mass media, each vying for control of the cultural arena. Television's democratizing reach is dangerous to the novelist in part because of the power it wields to level disparities in access to cultural products, exposing the writer to the scrutiny—and, indeed, the judgment of others who may not be like-minded" (205). This interplay between gender difference and a "like-mindedness" dependent upon intellectual class distinctions explains Franzen's reluctance to appear in the wrong sort of reading community and observe its protocols, a context in which he might have served as oral performer but not a codiscussant.

The incommensurability of these two different reading communities becomes apparent in Franzen's admission: "I'll encounter two kinds of readers in signing lines and in interviews. One kind will say to me, essentially, 'I like your book and I think it's wonderful that Oprah picked it,' the other kind will say, 'I like your book and I'm so sorry that Oprah picked it.' And because I'm a person who instantly acquires a Texas accent in Texas, I'll respond in kind to each reader. When I talk to admirers of Winfrey, I'll experience a glow of gratitude and good will and agree that it's wonderful to see television expanding the audience for books. When I talk to detractors of Winfrey, I'll complain about the Book Club logo" (75). In her assessment of the book lovers' quarrel that erupted over *The Corrections* and Oprah, Laura Miller emphasizes the same opposition:

America's book culture too often seems composed of two resentful camps, hunkered down in their foxholes. Lobbing the occasional grenade at each other and nursing grievances. One side sees itself as scorned by a snotty self-styled elite and the other sees itself as keepers of the literary flame, neglected by a vulgarian mainstream that would rather wallow in mediocrity and dreck. Each side remains exquisitely sensitive to perceived rejection from the other and the fact that one is often characterized as female and the other as male resonates with the edgy relations between the sexes of late. This divide in the reading public is also the place where submerged class anxieties of American life flare up. Conversations about books are often rife with silly agendas, each speaker intent on indicating how high (or, in the case of contrarians, low) his or her brow can go. ("Book Lovers' Quarrel," 2)

Miller delineates effectively where the battle lines are drawn here, but the ability that each camp has to see itself as superior is due to the fact that each is empowered by its own metanarrative, in Lyotard's conception of the term—narratives that legitimize their own authority in terms of the pleasures and goals of reading, and at the same time, delegitimize any conflicting metanarratives. In this sense, Oprah and Franzen are each powerful metanarrators of their respective grand traditions of Uplift and Oppositionality. Each promises a very particular sort of self-cultivation, because each produces its own type of knowledge about literature. Lyotard makes this crucial point:

> Knowledge is not only a set of denotative statements, far from it. It also includes notions of "know-how," "knowing how to live," "how to listen" (savoir-faire, savoir-vivre, savoir-écouter). Knowledge, then, is a question of competence that goes beyond the simple determination of and application of the criterion of truth. . . . Understood in this way, knowledge is what makes someone capable of making "good" denotative utterances, but also "good" prescriptive and "good" evaluative utterances. From this derives one of the principal features of knowledge: it coincides with an extensive array of competence building measures. (74)

Elite literary culture has had, since its institutionalization within the academy decades ago, a vast arsenal of such confidence-building measures, but popular literary culture, embodied by Oprah's Book Club, has been able to mobilize an impressive array of competence-building measures of its own within just the past decade, largely because it has outflanked traditional literary cultures in terms of its ability to deliver knowledge articulated in terms of knowing how to live and knowing how to listen.

Miller feels that it is unfortunate that the two book cultures cannot overcome their mutual animosity, but their mutual disrespect is inevitable, given the mutually incommensurable nature of these metanarratives of reading. While Lyotard may have famously defined the postmodern as the incredulity toward such all-encompassing metanarratives, I believe it is equally accurate to say that such incredulity is indeed omnipresent, except in regard to the metanarrative one subscribes to in order to give value to the way one improves oneself. Given the loss of respect for the academy as custodian of the gold standard of literary value by so many millions of readers outside the academy, and given the number of competence-building mechanisms mobilized by both popular and traditional literary cultures, incredulity is indeed endemic, but only toward the *other* literary culture, given how self-sufficient each metanarrative has become in empowering readers to feel fully engaged in the act of genuine self-cultivation. That the conflict between the two literary cultures should be a zero-sum game, rather than peaceful coexistence, is presented in no uncertain terms by Franzen in his essay "The Reader in Exile" (2002). The opening sentence makes this clear: "A few months ago, I gave away my television set." He felt this was essential because, as long as it was on the premises, he says, "I wasn't reading books." He pursues this either/or dichotomy even more forcefully in the next paragraph:

> For every reader who dies today, a viewer is born, and we seem to be witnessing here in the anxious mid-nineties, the final tipping of a balance. For critics inclined to alarmism, the shift from a culture based on the printed word to a culture based on virtual images—a shift that began with television and is now being completed with computers—feels apocalyptic. (165)

But for whom is it apocalyptic? What about the readers who are also viewers? Surely not the readers who think that giving away your television so you'll be able to read more is just too quaint for words. That we've reached another sort of "tipping point" not foreseen by Franzen's essay became overwhelmingly clear to me when I discussed the Franzen-Oprah controversy with the students in my postmodern narrative course in the spring of 2005. I had them read *The Corrections*, along with "Why Bother?" and "The Reader in Exile," and I showed them the *Anna Karenina* program. I want to conclude this chapter by discussing their reactions to both Franzen and Oprah, because I think their responses suggest a great deal about tipping points, given who they are and what they're in the process of becoming. Since I've been focusing on the roles played by the Reader, the Librarian, and the Author within popular literary culture throughout these first chapters, I wanted to bring back the Professor, or in this case the Professors-in-Training to get a sense of how they situate themselves in that controversy.

The class was a mix of graduate students in English and advanced undergraduates in film and television. Most of them characterized themselves as solitary readers, at least as far as literary fiction was concerned—few had come from homes where reading literary fiction was a modeled behavior. They all had two things in common: they had all been in AP English classes in high school and, while they had seen Oprah's television show from time to time, none of them had ever watched a Book Club episode. In the preliminary discussion before we began watching the episode, I asked them about their perceptions of the Book Club "going in." They were uniformly positive, if a trifle condescending. None of them ever contemplated becoming a member ("It's not intended for us, so why would we?"), but just about everyone had a mother, grandmother, aunt, or cousin who was a Clubber and they thought this was generally a positive development (e.g., "Anything that keeps my mother from watching *Fox News* is great, as far as I'm concerned"). The consensus that developed, then, was benevolent approval of Oprah and an affirmation of the "uplift" position. This is a good thing, and if it's not all that sophisticated, so be it— "She's getting people to read, and that's the toughest job we have to do."

As they began to watch an actual book club segment for the first time, their approval started to fade. Things began to go badly as soon as Barry Manilow sang (mispronouncing), "Anna, Anna Karen-ni-ni-na," and then Oprah did the same fool thing, apparently affiliating more with Barry than Leo at that point. As the segment progressed the students grew surly. Their comments:

"When are they actually going to get down to it and talk about the novel?"

"This is like watching a Weight Watchers infomercial. It's all about mutual affirmation and feeling good about yourself. What are they learning about reading literature?"

"It doesn't seem to make any difference whether they're jogging together or reading together—it's all about belonging. Tolstoy is just the McGuffin."

"I'm glad you showed us the video, because if you had just told us about the pajamas routine I would've thought you were making it all up."

"And now they're off to China! Bon voyage, girls! This isn't about reading, it's all about tourism."

By the end if the program, widespread skepticism replaced benign approval as the new consensus. As a discussion leader/oral interpreter extraordinaire, Oprah "wasn't doing it right," because they weren't "learning" anything about the book. But something else became just as apparent—this was not the students' taste culture. Reading here was intertwined so explicitly with tastes in music, clothing, and entertainment that they realized that what was called reading within that world was simply not the same activity as it was for them. My students were passionate readers too, but they wanted nothing to do with these Weight-Watching, Barry-Manilow-listening, Tolstoy-reading Clubbers. For reading to count as meaningful activity in their eyes, it couldn't become so thoroughly bound up with such bad taste in other forms of cultural expression. If *Barry Manilow's Scores* was in the CD player, their Tolstoy had already left the building.

The next class was the first day of the Franzen unit, and, given the way they'd reacted to the *Anna Karenina* show, I expected them to affiliate enthusiastically with Franzen, who was a member of their taste culture—or so I thought. But the more we discussed these essays, the more they *dis*affiliated from him. They certainly couldn't see themselves in one of those "I'm Not Scared" T-shirts chanting along with the rest of the Clubbers, but they couldn't see themselves in the team photo of Franzen's imagined community of book lovers either. If anything, they were even more determined to put distance between themselves and Franzen when we discussed "The Reader in Exile." I had expected the film and television majors to go after him, and they did, knives out. They zeroed in on the elitist assumptions about how mass culture allegedly worked and reserved special scorn for his dismissal of the visual ("I'm supposed to think that *The Corrections* is a greater work of art than *Eternal Sunshine of the Spotless Mind* because it's in print instead of these evil images?!"). What I didn't expect was that the graduate students in English, the most professionalized, sophisticated readers in the class, would be even more critical of what they considered an antiquated notion of literary writing:

> "This guy writes a novel that Updike could have written twenty years ago and he's carrying forth the torch of the high-art literary tradition?!"
>
> "This was a perfect choice for the Oprah's Book Club. It's a middlebrow novel about a dysfunctional family. Of course she loved it!"
>
> "He gave away his television set so he could read? Is this guy caught in a time warp or what? He sounds like the deposed Crown Prince of Modernism, waiting to be restored to the throne."

What I found particularly interesting in their reactions was that, on the one hand, they were employing the evaluative criteria that graduate students specializing in contemporary fiction have always used—the only thing really worth talking about is the cutting edge. On the other hand, they had no desire whatsoever to restrict that experience to print-based texts. They wanted to talk about literary novels, but they also wanted to discuss Chris Ware's *Jimmy Reardon: The Smartest Boy in the World*, Frank Miller's *Sin City*, Quentin Tarantino's *Kill Bill* saga, Alfonso Cuaron's *Y Tu Mamá También* and David Lynch's *Mulholland Drive*. Many of the factors associated with the reading of literary fiction, as opposed to popular visual media, were now being detached from literary experience and transferred to texts coming from the heart of that visual culture; that is, texts that demanded close reading possessed the density to justify repeated readings, and also required the specialized knowledge that came with professionalized reading. This is not to suggest that there hasn't been something called film studies solidly in place for the past four decades that hasn't been doing exactly that. This was, however, the first generation of English graduate students I had encountered who were in hot pursuit of exactly those kinds of cutting-edge texts that called out for professionalized reading protocols, but they saw no need whatsoever to restrict their search to the literary fiction as such. The sort of scholarly reading formerly reserved for the high-art literary tradition that Franzen affiliated with was now uncoupled from that tradition and applied with equal success to a wide range of print-based *and* visual texts. In other words, what was formerly thought of as a "literary experience," in terms of the sophistication of both the texts involved and the manner of reading needed to appreciate them no longer depended on print. The "literary experience" could be enjoyed just as easily with visual media. Since the foundation of Franzen's *je refuse* oppositionality was his opposition to the virtual images generated by television and computer screens, he was as foreign to their taste culture as Barry Manilow, and no one wanted Franzen's "Reader-in-Exile Blues" in their iPod either. Why, indeed, bother?

At the end of the class, I asked them where they were now. Were they comfortable picking a side in the controversy? There was widespread reaffirmation of the uplift position ("Bring on the book bait, even if it's *The Corrections*"), but two other positions were advocated with greater fervor. What was really worth pursuing about the relationship between print culture and visual culture was the fluidity between them, not endlessly rebuilding the same old worn-out fencing. And please don't ask us to watch the Oprah Book Club again — endorsing the uplift position doesn't mean we have to like the show. In order to get a better perspective on the nature of popular literary culture then, two questions still need to be explored in greater detail in the remainder of this book: What is the relationship between print and visual culture in terms of what now constitutes a "literary experience"? And how *does* taste culture determine what counts as quality reading and what is recognized as quality writing?

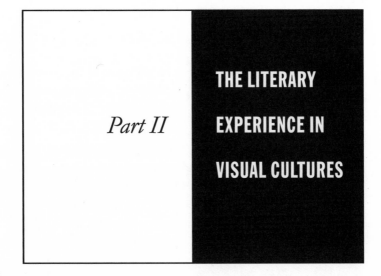

Part II THE LITERARY EXPERIENCE IN VISUAL CULTURES

3

THE *MOVIE* WAS BETTER

The Rise of the Cine-Literary

One of the most visible forms of both the popularization and relocation of literary culture has been the high-profile adaptation films produced by Miramax, Sony Pictures Classics, Fine Line, and Focus Features. Harvey Weinstein's explanation of the success of Miramax in a Hollywood dominated by high-concept blockbusters—"our special effects are *words*"—suggests just how important literary values were in that success story. But why do *literary* words function as successful special effects within what are alleged to be image cultures? Evidently, the literary creative process must hold some fascination for quality-film viewers. It's one thing for Shakespeare to be in love, but when the print advertisements for the film in which he does all this loving promise the viewer, "A celebration of life, language, and the creative process that has critics and audiences across America laughing and crying, standing and cheering," and then that "celebration" brings in over $100 million, domestic box, it's abundantly clear that cinematic literary experiences of a very particular variety are being enjoyed on an unprecedented scale. A "Stand Up and Cheer" movie about the creative process?

This would seem, on the face of it, to be an unusual development, given the persistent demonization of the film industry by novelists and literary critics throughout the twentieth century. Hollywood was allegedly the pure distillation of the vulgarity of American culture, endlessly cast as the mass-cultural villain whose popular appeal and utter lack of artistic standards threatened to eliminate the audience for all things literary. Literary adaptations have been around for over a century, so why have they become so popular within the past decade? In its annual "Power Issue" in 1996, *Entertainment Weekly* named Jane Austen one of the Ten Most Powerful people in Hollywood, featuring a photograph of the author, pool-side, complete with cell phone and fax machine at the ready. A decade later, in spring 2006, the adaptation film and the literary author appeared to be even more prominent. The film version of Annie Proulx's story "Brokeback Mountain," which had originally appeared in *The New Yorker*, garnered more Academy Award nominations than any other film, in addition to winning the Producers Guild Award, the Directors Guild Award, the Writers Guild Award, the Golden Lion at the Venice Film Festival; it was also named Best Picture by dozens of critics associations throughout the United States and earned more British Academy of Film and Television Arts (BAFTA) nominations than any other film. Kiera Knightly was nominated for Best Actress for her performance in *Pride and Prejudice*, and Phillip Seymour Hoffman was the runaway winner of all of the acting awards for his role in *Capote*, a film whose very title obviously bore witness to the status of the author within the category of the prestige picture. In 2008 the allure of literary adaptations hit a new level, with the high-profile releases of *The Jane Austen Book Club*, *Becoming Jane*, and *The Kite Runner*, culminating in the Academy Awards, when adaptations of novels by the Great American Literary Novelist (Cormac McCarthy) and the Great British Literary Novelist (Ian McEwan) were in head-to-head competition for Best Picture, and *No Country for Old Men* (McCarthy) eventually walked away with the grand prize. The film version of McEwan's *Atonement* may have finished as an also-ran, but even as those awards were being presented, the novel was the bestselling book in North America, sitting comfortably atop both the trade and the mass market paperback lists, with a cover photo featuring Kiera Knightly, now clearly "the face" of choice for *Vogue* magazine and British literary fiction of any vintage. Although McEwan was not in attendance for the Oscar ceremony, Cormac McCarthy was there, and television cameras cut to close-ups of his face every time the adaptation of his novel won an award throughout the evening. The intercutting between Joel and Ethan Cohen at the podium and McCarthy looking on approvingly in the audience was a perfect visualization of *cine*-literary culture—all three authors were copresent at the moment the film was recognized as Best Picture of the Year. The literary genius was no longer in Hollywood via a parody image in *Entertainment Weekly*—he was there on the Red Carpet as the source and guarantee of the film's greatness.

That interdependency of novel and film is secured by far more than an Academy Award program. While I was watching the telecast, I went to Amazon on my laptop to see how the competition was deployed there. The home page for *Atonement* (Wide Screen Edition) directed me to the "*Atonement* Movie Page," where I encountered a Related Video ready for viewing,

7. Kiera Knightly and "the Words," in the featurette "From Novel to Screen: Adapting a Classic," from the DVD edition of *Atonement* (2008)

a list of links to the trailer and behind-the-scenes featurettes, and images of the cover of the paperback edition of the novel, with Kiera Knightly and James McAvoy in vivid color. There I also found an extended interview with the screenwriter Christopher Hampton about the adaptation of McEwan's novel, and another feature, "From Book to Script to Screen," detailing Hampton's favorite adaptation films. The text above the paperback edition covers epitomized not just the interdependency of novel and film but their virtual interchangeability: "Read the Book, Then See the Movie, or Vice Versa." I then clicked to the paperback homepage of the book, where I found another special message box urging me, "Start reading *Atonement* on your Kindle in under a minute. Don't have a Kindle? Get yours here." And while McEwan may not have been in attendance at the Academy Awards, he was the featured player in the "From Novel to Screen: Adapting a Classic" featurettte in the DVD edition of the film, where he was joined by the film's director, Joe Wright, along with Christopher Hampton and Kiera Knightly, talking about how the novel was adapted. Throughout this featurette there were several extreme close-ups of passages from the novel and, at one point, the long dissolves between faces and text resulted in a momentary superimposition that is the very essence of cine-literary culture. Here literary prose and movie star face were completely imbedded one within the other, each elevating the other in a hybrid cultural entertainment that was as dependent on the words as it was on the glamorous image, each functioning as the "special effects" for the other. The seamless, simultaneous, interconnection of novel, film, featurette, Web site, and digital reading device is the foundation of cine-literary culture, and within this culture, reading the book has become only one of a host of interlocking literary experiences.

How did all this become standard operating procedure? We can begin to answer that question only by situating the recent evolution of the adaptation film in reference to the increasing convergence of literary and visual cultures. Their interdependency is attributable, to a great extent, to infrastructural changes within the entertainment industry. Miramax, itself a division of the media conglomerate Disney, produces films, but it also publishes Miramax Books and issues soundtrack albums, just like any media conglomerate; and Amazon, Barnes & Noble, and Borders provide all of the above at one location. Yet this realignment between the film and publishing industries does not entirely explain why cinephilia and bibliophilia have grown together, rather than keeping their usual distance. The adaptation mania that exploded in the nineties, and that appears to be only intensifying a decade or more later, depends on the reconfiguration of those pleasures in an expansive "cine-bibliophilia" that could be "authorized" only by realignments in taste cultures that suggest profound changes in the relative status of both reading and watching.

Within this cine-bibliophilia not all adaptations are created equal. Some are merely film versions of literary texts, and others are products of a particular reading/viewing culture, where they circulate as a singular kind of cultural experience that provides equal measures of literary and cinematic pleasure. Consider the profound differences between *Slumdog Millionaire* (2008) and *The Reader* (2008) as adaptation films in this regard. Both were among the most prestigious films of the year; both were nominated for Best Picture in the 2009 Academy Awards, as well as for Best Adapted Screenplay, Best Director, and Best Cinematography; and both films won major. acting awards at the Screen Actors Guild and the Golden Globes. On the face of it, those nominations and awards might make them seem roughly comparable as adaptation films, since they were grouped together in the same category so many times. Yet as adaptations they were circulated in vastly different ways. *Slumdog Millionaire* was based on a little-known novel by Vikas Swarup entitled *Q & A* (2005), which was retitled *Slumdog Millionaire* for its movie tie-in edition. The movie tie-in edition of *The Reader* on the other hand, sported a "#1 National Bestseller" sticker and needed no title change, which is not surprising, given the fact that the novel version of *The Reader* had already been a national phenomenon as an Oprah Book Club selection. It was a quality pre-sold concept for a massive, yet very particular reading/viewing community carefully cultivated and maintained by Oprah, Weinstein Pictures, Barnes & Noble, and Amazon, where two paperback editions of the novel were available during the film's theatrical release: the movie tie-in edition featuring Kate Winslet and the Oprah Book Club edition. But there was another essential difference between these two adaptations—their respective attitudes toward literary reading. In the case of *Slumdog Millionaire*, everything that counts for meaningful knowledge is gained through the main character's experience in the streets of Mumbai. *The Three Musketeers* is a key point of reference, but none of the main characters ever reads Dumas or any other novelist—genuine learning is not to be found in books. In *The Reader*, on the other hand, the narrator's relationship with Hanna is defined largely in terms of the books he reads to her so lovingly, first aloud and then on tape, with each and every title duly catalogued. In *Slumdog Millionaire*, the literary is irrelevant; in *The Reader* it represents a thoroughly transcendent realm. As an Oprah Book Club novel that details how an illiterate woman eventually learns about the transformative power of reading, it was a Miramax-Weinstein Picture waiting to be adapted, in this case by the usual Miramax subjects—the producer Anthony Minghella, the director Stephen Daldry, and the screenwriter David Hare.

Given the sheer volume of adaptations that have appeared over the past two decades, there is obviously no way one could do justice to their diversity except in an entire series of books. In these next two chapters I want to provide a framework for understanding the adaptation film as more than well-upholstered, pseudo-literariness for a niche audience. I will begin by charting the evolution of the adaptation, paying particular attention to how it was transformed from the *Masterpiece Theatre* public television phenomenon in the seventies, to the high-profile Merchant and Ivory films of the eighties, to the Miramax juggernaut of the nineties, which established an entirely new way of making and marketing adaptations that is still solidly in place and winning Academy Awards, year in, year out.

In order to identify the most significant changes that have occurred over the past two decades in a manageable way, I will look first at Merchant and Ivory's *A Room with a View* (1985) and then analyze the "Miramaxing" of the adaptation, placing special emphasis on three of the most high-profile successes, *The English Patient* (1997), *Shakespeare in Love* (1999), and *The Hours* (2002). I have chosen these particular films because they exemplify the main categories of the recent adaptation film—the canonical British novel, the "Shakespeare project," and the contemporary prize-winning British and American novels—and it is only through a close comparative analysis of the interplay between the aesthetic and commercial aspects of these adaptations that both recurring patterns and significant variations come into sharp relief. My goal is to delineate through close readings of these films what Merchant-Ivory and then Miramax came to mean as quality brand names, but I also explore how their success depended on the fashioning of a new *cine*-literary culture in which those films could resonate as "literary experience" and "prestige film" simultaneously.

In this chapter I also consider why academic film study in the United States has, until quite recently, been unable to come to terms with the proliferation of adaptations as a widespread popular phenomenon, except in terms of articles devoted to specific adaptations, most often written by professors of English and almost universally consumed with questions about the fidelity of particular adaptations that are judged, almost as universally, as inevitably inferior to the original. For all their apparent refinement in terms of stylistic analysis, far too many of these fidelity-based analyses have all the subtlety of a professional wrestling match in which Jane Austen battles Vulgar Adaptation in a steel-cage death match, and we all know it's going to be Jane who will be spinning her opponent around over her head before she slams him to the mat of legitimate literary culture. The main limitation of this approach is that it conceives of the adaptation process so one-dimensionally, as a direct transposition from page to screen. Between that page and the screen comes a host of intertextual networks — Web sites, television interviews, soundtrack albums, magazine feature stories, reading clubs, bookstore chains — which embody the increasing interpenetration of literary and visual cultures in terms of both delivery systems and the production of taste. Where the fidelity approach makes the intentions of the author the foundation of the adaptation process, I will examine how the author is used to *authorize* a host of pleasures that complicate the simple transfer from page to screen. This is not to suggest that the sort of stylistic concerns that have been paradigmatic within the fidelity approach (point of view, characterization, etc.) are not worth pursuing, but rather that they should be recontextualized in terms of what now shapes that adaptation process, especially now that literary classics are being "refunctioned" by film companies that lay claim to their own version of a genuine literary experience by asserting their own love of literature.

This inevitably involves matters of taste, and if there is anything academic film study has avoided more strenuously than the adaptation film it is the entire category of taste. This was an inevitable development in the sixties, when film studies as a discipline had to distance itself from the world of journalistic film reviewing with its stars, popcorn boxes, hankies, which made taste—who had it, who didn't—something that had to be checked at the door of the academy if film was to become an object of serious study. By making taste a category akin to alchemy or some kind of black magic outside the discipline (or more specifically, the discursive formation that became a university education in film), the war of legitimation was won, but the vestiges of that victory have come to haunt the discipline in the form of intellectual class prejudices that foreclose certain ways of making sense of film as popular culture. Coming to terms with the adaptation film is a difficult task, because these films represent such a significant challenge to the way film study is supposed to be conducted, largely because they are best understood as part of a broader countereducation project being offered within the realm of popular culture that stands in direct opposition to the academy.

Adaptation as Counterattraction:
From Anglophilia to Cinephilia (and Back Again)

Providing an adequate back story for the adaptation film since 1985 is a daunting undertaking, given that adaptations are virtually as old as the medium itself and have enjoyed global popularity throughout its history, as is evident from their recurring appearance within virtually every national cinema throughout the past century. One could argue, even more pointedly, that the medium, both as industry and as moviegoing experience, was massively shaped by the move toward adaptation films in the pivotal transitional period of 1908–14. In their masterful study of this period, *Reframing Culture* (1993), William Urrichio and Roberta Pearson analyze the changing profile of what going to the movies meant during this period of cultural instability, which had resulted from massive immigration and the burgeoning popular entertainment industry. The maturation of the industry from sideshow curiosity to solid middle-class entertainment was to a great extent accomplished through a series of artistic and exhibition strategies spearheaded by the adaptation film. Characterized by social reformers as a "moral contagion," nickelodeons had been placed in the category of enfeebling cheap amusements, along with sensational dime novels, dance halls, amusement parks, and so on. Uplift organizations such as The People's Institute, the Educational Alliance, and the Bureau of Lectures attempted to combat this moral turpitude by culturalizing the masses through a series of "counterattractions." The most visible form of counterattraction was the public lecture, dedicated to bringing the best that had been thought and said to an audience who, according to Henry M. Leipziger, director of the Bureau of Lectures, "responded to the yearning call for the higher life, who trudged willingly as pilgrims to the fountain of truth" (*Reframing Culture*, 36). When the New York mayor Frank McClellan bowed to public pressure and revoked the licenses of over five hundred nickelodeons in 1908, it became imperative for the industry to redefine itself in the public imagination, primarily by repositioning moving pictures, or at least a certain kind of picture, as a counterattraction.

This need to make "high-class educational pictures" inevitably depended on literary adaptations, because their cultural pedigree brought instant legitimacy. French and Italian film companies such as Pathé, Gaumont, Ambrosio, and Milano had already begun to produce literary-based quality films, commonly referred to as "film d'art," which were exported to the United States beginning in 1908 to exploit this need for uplifting subject matter. Vitagraph became the first American film company to produce this sort of quality film and, even though they represented a relatively small percentage of its overall production, they were skillfully promoted by the studio to give Vitagraph a distinctive profile, making *quality* a matter of brand recognition. Urrichio and Pearson detail Vitagraph's adaptations, particularly its ambitious Shakespeare productions such as *Julius Caesar* (1911), but perhaps their most significant point is that the move to adaptations was highly overdetermined. These films may have been promoted in terms of the industry's drive for respectability (the moving pictures could bring *culture* to the people just as well as the public lecturers), but this apparently altruistic, uplifting mission was also a matter of studio product differentiation for domestic and foreign distribution, made even more profitable by the fact that Shakespeare was a pre-sold concept whose works were in the public domain — "Shakespeare was not only respectable but free" (69).

The promotion of the adaptation during this period reflects a complicated interplay between financial and cultural capital. During this period, "high culture" was being marked off as such by cultural entrepreneurs who were determined to preserve it by moving it out of the realm of the marketplace. Paul Dimaggio's work on the Boston Brahmins and their attempts to exercise hegemonic control over a cultural life threatened by the onslaught of Irish immigration beginning in the middle of the nineteenth century is especially relevant here. In an essay published in 1991, he recounts how their success in framing culture in terms of a nonprofit profile, over and against the commodified pulp entertainments, was widely imitated throughout American cities, making the nickelodeon the seemingly natural enemy of genuine culture because it was so relentlessly for profit. The Brahmins' use of Shakespeare, Dickens, and company—all once unashamedly caught up in the concerns of the marketplace and only recently shorn of that taint through their relocation within the realm of Carnegie libraries, the legitimate theater, and the public lecture—led to a series of elaborate maneuvers by film companies and nickelodeon operators who wanted to pack the audience in with the sort of culture that wasn't supposed to be paid for at all, or at least not in those sorts of illegitimate venues.

Once the film industry's legitimation crisis subsided during the First World War, the rush to make adaptations cooled as well, but they retained the status of prestige picture during the classic Hollywood studio era, long after the battle to prove that movie going was an acceptable middle-class entertainment had been not only won but largely forgotten. If the Brahmins did not accept "the pictures" as legitimate culture, who cared, as far as Hollywood was concerned; movie going was a hugely successful entertainment for mass audiences that didn't subscribe to such taste distinctions, and the industry was happy to reign triumphant within the entertainment marketplace. When Hollywood faced another sort of image crisis in the early thirties, for its alleged sensationalizing of crime and sexuality, it responded with internal censorship in the form of the Hays Office, but also with a renewed emphasis on literary adaptations. The film education campaign undertaken by the industry, complete with direct appeals to teachers and film guides for movies such as *Little Women* (1934), has been carefully documented by Lea Jacobs (in an article in *Camera Obscura*, 1990) and Haidee Wasson (*Museum Movies*, 2005). The latter argues that during this crisis, "teachers became a regular aspect of marketing the rising number of classic literary adaptations and historical biographies that emerged during this period. Further, the names of Dante, Shakespeare, Dickens, and Tolstoy were used by industry spokespeople as transparent indices to industry goodwill in press releases and advertising campaigns" (12). In his study, published in 2000, of David Selznick's 1935 version of *David Copperfield*, Geurric DeBona details just how complicated, and internally conflicted, this campaign could become. He argues that, during the thirties, "prestige pictures played a crucial role in defining the public image of a company. Such films were especially important to the career of David O. Selznick, who was able to reap financial rewards and aesthetic dividends from overtly literary capital." The fact that MGM at first resisted the project as a "highbrow period piece [that was] . . . not only costly but a bit too much for the average viewer" (111) reveals how far the industry had moved away from the legitimation crisis of the Vitagraph period. Culture was expensive and probably over the heads of the middle-class audience Hollywood now considered its own. Selznick prevailed, but only by convincing MGM of the lucrative potential of adaptation films in terms of product differentiation and the expansion of domestic and foreign markets. In a telegram he sent to Arthur Loew in the Metro New York office in 1934, Selznick argued that *David Copperfield* would "add hundreds of thousands of dollars to British Empire gross while still giving us a picture that would be as good for this country, and at the same time do wonders for the entire *standing* of our British company" (111, italics mine).

Once the censorship crisis subsided, adaptation mania cooled once again, yet the adaptation continued to enjoy a vestigial force within the category of prestige picture, even when the Arnoldian social uplift mission had been finally abandoned by the film industry. The marketability of that still vibrant anglophilia has remained an enduring feature of the Hollywood prestige picture. In her appraisal of the evaluative criteria used by the Academy Awards since their inception, Molly Haskell cites Hollywood's love of "spectacle, epic and uplift" but also traces another current running alongside it, namely,

> the all-important genuflection at the shrine of Britannia. Anglophilia runs like a low-grade fever through seven decades of Academy Awards, testifying to a chronic American crush on England. In the early days, this hero worship reflected a touching display of aspiration on the part of moguls anxious to improve their immigrant audiences, if not themselves. But what was our excuse in the second half of what has been called the American century, when we were still fawning over the British?" ("When Oscar Is Bad," sec. 2, 1)

Haskell's question is well put, but she poses it rhetorically without offering any explanation of what might explain that enduring fascination, long after legitimacy of the industry had been secured. Indeed, since the vast majority of prestige adaptation films that have been nominated for Academy Awards have been based on British novels, what explains the persistence of anglophilia that appears to be inseparable from the adaptation film?

We can begin to answer that question only by examining in greater detail just when, and why that anglophilia has waxed and waned, particularly in regard to the evolution of another obsessive love—cinephilia. Haskell cites a number of representative examples of anglophilic fever, but she doesn't acknowledge the gradual diminishing of that fever in the sixties, and its virtual disappearance in the seventies—exactly at the same time that a cinephilic fever was rapidly spreading throughout Europe and North America. According to Susan Sontag ("The Decay of Cinema," 1997) cinephilia was

> a very specific kind of love that cinema inspired. Each art breeds its fanatics. The love that the cinema inspired, however, was special. It was born of the conviction that cinema was an art unlike any other: quintessentially modern; distinctly accessible; poetic and mysterious and erotic and moral—all at the same time. Cinema had apostles. (It was like religion.) Cinema was a crusade. For cinephiles, the movies encapsulated everything. Cinema was both the book of art and the book of life. (60)

Sontag's choice of words here is especially revealing. That films could be considered the *book* of life suggests that the power that books once had to instruct and inspire was now being taken on by cinema. Every religion needs its rituals, its sacred places, and its own specialized discourse. The cinephile experience at art house theaters, then, was not just a matter of going to movies at a different location but also the consecration of an emergent taste community. For Sontag, cinephilia meant that

> going to the movies, talking about movies, became a passion among university students and other young people. You fell in love not just with actors but with the cinema itself. . . . Its temples, as it spread throughout Europe and the Americas, were the many *cinémathèques* and clubs specializing in films from the past and director's retrospectives that sprang up. The 1960's and the early 1970's was the age of feverish movie-going, with a full-time cinephile always hoping to find a seat as close as possible to the big screen, ideally third row center. "One can't live without Rossellini," declares a character in Bertolucci's *Before the Revolution* (1964)—and means it. (61)

This exuberant cinephilia was profoundly anglophobic, because the formation of new taste hierarchies depended, to a very great extent, on the devaluation of British literary culture as a kind of international gold standard of educated taste. Among the university students Sontag refers to was a group of second-generation immigrants such as Francis Ford Coppola and Martin Scorsese, who formed the "film school generation," a group of directors who felt they needed to make no apologies for this medium and for whom the notion of culture installed by the Boston Brahmins to contain their ancestors was now there only to be challenged. Their cinephilia was defined in terms of the French New Wave; Italian directors such as Rossellini, Fellini, and Antonioni; and American genre auteurs — anything but the British adaptations, which were judged the antithesis of cinematic. While Coppola and company may have expressed admiration for Michael Powell or David Lean, cinephilia was dismissive of British film because, with very few exceptions, it appeared to be so dominated by a literary/theatrical cultural hegemony. This rejection of British film as somehow aggressively *un-*cinematic was neatly summed up by Truffaut's often-quoted formulation, "British cinema, that's oxymoronic, isn't it?" It is hardly surprising then that as this generation rose to prominence, anglophilic fever was virtually eradicated in terms of Academy Awards. After *Women in Love* was nominated in 1970 in the Best Director and Best Actress categories, no adaptations of British novels receive nominations in the major categories for a decade, except *Barry Lyndon* (1975), a film promoted heavily as a lavish historical film by the American director Stanley Kubrick, rather than as adapted from a novel by William Thackeray. The taste hierarchies of cinephilia were shaped by a fascination with European art cinema and Hollywood movies, including even pulp Hollywood auteurs such as Sam Fuller and Edgar G. Ulmer, who came to define the truly cinematic. Within this cinephile taste cartography, Jane Austen, E. M. Forster, and company exemplified the sort of antiquated social and intellectual class distinctions that had to be rejected in order for a popular, visual medium to gain ascendancy as a medium of genuine culture; at this point, *Kiss Me Deadly* trumped *Pride and Prejudice* any day of the week.

This declaration of independence from the literary, specifically the rejection of anything that suggested that film needed to go to literature to acquire prestige, was also a vital component of the professionalization of film studies within the academy. Adaptation was a central concern of the film classes offered in American universities during the fifties and early sixties, but these were taught primarily within English departments rather than in the relatively limited number of film or communication departments then available, at a handful of universities. As film studies evolved into a free-standing discipline, complete with its own departments, professional societies, conferences, and journals, the adaptation-based course became a vestige of an earlier prehistory, and as such was abandoned to English professors still keen to discuss whether Kurosawa's *Throne of Blood* or Welles's *Macbeth* was more faithful to Shakespeare, a scholarly game in which fidelity was the preeminent concern and the superiority of the literary host text was indisputable. As film theory began to pursue increasingly rigorous approaches to the study of "the film language" through semiotic, psychoanalytic, and ideological analysis in the seventies, the adaptation-based course became a cottage industry within English departments, particularly as the need to show students at least some film or television version of English classics became one of the taken-for-granteds of the profession, reflecting an instrumentality that only further diminished the allure of adaptation as an area of serious theoretical inquiry. Ginette Vincendeau summarizes the situation succinctly:

> Although auteurism has been challenged, there has been a continued drive, in film studies, to explore the specificity of film art and language. This explains, then, the conspicuous gap that exists between the abundant production of books and articles on film and literature—which derive mostly from a literary perspective and the low profile of the topic in film studies. Though we find an interest in film and literature reflected in journals like *Literature/Film Quarterly* and in a few manuals, the fact remains that the key textbooks ignore it. (*Film, Literature, Heritage*, xv)

In short, at no time in film history has the adaptation been more ubiquitous, and at no time has American film studies been so poorly prepared to make sense of the causes, functions, or ramifications of this phenomenon. In his introduction to his seminal collection, *Film Adaptation* (2000), James Naremore argues compellingly that, as long as adaptations continue to be such a significant aspect of global film production, they can no longer be ignored; but they can be productively revisited only if we can escape the tyranny of fidelity: "what we need instead is a broader definition of adaptation and a sociology that takes into account the commercial apparatus, the audience, and the academic culture industry" (10). The recently published collections by Robert Stam and Alessandra Raengo, *Literature and Film: A Guide to the Theory and Practice of Adaptation* (2004) and *A Companion to Literature and Film* (2007), have addressed this problem by vastly expanding the range of approaches employed in the discussion of adaptation films. The notion of a sociology of adaptation was first advanced by Dudley Andrew as a way of escaping the limited confines of fidelity analysis (1984). Andrew laid out the pivotal questions that are rarely posed, let alone answered, in adaptation analysis in American film studies: "How does adaptation serve the cinema? What conditions exist in film style and film culture to warrant or demand the use of literary prototypes? Although adaptation may be calculated as a relatively constant volume in the history of cinema, its particular function in any given moment is far from constant. The choices of the mode of adaptation and of prototypes suggest a great deal about the cinema's sense of its role and aspirations from decade to decade" (*Concepts in Film Theory*, 458).

To situate Andrew's questions within the historical context they demand: How has the adaptation served British and Hollywood cinema since the mid-eighties, first as a niche audience alternative to the high-concept blockbuster and, more recently, as a dominant force within the "great bifurcation" of American film production, in which major studios now specialize in high-concept franchises but the specialty divisions within major studios now appear to *own* the Academy Awards? What has occurred within American film culture, in terms of industry infrastructure and in terms of broader shifts in popular taste, for the adaptation to experience this unprecedented level of popularity? What has led to not just the use, but the near domination of literary prototypes with the category of the prestige picture? What happens, at the most fundamental level, to the relationship between film culture and literary culture when that occurs?

A meaningful sociology of adaptation should be able to at least begin to answer those questions, but it demands a theoretical framework that can incorporate textual as well as industry analysis, and place those issues within the wider context of the history of popular taste. In his essay "The Dialogics of Adaptation," Robert Stam lays out the foundation for an alternative approach to adaptation:

> Film adaptations can be seen as a kind of multi-leveled negotiation of intertexts. . . . The source text forms a dense informational network, a series of verbal cues that the adapting film text can then take up, amplify, ignore, subvert, or transform. The film adaptation of a novel performs these transformations according to the protocols of a distinct medium, absorbing and altering the genres and intertexts available through the grids of ambient discourses and ideologies and as mediated by a series of filters: studio style, ideological fashion, political constraints, charismatic stars, auteurist predilections, economic advantage or disadvantage, and evolving technology. (67–68)

The great advantage of Stam's intertextual approach is that it situates the adaptation within a specific set of contingent circumstances but, at the same time, opens adaptation analysis to a wide range of formal and cultural concerns. Most important, it allows for the consideration of the multiple determinations that shape adaptations and the multiple pleasures they provide, even for viewers who may be unfamiliar with the source text. In other words, Jane Austen would not have been a key figure in *Entertainment Weekly*'s "Power" issue if the audience for Austen films were limited to viewers eager to see just how faithful those adaptations of *Emma, Sense and Sensibility*, or *Mansfield Park* really were. Austen's celebrity cannot be even addressed by the old fidelity discourse because her popularity involves industry, audience, and taste considerations that have no place within that old interpretive game. The "mass audience" popularity enjoyed by such genteel literary figures as Austen, Henry James, and Forster can be explained only by exploring the other pleasures these films afford and the other uses they may be put to by both studios and audiences, many if not most of whom have not read the source texts in question and therefore find fidelity a nonissue.

The Merchant-Ivory Adaptation: Popular Culture as Finishing School

The culturalist, intertextual approach to adaptation study has been developed in sophisticated ways by British film scholars in the debates that have revolved around the "heritage film." Richard Dyer (2000), Andrew Higson (1996), John Hill (1999), Claire Monk (1995 and 2001), and Ginette Vincendeau (2001) have all examined the adaptations of British literature epitomized by the Merchant-Ivory films *A Room with a View* (1985), *Maurice* (1987), *Howards End* (1992), and *The Remains of the Day* (1992) in reference to the heritage industry that emerged in the United Kingdom in the 1980s. The number of museums in the United Kingdom doubled between 1960 and 1987, and a vital part of this expansion was the opening of country houses and estates through the National Trust and English Heritage foundations. Hill and Higson contend that adaptation film needs to be considered as part of a broader "museum aesthetic," embodying a fascination with uniquely British culture emanating from particularly glorious historical periods. Hill draws the parallel very precisely: "Just as the heritage culture permits Britain to carve out a niche for itself within the global tourist economy so heritage films may be seen to provide the British cinema with a distinctive product in the international media market-place. Heritage films, in this respect, have held a particular attraction for US audiences where they have often performed much better financially than they have in the UK. . . . *A Room with a View*, for example, earned $23.7 million in the United States and Canada while *Howards End* took in three times as much in the US (12.2 million pounds) as it did in the United Kingdom (where its gross was 3.7 million)" (79).

For Hill and Higson, the primary appeal of these cinematic adaptations depends on the visualization of a particular worldview that may be revisited touristically. As such, the style of these films is shaped by ideological factors that cannot be restricted to the intentions of Merchant-Ivory and others mining the same vein. According to Higson, the heritage films "offer apparently more settled and visually splendid manifestations of an essentially pastoral national identity and authentic culture: 'Englishness' as an ancient and natural inheritance, *Great* Britain, The *United* Kingdom." This nostalgic vision produces a singular type of mise-en-scène:

> Heritage culture appears petrified, frozen in moments that virtually fall out of the narrative, existing only as adornments for the staging of the love story. Thus the historical narrative is transformed into spectacle: heritage becomes excess, not functional, something not to be used, but something to be admired. . . . The effect is the creation of heritage space, rather than narrative space: that is, a space for the display of heritage properties rather than the enactment of dramas. In many respects, therefore, this is not a narrative cinema, a cinema of storytelling, but something more akin to that mode of early filmmaking that Tom Gunning calls the cinema of attractions. In this case, the heritage films display their self-conscious artistry, their landscapes, their properties, their actors and their performance qualities, their clothes, and often their archaic dialogue. The gaze, therefore is organized around props and settings — the look of the observer at the tableau image — as much as it is around a character point of view. ("Heritage Film," 1996, 118)

While Higson's opposition between narrative and heritage space is a compelling formulation, that relationship does not necessarily need to be cast as an either/or dichotomy. Martin Scorsese, a cinematic director normally thought to exemplify the opposite of the Merchant and Ivory picturesque style, has acknowledged the intensely visual nature of the latter's films: "I like the beautiful detail in a lot of Merchant-Ivory films that use

English settings. One wide shot says it all. When Jim Ivory shoots a period room, the eye is there. Perhaps it's more in his cultural make-up to understand the décor, so that when he places the camera, it's right for that room, you really see that room and all its detail. I feel more comfortable placing the camera in an Italian restaurant, or a church or club, or a Lower East side tenement" (Ian Christie interview, 2001, 67). Scorsese's contention that cultural makeup determines the eye is crucially important, because it suggests that the cinematic is not an abstract set of stylistic predilections but a way of seeing that can take a number of different norms. Using Gunning's distinction between narrative cinema and a cinema of attractions, one could argue that virtually every film style that has managed to distinguish itself within global film cultures of the past two decades depends on a comparable excess, a mise-en-scène that distinguishes it from the Hollywood high-concept, whether it be British adaptations, Danish Dogme films, or Bollywood extravaganzas. But what is especially distinctive about the interplay between narrative and spectacle in the adaptation film is that the attractions function as a new form of counterattractions, forming an entire taste culture that depends on a way of seeing that also includes the eyes of viewers with a very particular cultural makeup, or to put it more precisely, eyes in search of a cultural makeover that is no longer shaped by a traditional cinephile sensibility.

Within the excessive mise-en-scène of the adaptation film, the organization of space exceeds any one character's psychological space, because these films assume a shared psychological space in which characters and audiences converge in the same taste community, at which point culture becomes spectacularized, forming the set of special effects required for the proper delivery of all those words—rather an unexpected development in films normally thought to be so dependent on their literary sources. To return to Stam, here the literary adaptation exists in a dialogic relationship not just to the source novel but to a host of bestselling opera recordings, travel books, shelter magazines, and even cookbooks. Viewing pleasure in this case is not limited to traditional notions of character identification; the gaze of the touristic viewer appreciates the subtleties of character psychology à la Forster, but only as one of a number of interdependent pleasures within the tableau. The scene in *A Room with a View* in which Lucy goes in search of George during the picnic outing is a perfect case in point.

Here is the breath-taking star Helena Bonham Carter, wearing the exquisite costume, walking through the ever-popular Tuscan landscapes featured

8. Smorgasbord of cultural delights: Lucy Honeychurch (played by Helena Bonham Carter) in Tuscany, from the film *A Room with a View* (1985)

in bestselling travel books such as *Under the Tuscan Sun*, accompanied by a Puccini aria sung by Kiri Te Kanawa, from the singer's hugely successful recital disk of arias by Verdi and Puccini (a CD that will eventually sport the sticker "Featuring 'O Mio Babbino Caro' from *A Room with a View*"). Forster created the narrative situation, but he is in effect only one entry in the primer of tasteful living. The gastronomic delights that come with the Merchant-Ivory tour package have been promoted by Merchant himself in the companion cookbook, *Ismail Merchant's Florence: Filming and Feasting in Tuscany*, which includes his account of making the film, with behind-the-scenes photos alongside shots of Merchant in the local markets and lush still-life compositions featuring plates of Tuscan specialties and bottles of Tignanello deployed against the same breath-taking landscapes used in the film, the whole capped off by a recipe section with entries such as "Ismail's Explosive Pasta Sauce."

This simultaneous appeal to a number of rarefied tastes in which the literary and the cinematic become only two of a host of interdependent pleasures is the basis of this excessive mise-en-scène—but why is this particular excess, composed of what are seemingly such antiquated pleasures, so popular with contemporary audiences, especially in the United States, where the Merchant-Ivory films enjoyed their greatest box office success? In his essay "Anglophil(m)ia: Why Does America Watch Merchant-Ivory Movies?" Martin Hipsky argues: "What effectively allows one admittance to these movies is the proper accretion of what Bourdieu has called 'cultural capital'—the long-term social and educational investments that form the

9. Cover of Ismail Merchant's cookbook, from *Ismail Merchant's Florence: Filming and Feasting in Tuscany* (1994)

contours of one's cultural life and that, in accordance with their class affiliations, may concretely confer degrees of social status." What makes these
films popular with an American audience, he continues, is a crisis in that
system:

> For these films are the undergraduate literature or art history major's
> dream; they constitute a veritable survey course in the art of high cultural
> allusion. *Room with a View* alone features references to Dante, Giotto,
> Michelangelo, R. W. Emerson, Beethoven, Greek myth, Goethe, and
> Byron. . . . In short, I want to suggest that the act of viewing an Anglo-
> philic film may reaffirm one's accumulation of this type of cultural capi-
> tal, at a time when the professional–managerial class and its aspirants
> feel the need of that reassurance. These movies appeal to people who
> want their increasingly expensive college educations to pay some cultural
> dividends. (103)

Hipsky is correct in asserting that these films do involve elaborate transactions in cultural capital, but the currency of that college education has

undergone a significant devaluation. The appeal of these films for an American audience can be attributed to another crisis—the realization that their expensive college educations have failed to provide the lessons in taste that they need to pursue upward mobility.

In other words, the popularity of the Merchant-Ivory films can also be attributed to what this audience didn't learn in college and now has to look for in the finishing school of quality popular culture. An American university education may provide a knowledge of canonical literature but no sense at all of how to express one's taste in terms of a lifestyle, a widespread cultural anxiety that has been stoked and gleefully tended to by taste merchants available through a variety of different delivery systems.

This crisis in terms of just what that expensive college education fails to provide, and which therefore must be sought elsewhere, is articulated very succinctly by Dominique Browning, editor of *House and Garden* magazine, in a letter to her readers: "Okay, I'm ready to sign myself up, and eager to enroll about 50 people I can think of just off the top of my head. I think it is time to admit we got a little confused, a few decades back, when we decided that higher education should not include instructions in, well, what do we even call it? How to appreciate the finer things in life? How to behave like one of the finer things in life? It's time to bring back finishing school" (20). She condemns the vulgarity of the beneficiaries of "big and instant money," because they fail to appreciate that "the sense of the value of a thing—quite distinct from its cost—does matter. Much of the making of a home has to do with the making of a soul." Her complaint about the difference between having money and having the proper sensibility sounds remarkably like Forster's position in *Howards End* and, at the same time, exemplifies Bourdieu's distinction between financial and cultural capital—but with a key difference. Browning's diagnosis of the problem identifies the operative assumptions that animate this taste crisis: that the acquisition of taste, unlike money, is a matter of the right education, that no one receives those lessons in how to live tastefully from a secondary or university education anymore, but that knowledge has to be found *elsewhere*, specifically from various forms of popular culture that provide the goods and, just as crucially, the information needed to translate consumer decisions into expressions of one's inner being. The notion that the chief objective of a higher education should be the acquisition of taste has indeed been rejected by an academy that considers any such notion of refinement to be, at best, antique and, at worst, ideologically repugnant, because it carries vestiges of an educational system intended to maintain the hegemony of the upper-class values. But within this new evaluative dynamic advanced by *House and Garden*, along with a host of taste mavens like Martha Stewart, Terence Conran, and an entire design industry that labors to make décor an intensely personalized fashion statement, a higher education is judged essential but incomplete, in need of the finishing that only high-end popular culture can provide. Most tellingly, Browning locates the origins of this taste crisis "in the eighties," when everything began to go wrong — exactly the same period when the Merchant-Ivory adaptations began to enjoy the box office success that suggested that their appeal had extended far beyond the old *Masterpiece Theatre* niche audience.

The expansion of that audience depended to a great extent on changes in how canonical literature was to be read, or more specifically how the enjoyment of the classics was fundamentally refunctioned. Just as the bestseller status of Tolstoy and Faulkner novels may be attributed to the ways in which they have been redefined by Oprah Winfrey's Book Club, the cinematic versions of Austen and James novels represent a comparable reframing that changes the picture quite drastically — they *are* different novels, and not just because they have been transformed into images. They are different experiences now that they've been given value and function within a particular taste culture. In her study of how genre romance novels are read by their fans, Janice Radway found that it was not mere escapism that was the key to the success but rather another unforeseen use value: "Their attitude toward language . . . , rather than the text alone, is responsible for one of the most important claims about the worth and function of romance reading. Although the books are works of fiction, the women use them as primers about the world. The romance for them is a kind of encyclopedia, and reading, a process of education" (474). In much the same way, the adaptation film since the mid-eighties has become a kind of encyclopedia for a college-educated audience for whom viewing becomes a process of education in matters not addressed by that university education. The burgeoning popularity of the adaptation films in the eighties, which only continued to gather momentum throughout the nineties, was due to changes in attitude toward literary classics, which could now be read as taste primers in an education in graceful living that was becoming an entertainment industry unto itself outside the walls of the academy. The academy had sidelined itself by defining educated reading in terms of the appreciation of an author's vision or as a manifestation of a particular set of gender and class relations. Reading as a process of acquiring lessons in love and quality consumerism was clearly not a move on the board within an academic reading formation, but that sort of education was thriving within the realm of popular culture.

The "sociology of adaptation" called for by James Naremore (for example, in his collection *Film Adaptation*) and Dudley Andrew (*Concepts in Film Theory*) necessitates situating the appeal of the adaptation within this broader crisis in terms of where and how one would acquire the requisite cultural capital, because it reveals so much about the excessiveness of this mise-en-scène and, at the same time, suggests why film scholars from that academy have been unable to come to terms with the cultural forces that have shaped that excess. The avoidance of the literary adaptation is itself a significant part of that sociology. That academic film study was clearly on the "other side" in this taste crisis becomes especially clear when Higson, in his essay "The Heritage Film and British Cinema," admits his own ambivalence about these films. He acknowledges that he initially wanted to perform an ideological critique of the heritage films:

> But I had to take on board the fact that I also rather enjoyed these films, although I'm not sure I felt that I could admit as much, since this would reveal my own class formation, my own cultural inheritance, my attachment to the wrong sort of cinema for a Film Studies Lecturer. For Film Studies, it seemed to me, had established itself as a distinct discipline precisely by breaking away from respectable middle-class English literary culture, by celebrating the central texts of political modernism, by exploring what was seen as the specifically filmic, and by embracing popular culture. (238)

Higson's admission of this guilty secret is significant in two regards. It provides the historical explanation for why the discipline of film studies had to distance itself from the British literary culture in order to define its borders as a particular discipline with its own conception of "culture." And, just as important, this admission suggests a great deal about how that discipline was, and continues to be, a taste formation that defines the cinematic in ways that are cut to the measure of notions of cultural value determined in the 1970s, when the different forms of ideological analysis became increasingly prominent within that discipline.

The legitimation of film study, in both the American and the British academies, could not have been accomplished without challenging the literary as the international gold standard of cultural capital. Yet the inevitability of that challenge should not blind film studies to the fact that its institutionalization as a discipline was to a great extent the result of a taste war, a back story that can no longer be ignored, now that the vestiges of those conflicts have reemerged in the form of the high-profile literary adaptations that have become the dominant form of prestige picture for the past decade. We need to reexamine the entire category of the cinematic, which served as the central taken-for-granted in the dismissal of these adaptations. The hidebound assumptions about what is, and is not, cinematic still to a very large extent depend on distinctions made by *Cahiers du cinema* critics in the 1950s, when battle lines were drawn between the quasi-literary and the truly cinematic. I think it is far more productive to consider how aggressively cinematic these films really are in reference to what film-viewing pleasures might consist of within contemporary image cultures. The alleged lack of a genuinely cinematic quality in adaptation films rests on two interdependent assumptions: first, that the cinematic is a way of seeing formed by an auteur's signature or, more generally, by a type of film practice that is immediately recognizable as art cinema (e.g., *Memento, 2046, Requiem for a Dream*); and second, that adaptation film is a picturesque way of seeing, closer to other unauthorized visual regimes associated with interior design and travel. The former is considered a legitimate form of visual spectacle, because it is somehow transformative, where the latter is touristic presenting spectacle solely for the sake of the viewers' pleasure. That dichotomy clearly needs to be reexamined in cultures where the circulation between the two has become increasingly elaborate in the formation of cine-literary culture in which novels, films, museum shows, and style magazines now participate in an intensely intertextual, interlocking visual culture, sharing many of the same pictorial codes and values for the same taste communities.

That interconnectedness represents the popularization of tastefulness on a grand scale, at which point, the adaptation film is clearly no longer a niche audience phenomenon but rather a mass audience, quality viewing experience that is tightly imbricated in a sophisticated visual culture driven by a conglomerate-based entertainment industry. The Merchant-Ivory films of the eighties and early nineties signaled the emergence of a growing audience for quality alternatives to mainstream mass entertainment and a commercial infrastructure to serve that audience in combines like the one that produced *A Room with a View* (Merchant-Ivory Productions, Cinecom, National Film Finance Commission, and Curzon Film Distribution). The Miramax adaptations of the later nineties represent a fundamental transformation of that relationship between audience and industry as the making of adaptation films moved from the cottage industry of international art cinema into the arena of Hollywood conglomerate. If the Merchant-Ivory films were, so to speak, the cinematic analogues of Sargent paintings in terms of their depiction of a certain class of characters in lush painterly style meant to be appreciated by a right sort of select audience, the Miramax adaptations of the nineties exemplified the massification of both that visual aesthetic and its intended audience. They were the cinematic analogues of John Singer Sargent as blockbuster museum show, an exhibition that drew over 800,000 patrons to the National Gallery and the Boston Museum of Fine Arts in 2001, at which point, Sargent as court painter to the idle rich became something other than coterie painter known primarily by art historians and art history majors. The exhibition of his paintings became the subject of full-page ads in the Sunday *New York Times*, just as ads for the film versions of literary classics by Austen, James, Wilde, Shakespeare, and Woolf had become fixtures there as well. How did the tasteful niche entertainment become an aggressively tasteful entertainment machine?

4

"MIRAMAXING"

Beyond Mere Adaptation

Miramax Authors Quiz

Match the author with the writing hand:

(a) Will Shakespeare, (b) Virginia Woolf, (c) James M. Barrie

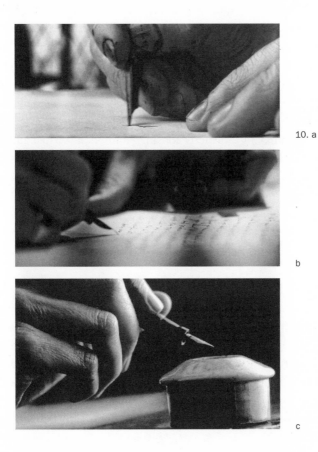

10. a

b

c

The success that Miramax films enjoyed in garnering Academy Awards from 1993, when it was acquired by Disney, until the Weinstein brothers left Disney in 2005 represents an unprecedented achievement in the history of film prizes—twelve consecutive years of at least one Best Picture nomination and 225 nominations overall. If one adds appearances on annual Ten Best Film lists, industry guild awards, and other critics' association prizes, that record looms even larger. No other production ever accomplished what Miramax did during this period—a virtual monopoly on prestige filmmaking, especially in those years when Miramax films won more nominations than all of the other studios combined. While Miramax made and/or distributed a wide variety of different kinds of films, their success in the awards game depended on the aggressive promotion of adaptations and literary-inspired projects, which came to define the contemporary prestige picture. The three close-ups that you see in figure 10, of hands of the author writing with quill or pen, are the "money shots" in Miramax Academy Award–winning films, in every sense of the term. Just as Amazon listmaniacs and television book clubs insist on their legitimacy within the realm of literary culture through their dedication to the love of literature, Miramax successfully realized a film version of that same passion by making the love of literature into one of its stable products—products paradoxically made profitable through the use of strategies developed within the world of high-concept filmmaking, formerly considered to be the virtual antithesis of all things truly literary. No studio has ever been this adept at transforming literary fiction into a cine-literary experience that transcended the category of mere "adaptation."

The Coming of Miramax, or How to Get from Art House to Multiplex via the Rose

In chapter 3 I established a context for the evolution of the adaptation film since the 1980s and then explored how the reception of those films inside and outside the discipline of film studies might form the basis for a sociology of adaptation. Here I concentrate exclusively on the Miramax adaptations and literature-inspired pictures that appeared between 1994 and 2004, exemplified by *Il Postino* (1994), *Emma* (1996), *The English Patient* (1996), *The Wings of the Dove* (1997), *Shakespeare in Love* (1998), *The Cider House Rules* (1998), *Mansfield Park* (1999), *Chocolat* (1999), *An Ideal Husband* (1999), *The Importance of Being Earnest* (2002), *The Hours* (2002), *Cold Mountain* (2003), and *Finding Never-*

land (2004). While Merchant-Ivory films like *A Room with a View*, *Howards End*, and *Remains of the Day* could garner multiple nominations and even win prizes in such categories as Screenplay Adaptation and Costume Design, and the occasional Best Actor Oscar, they were never in danger of winning Best Picture or enjoying blockbuster-caliber success at the box office. It was Miramax that made the literary adaptations that took over the category of Best Picture and exceeded the blockbuster threshold of $100 million domestic box office on a regular basis.

Until its acquisition by Disney in 1993, Miramax was emblematic of the state of foreign and independent film distribution within the United States—a small but savvy distribution company that, with very limited capital, managed quite skillfully to reach its niche audience: a reduced, but still viable art house circuit. As such, they came to represent the quality alternative to high-concept blockbuster filmmaking, a dichotomy that became increasingly visible after the summer of 1989—Miramax was *Sex, Lies and Videotape*, the industry was *Batman*; the former seemingly depended on cinematic genius, festival prizes, and strong word-of-mouth support, while the latter was conglomerate film production, complete with tidal waves of advertising, merchandizing, and ancillary markets. After the acquisition of Miramax by Disney, the relationship between high-concept blockbusters and the world of small, quality films changed profoundly. The "studiofication" of independent production and distribution was becoming a trend by the mid-nineties, and by the end of the decade, major studios had either acquired an "indie" company (Fine Line became part of Turner Entertainment) or developed its own in-house division for "specialty" pictures (Sony Pictures Classics). This diversification of the studio as purveyor of both blockbusters and art films was replicated even within Miramax as it formed Dimension Films (a unit dedicated primarily to exploitation films such as the *Scream* series, *From Dusk till Dawn*, etc.) and began to develop two different types of art films.

In the decade after the acquisition by Disney, Miramax became the preeminent broker of art cinema in the global film market, practically cornering the market in "hipster" films such as *Clerks* (1994), *Pulp Fiction* (1994), *Trainspotting* (1996), *Swingers* (1996), and *Kill Bill Volumes I and II* (2004), which represented a complete rejection of all things literary, at least in terms of traditional taste hierarchies that might privilege Jane Austen over Sonny Chiba. At the same time, they reinvented the adaptation film that came to dominate the category of prestige picture and dominate the Academy

Awards. According to Peter Biskind, "As much as the Weinsteins might love Tarantino, *Pulp Fiction* was never going to win an Oscar; it was just too weird. But *The English Patient* could. The Weinsteins would provide a steady diet of high-toned, Masterpiece Theatre-style, Oscar-grabbing pictures often adapted from prestigious literary works. Miramax mined Jane Austen like a truffle-sniffing pig" (*Down and Dirty Pictures*, 277). While Biskind's book is useful in terms of how it details the wheeling and dealing that made Miramax so powerful, he does not explore how these films became box office successes by appealing to an exponentially broader audience than the old PBS niche audience and, in the process, redefined the literary adaptation as anything but the stodgy, low production values associated with *Masterpiece Theatre*.

How did "Miramax" become shorthand for a very particular type of literary/film entertainment as well as an identifiable "taste formation," in the sense that it signifies a successful consolidation of industry product and audience expectation based on a set of shared values regarding the combination of literary and cinematic pleasures? In his study of the formation of the major independent film companies, Justin Wyatt argues that "Miramax films have thrived due to its marketing savvy, particularly the ability to apply 'exploitation' techniques to art house product" (83). More pointedly, Tim Corrigan, in his analysis of the Miramax public image, argues that its central distribution strategies are "positioning, platforming, and word of mouth, all of which work to generate a shared loyalty, trust, and faith between viewers and the film" (*Film and Literature*, 173). Alisa Perren, writing in *Film Quarterly* on Miramax's development of the "quality indie blockbuster," also stresses the importance of image: "The Weinsteins and their staff grew increasingly adept at selling positive images of themselves and their company along with their films" (31). Despite the proliferation of stories in the press about Harvey Weinstein's vulgarity and ruthlessness, the aggressive marketing of art house titles went hand in hand with the careful exploitation of a rhetoric of quality for the company itself and its audience, even as it was moving its product out of the one arena where quality cinema was recognized as such. Where Vitagraph positioned its quality literary adaptations as a counterattraction to the pulp cinema produced by the rest of the industry by importing literary classics and thereby giving the legitimacy of nonprofit culture to mere moviegoing, Miramax positioned itself as a counterattraction to the Industry, but only by taking the art house film (which was as close to quality nonprofit culture as cinema could get in the United States) out of that realm directly into the marketplace, namely, the multiplex. Miramax was able to preserve the vestiges of the art house pedigree while moving its films into the world of wide-release general exhibition, giving the product the aura that once came with the scarcity of availability, yet somehow maintaining it within a realm of ubiquitous access and saturation advertising. The copy in the print ads used for Miramax titles such as *An Ideal Husband* and *The Importance of Being Earnest* boasts that these films are "The Perfect Antidote to the Summer Blockbuster." Yet, when Steven Soderbergh delivered his trailer for *Sex, Lies and Videotape* to Miramax, it was rejected because it was judged so abstract that it could only result in "art house death" (quoted by Perren, 31).

The creation of this new terrain for quality cinema, between blockbuster movies and the art house cinema, involved more than just product differentiation and brilliant marketing—the success of Miramax depended on the creation of a new film culture in the nineties, in which traditional relationships between art and commerce, and literature and film, were redefined in unprecedented combinations. Miramax's enormous success in terms of both Academy Awards and box office returns may be attributable to high-concept promotion of art house titles, but that strategy was only part of a broader series of interconnected developments that changed the *location* of quality film in the nineties—location measured in terms of where one went to actually see these films, but also in terms of where these films were situated in the hierarchies of American popular taste. This involved nothing less than the transformation of art house film culture that positioned itself as the only alternative to blockbuster-driven Hollywood, a culture that was still dominated, to a great extent, by the vestigial force of the European art cinema of the sixties and the taste distinctions that circumscribed a quality film experience.

The Weinstein brothers have repeatedly described themselves as products of a sixties art house education, which has served as the foundation for their rhetoric of quality. In an article that appeared in the annual Academy Awards issue of *Vanity Fair* (April 2003), Bob Weinstein begins the Miramax story by saying that he and his brother Harvey founded their company in 1979: "Harvey is the public face of Miramax, a role born out of the necessity to win recognition for the 'art house' films we began our careers by distributing—films of high quality, but most of them sorely lacking in bankable stars. Harvey tapped into his inner showman and became the voice these small jewels needed to win the recognition they deserved." The combination here of "inner showman" and "jewels," is the basis of this re-formulation—artistic genius can only be delivered through the agency of marketing genius. That the art house experience, once it was rethought in terms of marketing potential, could become more than a holy place for cinephiles to gather becomes even more explicit in his account of their first "art film" adventure with their father. According to Weinstein, most of their moviegoing consisted of standard genre fare until

> Harvey started pressing to go to a foreign film. Being 15 and having been to a few on his own already, he argued that it was educational and cultural and a bunch of other things that made me think my brother had lost his mind. I was 13 and I didn't want to read my movie! Before I could protest too much and ruin the plan, he took me aside and explained: the name of the film was *I Am Curious Yellow*, a specially imported Swedish "art" film. We needed our father in order to get in because it was rated X. Suddenly foreign didn't sound like such a bad idea. . . . I know that Harvey has been quoted in many articles as saying *The 400 Blows* was one of his favorite foreign-language movies ever, but I can tell you what mine was at that moment in time—I was 13 after all! There was no chance of my falling asleep. But Harvey was just older enough to notice something else: a packed audience of "art-lovers" who never would have set foot in a movie with subtitles but for the fact there was a little something extra added. It was a lesson that would come into play years later. (44)

That "art films" were popular with crossover audiences as *adult films* is not in itself a revelation—the widespread perception that art cinema meant sexy cinema has been detailed by Barbara Wilinsky in her study of the art houses of the 1950s (*Sure Seaters*). What is especially significant here is the phrase "a little something extra" that explains the appeal—jewels alone don't pack the house. To return to Sontag's account of the art film experience during this same period, there is no mention of the something extra, and art film is referred to without quotation marks. One could argue that the something extra factor, that "x" which mainstream movies did not offer and art house did (in addition to all that cinematic artistry) has always been responsible for making certain art films appealing to the crossover audiences of non-cinephiles, whether it be sex in the case of *Blow-Up*, stylized violence in *Reservoir Dogs*, or high-toned martial arts in *Crouching Tiger, Hidden Dragon*. Miramax in fact, was very successful at presenting art films as high-class pornography in its promotion of *The Cook, The Thief, His Wife and Her Lover*

(1998), *Tie Me Up, Tie Me Down* (1990), and *Ready to Wear* (1994), particularly through its ability to manufacture a media circus around its battles with the Motion Picture Association of America over the x or NC-17 ratings given to these films. (Tellingly, at the press conference Miramax organized to protest the rating of *Ready to Wear*, it was represented by superlawyer Alain Dershowitz and supermodel Helena Christianson, who was featured, next to nude, in the poster for the film.)

Miramax had the perspicacity to see that there was another "little something extra" that would draw the crossover viewers in the nineties: *taste*, which had become the sex of the nineties. Taste, or more specifically how to get it, was as foreign to Hollywood action films and teen pix as adult sexuality had been in the fifties, despite the fact that it was otherwise ubiquitous in popular culture in the form of the gastro-porn and décor-porn that were becoming phenomenally popular through cable television and shelter, food, and lifestyle magazines. Tasteful romance, that is, romance between attractive, cultured individuals in the right sort of clothes and locations, whose own lifestyle could serve as a primer for a host of interdependent pleasures — sexual, literary, touristic, gastronomic — became the stable product of the Miramax films of the nineties, from the conflation of sex and food in *Like Water for Chocolate* (1992) and *Chocolat* (1999) to the explicit celebration of romantic hunk as taste machine in *Kate and Leopold* (2002), in which the hero has his showdown with his rival for Kate's affections in a fashionable New York restaurant and humiliates him by demonstrating that when it comes to taste, size matters. I introduce *Kate and Leopold* here even though it is not an adaptation film, because the character of Leopold is a creature of the nineties adaptation, the personification of the sort of romance promoted by these films and the sort of taste that serves as its foundation. Leopold knows everything about painting, opera, wine, and food but apparently has never been to "the pictures."

As a way of determining just how identifiable the Miramax style has become within American film culture, I asked the students in my contemporary Hollywood class in the fall of 2002: "Imagine a new Miramax adaptation is opening this Friday at the local multiplex. What would you expect it to be like?" I include their responses here because I was struck by how effortlessly they were able to sketch out a set of expectations. Despite the fact that many of the films that are considered to be emblematic of Miramax were first developed at other studios and then acquired by Miramax when financing stalled and most have been coproduced with other studios, an identifiable Miramax style has nonetheless been established within American film culture. According to my undergraduates, who have all come of age, cinematically speaking, during its rise to prominence, a Miramax adaptation had the following:

1. Big, passionate love story: involving quality characters who are attractive and articulate but not intimidating intellectually
2. Both prestige actors (mainly European, e.g., Binoche, Scott Thomas, Bonham Carter) and movie stars (Paltrow, Depp, Kidman, Affleck) in same casts
3. Lots of "classy" dialogue: obviously not contemporary American conversational speech, but perfectly understandable to current audiences
4. Visibly "literary" in some way: authors as main characters, characters shown writing, reading, close-ups of books or libraries
5. Geographic exoticism: featuring settings most appealing to American college-educated audiences — English countryside, Tuscany, the south of France, North African deserts
6. Historical exoticism: period pictures ranging between 1820s and 1940s
7. Lush visual style: showcasing the dialogue but never taking precedence over it or calling attention to stylistic experimentation ("not Aronfsky or Lynch, in other words")
8. "Foreign feeling": that is, foreign compared with mall movies but not really foreign as such ("art cinema lite")
9. Not age-specific in terms of audience appeal: "date movies" yes, but also the sort of films "you could go to on Christmas break with your mother and not feel too cheesy about it"
10. Widely advertised: "Your mother asks you if you've seen it yet," though she doesn't ask this of Miramax hipster films like *Swingers* or Miramax foreign films like *City of God*)
11. Extensively merchandized in quality formats: that is, adaptations currently in release likely to be immediately encountered upon entering at Barnes & Noble or Borders on new release tables at front of store, with poster for the film on the cover (also likely to see *making of* books, screenplays, etc.)

The list the students compiled within a matter of minutes suggests a number of very significant things about Miramax. In terms of brand recognition, it has an identifiable profile that most corporations spend millions to create. These films have so defined the category of the adaptation film that the brand has become synonymous with the category item. When *Sense and Sensibility* (1995) was brought up as an example during this discussion, and it was quickly pointed out by other students that it was not a Miramax product, the response was, "Maybe not technically, but it's still a Miramax movie." The authorship of these adaptations of works written by, or directly associated with, major literary figures, was framed by my students in terms of neither literary authors nor cinematic auteurs but of a film company that is a division of a major media conglomerate, Disney (even though Disney never entered the discussion).

The high-concept adaptation that Miramax hybridized so successfully depended on the combination of things formerly thought to be not just mutually exclusive, but mutually antagonistic within the dominant taste categories of American culture. In other words, Miramax made the twain meet. These films, according to my students' Miramax movie profile, combine actors and stars as a matter of course, seem both foreign and familiar at the same time, and are equally dependent on elegant words and beautiful images for their success. Yet perhaps the most important hybridization of what was formerly considered antagonistic is the way these films manage to radiate a quality *cultural* experience while being so intensively *marketed*. This ability to sustain in some sort of equilibrium the celebration of a literary experience on film and the marketing of that experience without invalidating it in the process was the key to Miramax's prestige formula. But that kind of equilibrium can be maintained only by appealing to transcendent values that can transform mere commodity relations into enlightened cultural exchange.

In the case of Miramax, this was founded on two interdependent combinations — the intertwining of sexual passion with a passion for the literary experience, and the collapsing of film company and audience into a shared community of book lovers. Just as the book club neutralizes the taint of the commodification of that reading experience, through the appeal to a community of passionate readers whose love of reading and love of belonging are thoroughly fused together, Miramax successfully fashioned its own kind of community, in which creative personnel and devoted fans are imagined as part of the same cine-literary club. The charge that Miramax films "Harlequinize" the complicated love stories found in the literary texts that have been adapted is an oversimplification, because it fails to recognize how *loving* in a Miramax adaptation is indeed a matter of overwhelming passion, but its manifestations are consistently expressed in terms of writing and reading for an appreciative audience that validates the transcendent nature of the experience. This conflation is nowhere more explicitly or succinctly expressed than in that advertising copy for *Shakespeare in Love*, which bears repeating here: "A celebration of life, language and the creative process that has critics and audiences across America laughing and crying, standing and cheering." Note here how the eroticizing of the creative process is inseparable from audience participation, a point made even more explicitly later in the same advertisement: "Prepare to be ravished by a movie that excites and entrances on so many levels that it takes your breath away."

The transcendent nature of this rapturous love of literature that appears to be nothing less than the most refined form of sexual passion is at the very heart of *Il Postino*. The figure of Pablo Neruda in this film is a paradigmatic example of the role of the author within cine-literary culture. The author is a cultural Titan because he or she is the singular voice responsible for all this passionate meaning, reigning supreme as love advisor rather than mere text function. The restoration of the author goes hand in hand with the revival of a premodern, decidedly Romantic aesthetic, in which literary achievement is measured more in terms of emotional impact than stylistic refinement. Neruda may be in this small town in Italy because he has been exiled from Chile due to his political activism, but once there, he becomes a *lover*, offering advice in affairs of the heart and dancing the tango with a degree of passionate intensity that convinces the viewer that political interests could only be a sideline.

That this kind of passion inspires a community, which then validates its transcendent power, is made explicit in additional material included on the original videotape release of the film. After the film and an extended advertisement for the soundtrack album, another trailer appears promoting an album of Neruda's *Love Poems*. The roster of readers includes prestige actors such as Ralph Fiennes, Rufus Sewell, Miranda Richardson, and Willem Defoe, as well as movie stars and pop star celebrities in the form of Julia Roberts, Sting, Madonna, Wesley Snipes, and Samuel L. Jackson. The experience of the film is multiplied in high-concept form through the production of these commercial intertexts—two different recordings as well as a volume of Neruda's love poetry published by Hyperion Books, a division of Miramax. But what distinguishes this from the merchandizing associated with blockbusters is the attempt to present stars like Wesley Snipes and Madonna, who are synonymous with the most mainstream commercial entertainment, engaged in what labors to be a noncommercial venture. The voice-over in the *Love Poems* advertisement informs us that "in order to pay homage to Neruda, these celebrities got together" to record these poems out of sheer love for his work. Rather than a mere spin-off product, the *Love Poems* appear to be a spontaneous gesture of passion for literature, a kind of ad hoc, Poetry Live-Aid in which Sting and Madonna do charitable work for a noble cause. The "pay homage" formulation represents a fascinating interplay between financial and cultural capital—the former made possible by Disney-style merchandizing, the latter dependent on literary aura—that suggests a purer aesthetic realm in which celebrities and fans spontaneously form a community of book lovers.

This determination to fashion a shared community as part of the promotion of film in a manner that intensifies rather than strips away literary aura is exemplified by the special event organized for *The English Patient*. In February 1997, approximately a month before the Academy Awards, Miramax, through Disney's book division, Hyperion Books, organized a kind of public reading that serves as a pristine example of cine-literary textuality. Using the poster for the film as its frame, this advertisement in the Sunday *New York Times* announced a charity event sponsored by two publishers, Vintage and Hyperion Books, for the benefit of the American Film Institute and the PEN American Center for Literacy (a division of the same organization that annually gives the prestigious PEN Faulkner Award, roughly comparable to the British Man Booker Prize). Here the figure of the actual author (Ondaatje) replaces the cinematic image of the author (Neruda) as a guarantee of cultural aura as he actually appears onstage. But this was not your ordinary author's reading—this featured Ondaatje reading from *The English Patient*, and the film's director-screenwriter, Anthony Minghella, reading from his *English Patient* screenplay. They were joined by the St. Luke's Chamber Ensemble, which played selections from the soundtrack of *The English Patient*, conducted by the composer, Gabriel Yared. Here the author's public reading, traditionally a uniquely literary ritual devoted to the celebration of the word, had acquired cinematic dimension, in terms of the sponsors, the charities, and the featured entertainers, resulting in an intertextual, intermedia form that was neither literary or cinematic but an unusual combination of the two. Within this context, the screenplay quite literally shares the stage with the novel, gaining in prestige as it is given equal footing with that novel; the fusion between the two is made complete when Minghella proceeds to read from the novel and then from his screenplay.

Here, the celebration of words appears to be as much a cinematic pleasure as a literary one, a point made quite vividly in the convergence of Miramax Films and Vintage Books, chief American broker of quality, award-winning novels that come accompanied by a sophisticated book club and reading guide apparatus. This shared community also includes the book lover and cinephile in an advertisement made to resemble an invitation to a charitable event: "Please join us for an evening of readings and conversation." This was indeed a charitable, nonprofit event, but at the same time it also functioned as a magnificent promotion for the film during the Academy Awards voting period, a time when the legendary Miramax treatment is in full swing and special events are arranged for Academy members across the country.

The hybridization of the literary and the cinematic, made possible by the convergence of the literary experience and the marketplace is at the very center of *Shakespeare in Love*. The first thing we are told in the opening graphics is, "In the glory days of the Elizabethan theater two playhouses were fighting it out for writers and audiences." This sets in motion an elaborate relocation of the glory of literature not just within a commercial context but within contemporary Hollywood. The combination of graphics that resemble a description of the film business and the period images they are laid over produces a dual-tracked temporality; the point is reiterated in the opening tracking shot through the Rose Theatre, where Shakespeare's company was based, and by another graphic: "Across the river was the competition, built by Philip Henslowe, a businessman with a cash flow problem. . . ." The tracking shot comes to rest on a poster for a play, *The Lamentable Tragedy of the Moneylender Revenged*, which is followed by a bullet track to backstage, where Mr. Fennyman the financier is torturing Henslowe for the money he's owed. After a short dialogue scene in which the profit motive for producing plays is again reiterated, the author appears, if only a piece of him. The first two shots of Shakespeare produce a neatly constructed discrepancy. In the initial close-up of his hand, he is writing away, but as that hand moves across the page we see superimposed across that image in bold red graphic the title of the film, apparently written in cursive script by the man himself at that very moment. Here the author, the author of authors, is writing *Shakespeare in Love* in his own hand, guaranteeing the authenticity of the

11. Variations on Shakespeare's signature, from *Shakespeare in Love*

film that is signed by none other than Shakespeare himself. Yet the next shot appears to demythologize the moment, through a point-of-view shot in which we see that same hand writing signatures that don't look anything like the autograph in the red graphic that is still emblazoned over the image onscreen—which now shows us the same hand writing an endless series of signatures, none of them *right*.

The film may be about Shakespeare, literary god, the author of authors, but at this point he is so far away from that status that he is still deciding what to call himself, alternating between Will and William and trying out a variety of spellings for his last name. The discrepancy between these signatures, one emanating from within the period image, the other one coming from the graphics that have been established as a voice in the twentieth century, sets in motion a process of demythologizing and simultaneously remythologizing Shakespeare throughout the rest of the film.

Throughout this first third of the film Shakespeare is characterized as hack screenwriter on the make, incorporating plot lines suggested to him by Christopher Marlowe and seemingly more worried about his own cash flow problems than artistic creation. His artistry is mere pose at this point, little more than an affectation he displays like the leather jacket—it goes with the role. After a dialogue scene with Richard Burbage, in which the production of plays is discussed only in terms of financial gain, the audience is apparently prepared to agree with Henslowe when he tells Will, "You see, *comedy*. Love and a bit with the dog, that's what they want." The fact that we see Queen Elizabeth laughing at the slapstick dog routine only validates Henslowe's "give 'em what they want" sentiment. Given the film's frequent recourse to a "wink-wink, this is really all about Hollywood" allegorical mode, Henslowe is the voice of the film business, the ironic deflator of any mystification of theater as Great Literature, telling us, in effect: "You see folks, it's always been an entertainment business." This approach goes unchallenged in the opening scenes of the film, because Shakespeare is devoid of *originality*, the indisputable requirement of genuine authorship, which is opposed to that marketplace—at least by the standards of the late twentieth century, which keeps elbowing its way onscreen.

And then everything changes, as Shakespeare finds not just his muse but also his collaborator/lover. The rest of the film remythologizes Shakespeare, not by restoring him to his former status as literary god, but by reinventing him as lover extraordinaire, his genius clearly depending on his ability to perform in bed and then write about it as quickly as possible, transcribing passionate conversation into literary dialogue. His originality is revealed to be the result of another collaborative process in which he no longer steals from Marlowe but fashions great literature directly out of his love life. This conflation of love life and literature, in which Shakespeare out-performs the tango-dancing Pablo Neruda in *Il Postino* is most explicitly visualized in the cross-cutting between the play rehearsal and the love scenes between Will and Lady Viola. Here the bedroom and the playhouse are fused into one continuous space through the repeated tracking shots, cross-cuts, and the very skillful use of bed posts and pillars accompanied by the continuous nondiegetic music, all of which make love talk and great literature seem indistinguishable.

In the midst of this intercutting, Will breaks away from his lover to go write, the script of *Romeo and Juliet* becoming an up-to-the-minute reporting of their love, as it is occurring. The shot of Shakespeare rushing to his writing table is obviously intended to echo the opening shot of him scratching out his signatures. Here, as we see the hand move across the page, the disembodied voice of Lady Viola seems to be speaking the line *as* he is writing it, a point reiterated by the quick cut to the pair in bed, where she is reading from the same page. Where the shots of the author's hand that open the film stress only discrepancy, now there is only perfect union—

12. "Co-creation": Will Shakespeare (played by Joseph Fiennes) and Lady Viola (played by Gwyneth Paltrow) turning love life into literature, from *Shakespeare in Love*

the hand writes and voice recites: "But soft! What light through yonder window breaks?" Writing the lines, reading the script, rehearsing the play, and performing the sex that inspires it all are all interdependent parts, the creative process becoming the enactment of pure desire, a point made most vividly at the end of the sequence as the cross-cutting between bedroom and playhouse accelerates, culminating in a tight close-up of Lady Viola's face in full orgasm, the moment when passionate conversation and *literature* are as fused together as the lovers. There may be, as Lady Viola tells Will after they make love for the first time, something better than a play, namely sex, but the best plays about love are transcriptions rather than mere *inventions*.

This scene may epitomize the successful fusion of passion and passion for literature, but that convergence, in a Miramax movie, needs an audience, a shared community. I refer here not just to the wildly appreciative audience at the Rose, whose rapture and then thundering ovation are offered as proof of the instant appeal of the play. The appearance of Queen Elizabeth in such deus ex machina fashion to decide the wager only confirms that this is what audiences really want, even back then—quality love stories. But there is another audience in the film that confers even greater power on the play.

13. Lady Viola and Fennyman (played by Tom Wilkinson) enraptured, from *Shakespeare in Love*

In the midst of the cross-cutting between playhouse and bedroom there are two shots of the *first* audience. We see the actors in attendance, apparently mesmerized by the play as Ned and the others come forward to the edge of the stage to listen attentively, seemingly struck dumb by all those words. Most interestingly, after cutting back to the couple now just approaching orgasm, the cut back to the playhouse shows us Fennyman by himself, the money-lender now mesmerized by the play, artistry apparently overwhelming all commercial concerns.

The film offers its own proof that literary passion can collapse the bar between commerce and art by creating an experience so transcendent that it takes the breath away from Lady Viola and audiences everywhere—Fennyman is so swept away that he becomes an actor desperate to take part in this enrapturing experience. This transformation epitomizes the Miramax image as maker of quality cinema, itself the Moneylender Enraptured. The marketplace yields to great art. Henslowe remains the fool who doesn't quite get it as he looks mystified while Fennyman and the actors are overwhelmed by the play. Fennyman is so appalled by Henslowe's money talk that he literally kicks him out of the theater and apologizes to the cast for the disruption, the commercial by this point having no place in the production of art, even for the financier.

Despite this celebration of literature that transcends the marketplace and this overt eroticizing of literary passion as the most refined expression of sexual passion, *Shakespeare in Love* was marketed so heavily that when it won the Academy Award for Best Picture, Miramax was accused of buying the Oscar through its massive advertising campaign. The day after the awards ceremony, in an article entitled "Mogul in Love with Winning" in the *New York Times*, Bernard Weinraub reported:

> Executives at Dreamworks, including Jeffrey Katzenberg, have said in recent weeks that Mr. Weinstein has upped the ante by spending millions to promote *Shakespeare*. Mr. Katzenberg's partners, Mr. Spielberg and David Geffen, were also known to be angry with Mr. Weinstein. . . . Bill Mechanic, chairman of Fox Entertainment, said, "It's like the process of trying to win an election. It's no longer about the material or the merit. It's about how much money you spend. It's not what the Academy founders set out to do." (B1)

Here Weinstein, the enlightened financier in the style of Fennyman, is portrayed as a mogul perverting the artistic process by buying prestige, absconding with cultural capital it somehow isn't entitled to in order to cash it in at the box office. This scenario reveals just how far Miramax had come, from distributor of alternative art cinema to a company that outspent all rivals in its relentless promotion of its films, to a point where the mainstream industry, exemplified by Spielberg and Katzenberg, are the injured parties invoking the Academy Awards as a measure of film quality, untainted by commercial interests. In a telephone interview with Weinstein conducted by Bernard Weinraub and reported in the same 1999 article in the *New York Times*, Weinstein provided a succinct formulation of the Miramax strategy,

> The overall campaign from beginning to end for *Shakespeare* is $30 million. It's a bit less than the overall campaign for *The English Patient*. I'm not doing anything different to market these movies this year than any other year. We began the movie with a small release. Went wide. Got to the academy. And then the blitzkrieg was really in support of the commercial release of the film. *Shakespeare in Love* was $38 million at the box office before the nomination. It's $66 million now. And it will be $75 million by the time of the awards.

O, she doth teach the torches to burn bright!
Her beauty hangs upon the cheek of night
Like a rich jewel in an Ethiop's ear;
Beauty too rich for use, for earth too dear!
So shows a snowy dove trooping with crows,
As yonder lady o'er her fellows shows.
The measure done, I'll watch her place of stand,
And, touching hers, make blessed my rude hand.
Did my heart love till now? Forswear it, sight!
For I ne'er saw true beauty till this night.

Romeo and Juliet (I.v)

14. Illustration from the Miramax Books edition of Shakespeare's love poetry,
Shakespeare in Love: The Love Poetry of William Shakespeare

"Getting to the Academy" is a crucial step in this process, because once the nominations are secured and the quality factor established, the nominations become the centerpiece of the two-pronged blitzkrieg aimed at the general audience and Academy voters with the expectation of exponentially greater box office returns. The extensive marketing of *Shakespeare in Love* involved more than just advertising, as Miramax merchandised the film in high-concept style through its simultaneous release of a number of ancillary spin-off products. The release of a soundtrack album and screenplay are, of course, standard operating procedure even for the most "independent" films, but Miramax Books also released *Shakespeare in Love: The Love Poetry of William Shakespeare*. This volume is another perfect example of cine-literary culture, since it so neatly hybridizes the literary and the cinematic, featuring excerpts from the plays and the sonnets accompanied by stills of Joseph Fiennes and Gwyneth Paltrow, which function as illustrations on the pages facing the poems.

These pairings of verse and film stills are punctuated with two-page spreads featuring slightly gauzier stills with Shakespeare's handwriting, the same handwriting we see in the film, now laid over the image as a kind of tasteful dialogue balloon. For example, there's a shot of Paltrow overlaid with "Good night, good night. Parting is such sweet sorrow that I shall say good night till it be morrow" in cursive script. The format of this volume is virtually indistinguishable from the standard gushy love poetry volumes that are so ubiquitous at Valentines Day, a point made rather conclusively by the fact that I purchased my copy of *Shakespeare in Love: The Love Poetry of William Shakespeare* at a Barnes & Noble bookstore here in South Bend, where it was displayed on the Valentines Day table in the center of the rotunda, alongside titles that did not share quite the same literary pedigree, *101 Nights of Greaat Romance*, *101 Nights of Greaat Sex . . .*

When I showed this book to the students who had assembled the Miramax movie profile, it was met with a round of laughs and shaking heads, one female student commenting, "I liked the movie but I wouldn't be caught dead with that thing." Their reaction suggests that Miramax was obviously appealing to another audience of readers/viewers, but what are the contours of that taste community? One would expect college educated, or college bound, since it is after all Shakespeare, but my college students recoiled from it in horror. The easy answer is romance reader types, who adored the film as a great love story and tuned out the fact that it was Shakespeare; only this book is filled with Shakespeare's verse—so what would explain an appeal so strong that it figures so prominently on the Love Table at Barnes & Noble, four years after the release of the film?

The success of any high-concept blockbuster depends not on the appeal to a mass audience but rather on a studio's ability to *mass* audiences, normally by targeting different audiences through diversified advertising and merchandizing strategies. In film business talk, this has been called "filling out the quadrant." The publication of Shakespeare's love poetry by Miramax demonstrates how successfully those strategies were applied to literary properties, but filling out the quadrant was complicated in this case because the massing of audiences involved the potential for profound taste conflicts that would not arise in the promotion of the average blockbuster. The merchandizing of *Lord of the Rings*, for example might involve action figures for children and special edition books for teenage and adult readerships, but the presence of Gandalf as action figure does not negate the pleasures taken by the more mature readers/viewers who want to consider Tolkien's opus a literary masterpiece. For Miramax to fill out the quadrant sufficiently for a literary prestige picture to become a box office smash, taste cultures that might otherwise view each other antagonistically had to be encouraged to not just enjoy the same film but somehow regard it as *their own*.

To return to *The English Patient*, the gala authors' reading event staged by Miramax and Vintage and Hyperion Presses at Town Hall in March 1997 was aimed at a sophisticated taste culture, one that read their Sunday *New York Times* religiously, attended authors' readings, and would know automatically where Town Hall was and be familiar with the sort of protocols involved at such events. That audience was not likely to buy *The Love Poetry of William Shakespeare*, and the suggestion that they might read romance novels would produce the same sort of giggling that my students displayed. Yet when Ondaatje was featured in a profile in the *New York Times* after the event, another audience came into play. The interviewer, Ben Ratliff, describes the Indian lunch he and Ondaatje are enjoying during their conversation:

> The restaurant is a block away from the Ritz, his base during a quick visit to New York to give a reading at a sold-out Town Hall, along with Anthony Minghella, the screenwriter and director of *The English Patient*. One spectator was Kathryn Falk, the editor of *Romance Times*, the trade magazine of the romance novel business, whose February issue had an article pronouncing *The English Patient*, "greatest romantic movie of the decade." "Oh my god," he (Ondaatje) said with an uneasy chuckle. "Mmmm . . . *Romance Times*. I hadn't realized it had got to that level." (sec. 1, 47)

The English Patient: *Getting to "That Level"*

How did it get to that level? And what exactly is *that level*? Certainly, few adaptations have ever appealed across so many different taste cultures that were formerly thought to be mutually antagonistic. The awards that *The English Patient* has won in novel and film incarnations demonstrate that range, from Booker Prize to Academy Awards to *Romance Times*, a range that translates quite easily into the traditional high-brow, middle-brow, and low-brow culture hierarchy. Yet the successes that the novel and its adaptation have enjoyed also reveal how antiquated that hierarchy has become, now that formerly elite pleasures have become so successfully *massified*. The work of Arjun Appadurai (in particular, his introduction to *The Social Life of Things*) is especially useful in describing the contours of this transformation. Appadurai argues that value is determined within consumer societies by "regimes of value" that establish the customary paths through which a specific commodity circulates. Within a given path, an entire network of institutional frameworks and protocols maintain the value cohesiveness of that particular regime. But the value of commodities can be changed fundamentally through what he calls diversions, in which an object begins to circulate in a different orbit. An example of this sort of diversion, according to Appadurai, is the way that objects which function as tools within one path (Masai spears, Dinka baskets, etc.) become objets d'art through a very specific form of aesthetic diversion. Appadurai insists, "Diversions are meaningful only in relation to the paths from which they stray" (28). In the case of *The English Patient*, the move from Booker Prize to film adaptation is not without precedent—since its inception in 1969, thirteen novels that have been short-listed for the Booker Prize have been made into films, two of them by Steven Spielberg: Thomas Kenneally's *Schindler's Ark* (1982) and J. G. Ballard's *Empire of the Sun* (1984). These adaptations may represent a shift in paths but not real diversions, since the cultural capital that comes with the Booker is incorporated in the promotion of the important picture. The event at Town Hall exemplifies the merger of literary culture into quality film culture, as though the latter were simply an extension of that former path, which might involve massive changes in the geography, capital, and delivery system but nonetheless appears to be an extension rather than a diversion, because it subscribes to the same regime of value by celebrating the transcendent power of all those words.

Adapting a novel in such a way that it moves from Booker Prize to *Romance Times*, on the other hand, involves a genuine diversion, because it is predicated on a change in regimes of value, specifically in regard to the relationship between pleasure and quality. The Booker, like the PEN Faulkner, is a recognition of superior achievement within the realm of serious fiction, a regime of value that privileges the appreciation of literary craft as a pleasure unto itself, and therefore rather dubious about any pleasures that fictional texts generate that aren't authorized as such. *Romance Times* and its readers aren't bound by the same covenant—the pleasures that the film version of *The English Patient* offers depend on a particular way of envisioning love, in which case the impact of the stars far outweighs that of the author. The two different covers of the novel visualize this neatly. The original dust jacket and paperback cover featured a black-and-white photograph of a figure enshrouded by a misty landscape, its face completely indiscernible. The cover of the American paperback edition that appeared after the release of the film was the poster for the film—a tight close-up of the beautiful couple in passionate embrace. The television spot advertisement reiterated this focalization on the couple virtually to the exclusion of everything else except a few all-purpose combat shots taken from the Tobruck sequence. The faces of Katharine (Kristin Scott Thomas) and Almasy (Ralph Fiennes) dominate the ad, and only four lines of dialogue from the film are quoted in alternation with the voice-over listing the Academy Awards the film had just won, lines that encourage the readers of *Romance Times* to think of the film as their own:

> *Katharine*: Promise me you'll come back for me.
> *Almasy*: I promise I'll never leave you.
> *Voice-over*: Winner of. . . .
> *Katharine*: We didn't care about countries, did we? None of that mattered. There's something finer than that.
> *Voice-over*: [continues to enumerate awards]
> *Almasy*: We're the real countries. Not the boundaries drawn on maps. As God wanted, to walk in such a place with you.

This television advertisement obviously may Harlequinize the love stories found in Ondaatje's novel, but it does not completely misrepresent the sort of passion that is so all-pervasive in Minghella's film. How it got to "that level" can be explained in terms of marketing, but filling out the quadrant necessarily involves particular adaptation strategies that need to be examined more closely in order to delineate the relationship between literary and cine-literary.

The English Patient is a revealing case study in this regard, because the adaptation was so self-consciously "literary," yet its literariness is so at odds with the overtly literary aspects of the novel. Ondaatje's novel includes a wide array of intertexts that are used repeatedly to establish both the historical stage for the action and the relevant antecedents for Ondaatje's own writing. He makes the two main landscapes for the novel, northern Italy and the Sahara, hum with the echoes of past inscriptions, the intertexts referred to repeatedly by both characters and narrator. Almasy says, while watching Katharine read the story of Candaules and Gyges by the fire: "I would often open Herodotus for a clue to geography. But Katharine had done that as a window to her life" (233). The echoes of previous inscriptions that become figurations for the characters in the present are just as resonant when the action moves to Italy. As Hana reads aloud to Almasy from the books she finds in the library, passages from Stendhal and Tacitus are quoted in the text, forming a chorus of voices, each envisioning this same landscape across the centuries. At one point, Kip looks up into the cypress trees, whose middle branches had been shelled away, and muses, "Pliny must have walked down a path like this, or Stendhal, because passages of the *Charterhouse of Parma* had occurred in this part of the world too" (72). Almasy is convinced that this isn't just any old ruined palazzo, telling Hana, "I think this was the Villa Bruscoli. . . . Yes, I think a lot happened here. . . . Pico and Lorenzo and Poliziano and the young Michelangelo. . . . They sat in this room with a bust of Plato and argued all night" (57). Ondaatje makes the commonplace book an explicit intertextual model for his own project. The most visible form of this sort of intertextuality as palimpsest is Almasy's copy of Herodotus, which "he added to, cutting and gluing in pages from other books or writing in his own observations — so they all are cradled within the text of Herodotus" (16). Katharine's drawings are also glued into the book by Almasy, and she later writes in it as she lies dying in the Cave of Swimmers, adding still more layers of inscription on top of Herodotus. The end result is an elaborate intertextual web, a novel in which characters' words and images intermingle with those of Herodotus, Tacitus, and Giotto, as well as Stendhal, Fenimore Cooper, and Kipling, all of which are cradled within the text of Ondaatje. Almasy formulates the intertextual project of the novel succinctly: "We are communal histories, communal books" (261).

Minghella's version of *The English Patient* epitomizes the distinctive characteristics of *cine*-literary textuality in terms of what it transposes from the novel to the screen in order to advertise its own literariness, and in terms of what it omits in its pursuit of quality passion. The film focalizes on Almasy's copy of Herodotus as the principal signifier of the film's literary affiliations. There are a number of shots of the book itself, and we see both Almasy and Katharine adding their inscriptions. Hana reads from this book extensively, her words often becoming a voice-over, which at times gives way to the voices of Almasy and Katharine, speaking aloud what they've written. This voice-over resonates as arch-literary, because it isn't Hana's account of the action, told to the reader in a conversational manner à la *Virgin Suicides*, nor is it the voice of the disembodied author, à la *Tom Jones*. It is instead a *reading* of a text composed by other characters, written in an intensely poetic style of prose, filled with figures of speech, cast in rhythmic, repetitive cadences as they try to describe their love and loss. They caress the words they use to accomplish this, and the film does all it can to continue that caressing of the written word, making reading a privileged activity within the film, both in terms of onscreen action and the soundtrack, which repeatedly focalizes on the words.

While the layers of Tacitus, Stendhal, and company do not appear in the film, the omission that really differentiates the literary from the cine-literary concerns Kip's relationship to all these words and the passion they convey. I'm referring here to the profound ambivalence he feels toward his European education and the sort of political tension that his character creates within the novel, neither of which has a place within the world of the film. One of the principal features of the cine-literary is the equation of quality literature with quality passion—great literature *sweeps you away*. But the displacing of Kip reveals exactly what has to be swept aside, in order for the cine-literary to sweep you away. At the end of the novel, he reacts violently to the news of the bombing of Hiroshima, an event not even alluded to in the film. His reaction throws into question all of the refinement and good taste that come with the literariness that Miramax promotes so unequivocally. Upon learning the news of the bombing, Kip rushes into Almasy's room and takes aim with his rifle, firing at the last moment at the fountain instead of at the English patient. In what the novel constructs as a point-of-view shot from Kip's perspective, looking down the barrel of the gun at Almasy's face, he screams:

> I sat at the foot of this bed and listened to you, Uncle. . . . I believed I could carry that knowledge, slowly altering it, but in any case passing it on beyond me to another. I grew up with the traditions from my country, but later, more often, from *your* country. Your fragile white island that with customs and manners and books and prefects and reason somehow converted the rest of the world. You stood for precise behavior. . . . Was it just ships that gave you such power? Was it, as my brother said, because you had histories and printing presses? (283)

This rejection of the ideological baggage that comes with all the books and good taste reflects the tension in the novel between desire and global power relations. When Caravaggio tells Kip not to blame Almasy because he isn't English, his response throws their national differences into sharp relief: "American, French, I don't care. When you start bombing the brown races of the world, you're an Englishman. You had King Leopold of Belgium and now you have fucking Harry Truman of the USA. You learned it all from the British" (286).

The conclusion of the film version of *The English Patient* sweeps all this away in a grand romantic ending that seems more in keeping with the recording of Pablo Neruda's *Love Poems* or *Shakespeare in Love: The Love Poetry of William Shakespeare*. Just as the value of all things literary is never questioned, the tension between desire and national identity is collapsed— everything is subservient to quality passion. The characters whose love defies all maps get the last word, primarily because the complications of racial difference are nowhere to be found on this cinematic map that is so unblemished by postcolonialism. Two brief scenes near the end of the film reveal what gets swept away. The first is a scene in which Kip reacts to the death of his partner, Hardy, which takes the place of Kip's speech about bombing the brown races of the world. As he packs up his belongings he tells Hana: "I was thinking yesterday, the Patient and Hardy, they're all that's good about England. And I couldn't even say what that was. We didn't exchange two personal words and we'd been together through some terrible things. He was engaged to a girl in the village. And us, he never once, he didn't ask about whether I could spin the ball at cricket, or the karma sutra . . . *I don't even know what I'm talking about*" (emphasis mine). To which Hana replies simply, "You loved him." Kip only stares off into the distance, overcome by his grief. Here, solidarity in arms replaces outrage as national differences are overcome through love, a position entirely contradictory to the climax of the novel. Kip's impassioned speech is not just omitted but replaced by his inability to even know what he is saying. The overpowering nature of quality passion acquires mythical proportions in the last scene featuring Almasy and Katharine. After we have heard Hana's, and then Katharine's voice recount her death, and seen Almasy die in the villa, the couple reappear in their glistening silver biplane, now in some sort of mythical realm where they fly out into a world without maps, where they linger yet.

Ironically, the last scene in Ondaatje's novel is arguably more cinematic, for it tells the reader something quite different about the nature of love. The novel concludes with a cross-cut that visualizes their connection: "And so Hana moves and her face turns and in a regret she lowers her hair. Her shoulder touches the edge of the cupboard and a glass dislodges. Kirpal's left hand swoops down and catches the dropped fork an inch from the floor and gently passes it into the fingers of his daughter, a wrinkle at the edge of his eyes behind his spectacles" (302). Ondaatje creates a "match on action" cut—Hana knocks the glass toward the floor, and through the "cut," it becomes the fork caught by Kip in his kitchen in India sitting amidst his family, married and raising children with someone else. In his analysis of this concluding scene Raymond Younis, in an essay in *Literature and Film Quarterly*, argues: "The novel's end suggests that it is the things that bring two nationalities or two people together, and not the things which separate them, that are ultimately of the greatest value." But they are apart despite that connection. This "cut" crystallizes the exquisite agony of the moment—they may well have been the great love of each other's lives, but they are on opposite sides of the world, following lives that will never allow them to meet again because of the geopolitical factors that blew them apart. Love, in the case of this couple, cannot overcome maps.

In her reading of *The English Patient*, Jacqui Sadashige, also writing in *Literature and Film Quarterly*, argues that the film "de-postmodernizes" the novel:

> Whereas Ondaatje's treatment of his characters suggests that there are multiple subjectivities located in myriad and simultaneous loyalties to structures such as family, nation, and race, Minghella's film constructs and fetishizes an essential interior self. . . . More specifically, the film implies that selfhood is located in a person's ability to love and is evidenced by acts inspired by such sentiments. As a result, the "lover" emerges as the true subject—set against the fleeting and mutable identities associated with race or nationality. (255)

Ondaatje has indeed been considered one of Canada's foremost postmodern writers, figuring prominently in Linda Hutcheon's *The Canadian Postmodern*. Yet this notion of an essential self as lover, transcending mere nationality was not invented by Miramax and company because it is so prominently advanced throughout the novel by Almasy and Katharine. This notion of love overpowering the map is set in direct opposition to Kip and Hana's relationship, in which the reverse is true—sometimes the map is inescapable. The dialogic relationship between these two ways of imagining love and nationality, one a vestige of European Romanticism, the other shaped by a South Asian postcolonialism, is the central tension in the novel, a point made quite succinctly in Ondaatje's invocation of the fresco and the parable to describe these characters. Late in the novel the narrator says of Kip: "The naive Catholic images from those hillside shrines that he has seen are with him in the half-darkness. . . . Perhaps this villa is a similar tableau, the four of them in private movement, momentarily lit up, flung ironically against this war" (279). The connection between the religious art and the characters in the villa is reiterated on the next page, when an explicit comparison is made between the statuary in the church and Hana, Kip, and Almasy: "these creatures that represent some parable about mankind and heaven" (279).

Ondaatje's novel is a postmodern parable that offers the reader two different lessons about the relationship between love and nationality, notions that remain suspended in a dialogic tension. Hutcheon's contention that one of the distinguishing features of postmodern textuality is the rejection of the either/or dichotomies of high modernism in favor of a both/and aesthetic is particularly relevant here. Neither Almasy nor Kip serves as the *raisonneur* in this novel, because they both do, given the novel's consistent endorsement both of their perspectives. Almasy's insistence that he wants to live in a world without maps is articulated in some of the most poetic passages in the novel, the very beauty of the language giving those sentiments not just credibility but also an extremely seductive power. Within this dialogic parable, however, Almasy's internationalism is also undermined by the presence of Kip, whose impassioned speech about Hiroshima makes Almasy's "citizen of the world" perspective seem hopelessly naïve, a position that only an old-world European aristocrat could advocate. The novel's final cross-cut concludes the parable by emphasizing both the connection that grand passion produces and the separation that the world of nationalities still enforces.

Minghella's film exemplifies the Miramax movie style in terms of its celebration of an intensely literary passion, but questions concerning the fidelity of this adaptation can be oversimplified. The film is, in many ways, a meticulous envisioning of Almasy's worldview. Walter Murch's sound design and editing create a filmic equivalent of the meandering narrative voices in the novel, which "slip from level to level like a hawk" (4). The credit sequence, which serves as a kind of overture to the film, visualizes quite brilliantly Almasy's obsessions with the desert, Katharine, and inscription. The backdrop for the credits appears to be sand until it is revealed to be a parchment, when the brush begins to paint the swimming figure, at which point the paper dissolves into desert, which resembles in its contours the curves of a human form, thereby neatly visualizing the interdependency between

15. "Air Pottery Barn": the biplane carrying Amasy and Katharine, from the film *The English Patient*

the book, the desert, and the woman's body, which consume Almasy. But this series of dissolves is interrupted by the introduction of the gleaming silver biplane carrying Almasy and Katharine.

What was a hunk of junk in the novel is here transformed into "Air Pottery Barn," the biplane as stylish accent piece that is the perfect mode of transport for "Swept Away Romance," as the film fades into the land of a Ralph Lauren "Safari Collection" advertisement. By focusing on the European lovers and celebrating their belief in the transcendent power of a love that sweeps away all maps, only half the fresco comes into view, and as a monological fragment, it changes the parable completely. The film, like the novel, concludes with cross-cutting, but here the alternation is between Hana leaving the villa and the images of Almasy and Katharine flying across the desert, which open the film. Hana becomes the *reader* of their story rather than a lover herself (see Patrick Deer's "Defusing *The English Patient*" for an especially compelling analysis of this transformation). Like Mr. Fennyman, she plays the role of audience member transformed, a member of the ad hoc community that has been drawn together by the power of the words that tell this transcendent love story.

The Hours: *The Genius of the* Quality *System?*

I want to conclude with a discussion of the Miramax/Paramount adaptation of *The Hours*, because it complicates the sociology of adaptation that I have been tracing throughout this chapter. How that Miramax formula (whether applied by Miramax, Paramount, or a combination of the two) works in Stephen Daldry's adaptation represents a significantly different incarnation of the cine-literary, specifically in the ways it envisions the relationship among love, literary life, and imagined community of readers/viewers that is the foundation of the Miramax adaptation. In many ways, the film fits the Miramax movie profile sketched out by my students by making authors and avid readers the central characters. Michael Cunningham's novel is about Woolf's writing of *Mrs. Dalloway* and also how that novel is read by another character, Laura Brown, whose experience of the novel appears to be as intense and formative as the writing of the book was for the author. The third character, a literary editor named Clarissa Vaughan (dubbed Mrs. Dalloway by her former lover, Richard, in their younger days as undergraduate English majors), is a character two times over. She is the contemporary Manhattanite version of Woolf's character, in the process of organizing her own dinner party, as well as the model for the main character in the one novel that Richard has written—thereby incarnating one character while serving as the inspiration for another. Richard is the esteemed poet, about to receive a prestigious literary prize ("The Carruthers"), whose poems we learn late in the film are addressed to the mother who abandoned him, who happens to be the same Laura Brown—at which point, Laura becomes not just an avid reader of Woolf's novel but also the inspiration for her son's literary creations. We also see Leonard Woolf, Virginia's husband, actively engaged in the copy editing and printing of books at the Hogarth Press office, just as Clarissa works as an editor at an (unnamed) press specializing in literary books. This all-pervasive literariness naturally results in dozens of shots of writers writing, readers reading, and repeated dialogue sequences about the all-consuming power of both. Most important, the film's opening sequence features repeated extreme close-ups of the author's hand, as in *Shakespeare in Love*—here is the very act of writing from which everything we are about to see flows.

The creative personnel brought together to make the film and the eventual promotion of the film also exemplify the Miramax adaptation formula in paradigmatic form. Cunningham's novel had achieved both literary pedigree (it won the Pulitzer Prize and the PEN Faulkner Award) and bestseller status. As a literary bestseller it was very successfully marketed as a book club darling and became a mass market phenomenon, featured prominently at superstores like Barnes & Noble and Borders but also as a Recommended Book on end-cap displays in Target stores, alongside *Bridget Jones's Diary* and *The Girl with a Pearl Earring*. That pre-sold "quality" concept was further amplified by involving Philip Glass, Davis Hare, and Stephen Daldry (all

Academy Award timber), as were the players who were assembled, Meryl Streep and Julianne Moore having already achieved "fine actor" status, joined by an acknowledged movie star, Nicole Kidman. The film was given massive advertising support, Kidman became a fixture on daytime television chat shows promoting the film, and all three principals appeared together on the *Oprah Winfrey Show* (on November 8, 2002).

The promotion of *The Hours*, however, involved a different strategy from *The English Patient*. Instead of filling out the quadrant in terms of massing disparate audiences, it took the form of a saturation campaign aimed at a particular taste culture. Consider how the film was promoted within the various sections of the *New York Times* national edition, a favorite venue of Miramax advertising outside of trade publications like *Variety* and *The Hollywood Reporter*. I say "various sections" because, unlike the full-page and two-page spreads for *Shakespeare in Love* and *The English Patient*, which had appeared in the Arts and Leisure section alongside the rest of the film ads, *The Hours* was ubiquitous throughout the newspaper. The full-page and two-page spreads for *The Hours* were there in the Sunday edition, and substantial ads appeared regularly in the daily national edition as well (another standard venue for Miramax ads). What distinguished the promotion of *The Hours* was its inescapability throughout the paper. In the Sunday, January 19, 2003, edition for example, there was a full-page ad for the film in Arts and Leisure section ("The Most Nominated Drama of the Year," complete with appreciative blurb from the *Times*'s own critic, Stephen Holden), another smaller ad in the *Book Review*, and yet another half-page ad in the Sunday Style section, this one advertising "Virginia Woolf and *The Hours*, a Sponsored Archive of *The New York Times*," complete with another series of photos of the three stars. In addition to these advertisements, an article by Michael Cunningham about the adaptation was featured on the front page of the Arts and Leisure section: "The Novel, the Movie: My Baby Reborn," in which the author states: "I find myself in an enviable if slightly embarrassing position as one of the only living American novelists happy with his experience with Hollywood" (22); a full-page ad for the film appeared on the facing page. The adaptation appeared to be both a literary/film achievement and a lifestyle phenomenon, the latter point reiterated by further ads for the film in the Thursday House and Home section of the *Times*, a recently added section modeled after shelter magazines. Another article about Cunningham, "This Is the House the Book Bought," appeared in a later House and Home section (October 24, 2003), in which Cunningham recounted how the success of his novel had allowed him to buy his beach house on Cape Cod.

These ads and articles demonstrate two things. First, the distinction between advertisement and newsworthiness all but collapses—the ultimate proof that a successful buzz has been generated around a high-concept blockbuster, only in this case, it is a quality, high-concept adaptation. Second, reading the novel, seeing the film, and lusting after beach houses all become interrelated, even interdependent pleasures within the same taste culture, since the need to be in the know about this particular adaptation seems to be inescapable, given its coverage in the literary, film, fashion, and shelter sections of the same national newspaper. If, as I argued earlier in this chapter, the Merchant and Ivory adaptations of the late eighties and early nineties were primers in the art of gracious living, comparable to similar lessons being offered in shelter, travel, and fashion industries, Miramax/Paramount formalizes those connections into a series of tightly integrated intertextual arcs that form an elaborate taste synergy that link the novel, author, adaptation, film company, and audience within the same sensibility. For the Laura Browns of 2003, *The Hours* was inescapably the must-see quality film of the moment.

Given this relentless promotion of the film, how good could such an adaptation be, especially if we pose the traditional questions about fidelity in regard to such an overtly literary novel? The answer is, amazingly successful—a fact that complicates any hard-and-fast equations regarding the relationship between marketing strategies and adaptations strategies. While *The Hours* enjoyed the sort of advertising campaign that rivaled any high-concept prestige picture, its complicated narrative structure and intricate editing patterns represent a completely different kind of cinematic aesthetic than the "art cinema lite" style used in other Miramax adaptations. Rather than simplifying the novel's interlacing of three distinct narrative strands, which transpire in three different historical periods, the film actually makes the interplay ever more intricate, creating complicated patterns of mutuality that are possible only through cinematic means. Where Cunningham's novel cuts back and forth between three main characters in alternating chapters, each approximately ten to fifteen pages long, the film often cuts between them on a shot-by-shot basis in montage sequences where each one appears to either be engaged in the same activity or completes the other's actions.

When Laura Brown checks into the Normandy Hotel to take her own life, she lies down on the bed and begins reading her copy of *Mrs. Dalloway*. In Cunningham's novel, she speculates about Woolf as she reads:

> It seems, somehow, that she has left her own world and entered the realm of the book. Nothing, of course, could be further from Mrs. Dalloway's London than this turquoise hotel room, and yet she imagines that Virginia Woolf herself, the drowned woman, the genius, might in death inhabit a place not unlike this one. . . . She strokes her belly. I would never. She says the words out loud in the silent room: "I would never." She loves life, loves it hopelessly, at least at certain moments; and she would be killing her son as well. . . . She imagines Virginia Woolf, virginal, unbalanced, defeated by the impossible demands of life and art: she imagines her stepping into a river with a stone in her pocket. Laura keeps stroking her belly. It would be as simple, she thinks, as checking into a hotel. It would be as simple as that. (152)

In the film Laura Brown reads her copy of *Mrs. Dalloway* at the Normandy, and Woolf's voice-over speaking the words of the novel binds them together sonically as well as visually. But the film adds another even more sophisticated relationship between the two characters through the cross-cutting. This scene at the hotel occurs during Woolf's speculation about what to do with her character Mrs. Dalloway. As Brown reads her copy of *Mrs. Dalloway*, we hear the voice-over say, "It is possible to die," at which point, according to the screenplay, "suddenly brackish water floods from underneath, washing up over the sides of the bed. LAURA, in her imagination, sinks under the water, strewn with weeds, and then drowns" (Scene 61). As such, this shot is an elegant visualization of Brown's imagining herself as Woolf drowning.

But in the very next shot we see Woolf in 1923, again saying, "It is possible to die," this time, completely lost in thought during her sister Vanessa's visit. Vanessa responds by telling her daughter Angelica: "Your aunt's a very lucky woman, Angelica, because she has two lives. Most of us have only one, but she has the life she leads and she also has the book she's writing." She then addresses Virginia, "What were you thinking about?" Virginia replies, "Oh. I was going to kill my heroine. But I've changed my mind." At this point, the images of Brown at the Normandy are made to appear—retroactively, through the cross-cutting—to have been not just of her reading *Mrs. Dalloway* but also as a visualization of Woolf's own speculation about what to do with her character Mrs. Dalloway as she is writing *Mrs. Dalloway*. Brown is so taken with the novel because she *is*, in effect, Mrs. Dalloway,

16. Laura Brown (played by Julianne Moore) engulfed: the effect of water washing over Laura's bed in the Hotel Normandy, from the film *The Hours*

17. Laura Brown and Virginia Woolf (played by Nicole Kidman) as one: the scene with Laura, in her room at Hotel Normandy, cutting to Virginia, speaking to her sister, from the film *The Hours*

and can therefore serve as a possible future for that character, just as Woolf functions as the possible future Brown considers for herself. This particular dimension of the interplay is intensified even further in the next two shots.

After Woolf says she has decided not to kill her heroine, we see Laura back in the hotel room lying on the bed as it was before the flood waters came, closing the book, rubbing her stomach, and saying, "I can't. I can't," seemingly as a direct result of the author's decision about her heroine. This is followed by a cut back to Woolf, still in conversation with Vanessa: "I fear I might have to kill someone else instead." The creation of this sense of mutuality, in which these women appear to be so intimately attuned to each other's perspectives, despite their geographic and historical differences, is accomplished by the most *cinematic* of techniques — parallel editing and a mise-en-scène that emphasizes the inherent plasticity of the image.

Conceived of in this way, *The Hours* seems like a radically different kind of adaptation. Yet to what should we attribute these differences? To the fact that Scott Rudin, and not Harvey Weinstein, was the producer and Miramax was brought in to coproduce at a later point in the film's development? Or to the fact that the film did not attempt to capture the *Romance Times* readers and therefore fill out the quadrant, but instead appeared content to appeal to a relatively homogeneous audience, which had at its center the Laura Browns and Clarissa Vaughans of the world, who form the dominant readership for quality fiction in the United States? Or did a story about three women, all either bisexual or homosexual, already delimit the potential audience for the film and therefore establish a built-in horizon of expectations that made a more sophisticated stylistic treatment possible? And why, despite that more sophisticated approach, did *The Hours* (though nominated for seven awards, including Best Picture) fail to win as many Academy Awards or enjoy the box office success of *The English Patient* or *Shakespeare in Love*? Was it because *The Hours* was never given as wide a release as *Chicago* and had practically disappeared from multiplexes outside major cities in the weeks immediately preceding the Academy Awards, despite being released in the same slow roll-out fashion at approximately the same time as *Chicago*? Or because Miramax decided to put its promotional might behind *Chicago*, a film with far greater mass market appeal, despite its lack of comparable prestige as a literary adaptation? Underlying this last explanation is the suspicion that Miramax had become so mainstream that it no longer needed to position itself as a quality alternative, now that it could make a classic genre film into

Best Picture the way major studios had done for decades with big splashy musicals such as *Gigi* (1958), *My Fair Lady* (1962), or *The Sound of Music* (1965).

The answer is, all of the above, because no one auteur-director, producer screenwriter, actor, or composer defines the Miramax prestige picture style. No matter how much the popular press may portray Harvey Weinstein as a combination of Leo B. Mayer and Irving Thalberg, ostensibly controlling all decisions as *the* contemporary movie mogul, an auterist approach (even if centered on the film executive) misses the uniqueness of this particular production system. Since the advent of cinephilia in the 1950s, the category of art film has been defined against the constraints of the studio system, a scenario in which "personal vision" prevailed against the industry only in rare cases that were to be celebrated as a victory of artistry over commerce. In his seminal study *The Genius of the System* (1990), Thomas Schatz argues that this category of genius needed to be redefined in reference to classic Hollywood, because the production of so many films now considered masterpieces was attributable not to the determination of a few brave mavericks but a very particular production system: "The quality and artistry of all these films were the product not simply of individual human expression but a melding of institutional forces. In each case the style of a writer, director, star—or even a cinematographer, art director, or costume designer—all fused with the studio's production operations and management structures, its resources and talent pool, its narrative traditions, and market strategy" (604).

For Schatz, that production system ended when the classic studio system faded away in the sixties, but I think it can be a very useful template for delineating the Miramax profile. This is not to suggest that their success is simply a matter of reestablishing the classic studio model, but rather that it represents both a restoration and reformulation of that mode of filmmaking by adapting it to a production system based on *packaging* quality film properties. The establishment of a relatively stable group of directors, stars, screenwriters, editors, and composers, none under the sort of exclusive contract demanded by the major studios during their golden age, but all nevertheless coming together on a regular basis to form remarkably similar packages based on literary bestsellers, which will then be heavily marketed using remarkably similar promotional strategies, sounds a fair amount like that whole equation of pictures Schatz describes.

The genius of this system may resemble that of a traditional studio, but with crucial differences. Miramax in the nineties and MGM during the golden age of the studio system each developed a rhetoric of quality that was laid over a highly diversified group of films by different production units. But MGM was never perceived to be anything other than a movie studio, while Miramax was able to *brand* its literary adaptations, even as it privileged the uniqueness of each prestige picture in terms of the singularity of the literary work and the creative genius of director, screenwriter, stars, and composers, all seemingly getting together to produce masterpieces on a one-off basis. The high-concept adaptation developed by Miramax then rests on another hybridization—the classic Hollywood studio system and the traditional European film production company, which would seemingly form, only to dissolve after the masterpiece was realized. By combining the factory and the boutique, Miramax gave its audience what it expects in a world of "good-design" chainstores, superstore bookstores, and Starbucks cafés—increasingly easier access to what were formerly considered elite pleasures, which are carefully cultivated to retain the vestiges of exclusivity, even as they become increasingly ubiquitous.

So, ultimately, how does one judge the effects of this mode of quality film production, which has made cine-literary culture such an enormous success in terms of the financial and cultural capital it continues to generate? Easy answers to that question are invariably wrong, simply because the effects are multiple and conflicting. Close-grain qualitative distinctions can, indeed must, be drawn in order to appreciate the possible moves that can be made within this whole equation of quality pictures that is the Miramax formula. While all of these films create a *quality* cine-literary experience for appreciative audiences, a comparative analysis of the adaptations *The English Patient* and *The Hours* reveals both the formula and the variations. Both novels are pedigreed exemplars of contemporary literary fiction. Both film versions involved a world-class array of directors, screenwriters, actors, composers, cinematographers, and editors. Both were given very substantial advertising and promotion. Yet one so simplifies a narrative universe in search of a grand love story that it becomes an instant classic for pulp romance readers, while the other only further complicates an already sophisticated narrative structure that concentrates on anything but traditional heterosexual romance.

This analysis of the interplay between textual and promotional strategies, no matter how carefully situated in reference to broader changes within the infrastructure of the entertainment industries and the evolution of American popular taste, still cannot determine, once and for all, the decidability of effect. I am convinced that *The Hours* is a more compelling cine-literary hybrid than *The English Patient*, and one could conclude that it is the far more "faithful" adaptation, in terms of how the film develops intensely cinematic ways to visualize such an arch-literary novel. Yet many Woolf scholars have vehemently attacked *The Hours*, not for the film's lack of fidelity to Cunningham's novel, but Cunningham's lack of fidelity to the *real* Virginia Woolf. Despite the lack of that fidelity, the promotion of the film version of *The Hours* made *Mrs. Dalloway* a bestseller in the United States for the first time, in February 2003, during the height of the Academy Awards season, becoming the number 1 paperback on the Amazon.com sales list on Valentines Day. Both my local Barnes & Noble and Borders were sold out of copies the same day I encountered *The Love Poetry of William Shakespeare* on the featured "romance" table at the center of the rotunda. When *Mrs. Dalloway* reappeared the following week, the books were not on the shelf in the Woolf section in Literature and Fiction; dozens of copies came in their own free-standing cardboard display at the front of the store, bearing a new cover featuring a heritage-style photo, complete with women in white linen dresses and sun hats, along with two stickers on the front cover: "The Novel That Inspired *The Hours*" and "Harvest Reading Guide." The film version of *Mrs. Dalloway* (1998) had no such impact on the sale of the novel, but then it played in very limited release within the art house circuit. In this case at least, the argument that adaptation films lead viewers to become readers of the novels adapted is rather overwhelmingly true.

That one of the chief goals of the film version of *The Hours* was to turn viewers of the film into readers of *Mrs. Dalloway* (if they were not already a member of Woolf's fan base) becomes particularly clear in the "Special Features" on the DVD version of the film, which presents a host of novel-to-film interrelationships in a sophisticated form of cine-literary textuality. In the segment "The Mind and Times of Virginia Woolf," scholars (Hermione Lee, Molly Hite, Francis Spalding) are introduced as authoritative talking heads profiling the author and, at the same time, validating the film's fidelity to that life. Attestations to the scholarly legitimacy of the adaptation thus come along with the film, serving as a Readers/Viewers' Guide included in the same box instead of at the back of the book. Like the Readers' Guide, the Special Features take as a given the viewer's thirst for more authoritative inside information about the Author. In another special feature, "The Lives of Mrs. Dalloway," Woolf is joined by three more authors (Cunningham, Daldry, and Hare, who elaborate on how they tried to do justice to the masterpiece). Their commentary is intercut with close-ups from the film of

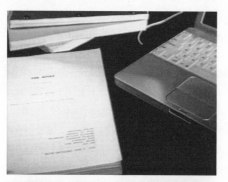

18. How a film script derives from a book about another book: the adaptation process, as shown in *The Hours*

Woolf's hand writing furiously and more close-ups of a copy of *Mrs. Dalloway*, which is given reliquary status, with the camera tracking up to the book exactly as the camera is used to move across the table to "find" the book in the title sequence of *Masterpiece Theatre* productions, only here the key passages are highlighted by accent lighting.

The interdependency of the film script, Cunningham's novel, and *Mrs. Dalloway* is visualized very efficiently in a concluding pan across all three—the viewer is shown in explicit terms how the script was derived from the novel, which was derived from the original masterpiece. The authors' reading organized by Miramax at Town Hall and featuring Ondaatje and Minghella has become, by this point, a featurette in the DVD package— the shared community of appreciative writers/readers/viewers that form part of the text that is *The Hours*. That the ultimate value of the film still depends on its ability to lead viewers to become readers reaches its zenith in the audio commentary on the feature by both the director and novelist. At the point when the waters rush up around the sleeping Laura Brown in bed in the hotel room, we hear:

> *Cunningham*: I just have to pause to mention it. It's a hugely successful movie about people reading a book. Imagine!
>
> *Daldry*: Well, there was a moment, wasn't there—I know we've discussed this in the past—that books change your life. Everyone used to believe that. Now, perhaps not so much.
>
> *Cunningham*: Not so much. I hope this movie is doing something to reestablish that notion!

In the case of *Mrs. Dalloway* and *The Hours*, Daldry's film undoubtedly attempts to reestablish that notion, since the cinematic and literary experiences are thoroughly interdependent, and reading and watching are made to appear just as tightly interdependent. Any sort of taste hierarchy that might have insisted on qualitative differences between the two no longer holds sway—quality reading and quality viewing have equal footing within cine-literary culture. Because of this equal footing, "adaptation talk," has apparently acquired an entertainment value unto itself for a quality readership/viewership. Where the discussion of how successful a given adaptation was formerly *entered the picture* only at a later point during the interpretive process, when avid fans or professors of English weighed in with their evaluations, now the viewer of the DVD boxed set enters a conversation already under way, a conversation between members of a shared community that establishes the utmost seriousness of all parties. The popularization of not just the adaptation film but of adaptation talk was an inevitable development, given the ever-expanding number of adaptation films, the refinements of DVD technology, and the cultivation of quality audiences for Readers' and Viewers' Guides, which provide specialized information, the "something extra," needed to really appreciate the text from an informed position. Here we're encouraged to believe that the movie is better because everyone involved in the preparation of both the film and the featurettes loves the novel just as much as you do, and in the case of Hermione Lee and company, they know them better than you do—and they are still ready and eager to join this cine-literary community.

The boom in adaptation films in Hollywood in the nineties depended on a complicated interplay between aesthetic pleasure and commercial interests. The transformation of the adaptation from *Masterpiece Theatre* marginality to Miramax ubiquity was the result of unprecedented developments in the business of culture and the hierarchies of popular taste. The formation of a massively successful cine-literary culture cannot be accounted for by the actions of any one director or studio head, although the efforts of Merchant and Ivory and the Weinstein brothers all had a profound impact in shaping that success. Perhaps the most revealing indication of how completely the Miramax equation came to redefine the category of the adaptation was the cover of the *New York Times Magazine*'s Annual Movie Issue (November, 9, 2004). There beneath a cluster of a number of A-list movie stars was the caption: "'Tis the Oscar-scheming, novel-adapting, release-date-juggling, upper-mid-brow-seducing, period-recreating, art-budget-breaking, grown-up-pleasure-making prestige film season." The Miramax formula had become, by this point, programmatic for the entire prestige film business, and the cine-literary so successfully hybridized that it had become part of the infrastructure of American culture.

Part III

POPULAR

LITERARY

FICTION

5

SEX AND THE
POST-LITERARY CITY

"What on earth were you talking to Comstock Dibble about?"
Selden asked in the limo on the way home. Janey shrugged,
"Movies, what else. I was telling him that he should make Edith
Wharton's *The Custom in the Country* into a movie. It's never been
done before and he'd be good at it."
—Candace Bushnell, *Trading Up* (2002)

"You wrote that. You *wrote* that."
It's a statement, not a question. Daisy stares at him, waiting.
He says again, "You wrote that." And then hurriedly, "It's beautiful.
You know that, don't you. It's beautiful. And you wrote it."
—Ian McEwan, *Saturday* (2005)

In earlier chapters I explored how a popular literary culture began to emerge
in the nineties because of changes in delivery systems and connoisseurship.
The advent of chain store and Web site bookshops, high-concept literary
adaptation films, and television book clubs have all changed where and
how a literary experience occurs. They have also changed the ways in which
one talks the talk of literary appreciation with a high degree of authority,
largely by making reading a process of self-empowerment that no longer
depends on acquiring the right sort of pedigree or professional training.
Novels by Tolstoy, Forster, Woolf, and Austen have acquired a high degree of visibility because reading pleasure itself has been so thoroughly
redefined. They are different novels now, because readers are encouraged to
read them as primers or guidebooks rather than expressions of transcendent
literary genius—it's all about how you *read* them.

But it is also a matter of how you *write* them, and the sort of people you write them about, especially when the novels in question are written for and about that popular literary culture. The first epigraph to this chapter comes from Bushnell's novel about Janey Wilcox, a Victoria's Secret model who circulates through many of the key locations of Bushnell's *Sex and the City*, drifting from Manhattan to the Hamptons, as the narrator details meticulously the social scene she encounters every step of the way until she comes to rest in Hollywood. The parade of celebrities she encounters does indeed seem to be, as the book jacket claims, "like characters who could have come from the pages of *Vanity Fair*." But which *Vanity Fair*? The celebrity lifestyle magazine whose Academy Awards party Janey is attending in the last chapter, or the novel of manners by Thackeray? The answer is clearly meant to be either, or better yet, both, since the same jacket assures us of two things — "Not since Candace Bushnell created Carrie Bradshaw and *Sex and the City* has there been a heroine like Janey Wilcox," and "Like Jane Austen or Edith Wharton, Bushnell lovingly skewers a society she knows well." This comparison, however, was not simply invented by the marketing department at Hyperion Books in an attempt to tart up a chick-lit book by accessorizing it with a literary status brooch. The entire novel is very self-consciously modeled on Wharton's *The Custom in the Country* (1914), a point made explicitly in the exchange, quoted in the epigraph, between Janey and Selden, her media mogul husband.

Why is this particular incarnation of Carrie Bradshaw writing a screenplay about her life modeled after a Wharton novel? And for a studio head obviously meant to be recognized as the former Miramax head Harvey Weinstein, since he is characterized as an overweight, New York–based mogul, head of Parador Pictures, acknowledged to be a genius in the movie business but "equally known for his irrational displays of temper" (34)? And why, when she tires of her boring movie producer husband, does she begin to lust after Craig Edgers, a literary novelist who has just published a five-hundred-page literary bestseller to great media acclaim, a character who is based just as obviously on Jonathan Franzen? It's one thing for Bridget Jones to be in love with Charles Darcy, but when Carrie Bradshaw has the hots for Jonathan Franzen, and counts Harvey Weinstein among her former lovers, we clearly have a hybrid phenomenon that is as central to understanding popular literary culture as *The Corrections* or *Shakespeare in Love*. Here, yet again, literary, film, and television cultures are intertwined within a book that, even before it is adapted, is always already an HBO television series, or an article in *Vanity Fair*, or, just as insistently, an Edith Wharton novel for the early twenty-first century.

Ian McEwan's *Saturday* would seem, at first blush, to come from not just another country but another planet. It is, after all, composed by a novelist that even *Entertainment Weekly* recognizes as *the* most important English writer, someone whose novels seem to be listed automatically for the Man Booker Prize upon publication. And the narrative circumstances would seem even further removed from the world of *Trading Up*. The main character, Henry Perowne, is a neurosurgeon who, in the course of his day, has a fender-bender with thugs who track him to his home that evening. They have his family captive and are about to brutalize his daughter until she recites Matthew Arnold's "Dover Beach," at which point, their leader is stunned by the beauty of the words ("You *wrote* that") and abandons his evil plan.

Why does Bushnell need Wharton? And why are McEwan's thugs mesmerized by Arnold? And why have both Bushnell and McEwan been referred to as the contemporary Jane Austen? The dust jacket for *Trading Up* makes this claim, and on my copy of *Saturday* the back-cover blurb from *Esquire* insists, "McEwan could be the most psychologically astute writer working today, our era's Jane Austen." Can they both be our Jane Austen? Or are we talking about very different "ours" here?

What constitutes a literary experience has been transformed by high-concept adaptation films but also by novels that either instrumentalize or sanctify quality reading for those readers who hang out at superstores, make lists at Amazon, go to their book club, watch Oprah's Book Club, or do their literary classics in the Miramax, Focus Features, or Weinstein pictures versions at the closest multiplex. Popular literary culture has been consolidated by those shared modes of consumption, but it has also been exuberantly celebrated by novels that have transformed that culture into narrative universes in novels as diverse as Melissa Bank's *The Girls' Guide to Hunting and Fishing* (1999) and *The Wonder Spot* (2005), Kate Christensen's *In the Drink* (1999), Helen Fielding's *Bridget Jones's Diary* (1996), Suzanne Finnamore's *Otherwise Engaged* (1999), Karen Jay Fowler's *The Jane Austen Book Club* (2004), Alan Hollinghurst's *The Line of Beauty* (2004), Nick Hornby's *High Fidelity* (1995) and *A Long Way Down* (2005); Diane Johnson's *Le Divorce* (1997), *Le Mariage* (2000), *L'Affaire* (2003); Jennifer Kaufman's and Karen Black's *Literacy and Longing in L.A.* (2006), Emma McLaughlin's and Nicola Kraus's *The Nanny Diaries* (2002), Elizabeth Noble's *The Reading Group* (2004), Tom Perrotta's

Little Children (2004), Irina Reyn's *What Happened to Anna K: A Novel* (2008), Cathleen Schine's *She Is Me* (2003), Curtis Sittenfeld's *Prep* (2005), Katharine Weber's *The Little Women* (2004), Alex Wichel's *Me Times Three* (2002), and Hilma Wolitzer's *Summer Reading* (2008). While these novels may differ quite dramatically in terms of their literary aspirations, they all have two things in common — first, they offer lessons in self-cultivation, now defined as an *informed consumerism* about love, culture, and material goods, and second, they make extensive use of canonical novels by Trollope, Flaubert, Tolstoy, Austen, James, Wharton, Forster, Alcott, and Charlotte Brontë as they very self-consciously reinvent the novel of manners for contemporary audiences. These authors and their characters may be driven to find meaningful sex and make the right purchases, but they've read books, by God, and they're determined not to let you forget it. But why won't they let you forget it?

The list of titles I've assembled above may seem like a wildly, even perversely, disparate grouping, since it includes everything from the greatest hits of chick-lit to arch-literary bestsellers. My grouping of these titles is not pure invention on my part, a product of a feverish critical imagination determined to identify a genre of fiction that I have "discovered." I got a lot of help, from Target superstores, *Vogue* magazine, Amazon.com, and Barnes & Noble, all of who make these sorts of groupings and connections on a regular basis. When I began writing this chapter, I went to my local Target superstore to see what I'd find in the Target's Recommended Reading section (a subsection within the Media department across the aisle from Best-Sellers). There I found a remarkably similar array of titles: *Trading Up*, *Fashionista*, and *The Devil Wears Prada*, intermixed with *The Jane Austen Book Club*, *Atonement*, and *Life of Pi*. The June issue of *Vogue* (2005) featured a similar grouping in its "People Are Talking About: Books" department ("*Vogue* picks summer's most provocative reads"), which included *The Wonder Spot* and *A Long Way Down*, along with Michael Cunningham's *Specimen Days* and Umberto Eco's *The Mysterious Flame of Queen Loana*. I went to Amazon to see if similar arrays were being assembled, and when I checked *The Wonder Spot* home page, the "Customers Who Bought This Book Also Bought" list included *A Long Way Down*, along with *The History of Love* by Nicole Krauss, *Prep* by Curtis Sittenfield, and Gigi Levangie Grazers's *The Starter Wife*. I then clicked directly to *A Long Way Down*, where the "Customers Who Bought This Book Also Bought" list included *The Wonder Spot*, along with McEwan's *Saturday* and Cunningham's *Specimen Days*. At the *Saturday* home page, the "Customers Who Bought This Book Also Bought" began with Roth's *Plot against America*, which was paired with *Saturday* as a "better together" package deal, but it also included *A Long Way Down*. Hornby was coupled with Bank and McEwan, and McEwan was coupled alternately, but simultaneously, with Hornby and Roth. And Barnes & Noble made the identification of these titles as a particular type of book even more pointedly—*The Wonder Spot*, *A Long Way Down*, *Saturday*, and *Specimen Days* were all "stepladder" titles featured during the week of their release on the stepladder display just inside the front door; the Hornby and Cunningham novels, enjoying the privilege the same week, sat side by side as featured novels of the week.

The point of this exercise is not to play a kind of literary version of the Kevin Bacon movie trivia game, in which I prove that I can get from Levangie Grazers's chick-lit to Roth's important literary novel in just two clicks. Nor am I just trying to show what an amorphous category "Recommended Fiction" has become. Important distinctions can, and indeed need, to be made within that range of titles if we hope to gain a better understanding of popular literary culture and the very different needs it serves for divergent audiences. In his benchmark study of the Booker Prize and the impact it has had on British fiction, *Consuming Fictions* (1996), Richard Todd delineates the ways in which prize-winning novels have almost automatically become literary bestsellers. While this chapter owes a great debt to his work, here I want to explore the spectrum of quality fiction rather than make categorical distinctions about what is, and isn't, a literary bestseller, because it is the fluidity of this continuum that is most significant. In this chapter, I provide a kind of tracking shot across popular literary culture, a scene filled with masses of readers who read quality fiction passionately, a publishing industry who caters to them just as lustily, and legions of novelists who are determined to prove the value of their novels for audiences in search of quality reading that will provide useful information.

My goal in these last two chapters is to delineate two adjacent, often overlapping types of bestselling fiction within this range—the Post-Literary Novel and the Devoutly Literary Novel. I use the term "post-literary" to characterize novels such as *Bridget Jones's Diary*, *The Girls' Guide to Hunting and Fishing*, *The Wonder Spot*, *The Nanny Diaries*, *Little Children*, *Trading Up*, and *A Long Way Down*, because they all make elaborate use of canonical literary fiction as they turn the traditional novel of manners into a guide to romantic consumerism, yet, at the same time, they distance themselves from contemporary Serious Fiction that is thought to be of no help at all in negotiating the complexities of contemporary desire. The Devoutly Literary novels I will discussing in detail in the next chapter—*Author, Author*, as well as *The Jane Austen Book Club, Balzac and the Little Chinese Seamstress, Literacy and Longing in L.A., The Master, Saturday*, and *The Thirteenth Tale*—insist on the transformative power of reading as an explicitly aesthetic experience within, but also somehow apart, from mere consumerism. In the former, books are relentlessly referred to by characters that also reference, with equal frequency and fluency, movies, television programs, rock bands, and fashion designers. In the latter, Henry James, E. M. Forster, T. S. Eliot, and Balzac circulate as central figures and copies of books take on a magical, transformative power. Both reject the traditional distinctions between popular and literary fiction. The post-literary novel dismisses the avowedly literary in pursuit of a new kind of quality fiction, while the devoutly literary sanctifies the reading experience, but in doing so turns the most "bookish" sorts of pleasures into the stuff of literary bestsellers. Both take for granted readers with a literary education of varying degrees; both appear on the same stepladders at Barnes & Noble. Both are all about *love*—of books, material goods and significant others. They all take self-cultivation as a given, and then blur the line between self-cultivation and self-help. Both feature characters who define themselves through their obsession with making taste distinctions and having firsthand experiences with *beauty*. Consequently, each reimagines, at the most fundamental level, the use value of reading fiction. If we hope to gain a better understanding of why people who read contemporary fiction passionately continue to do so, we need to look very closely at the novels that are providing them with the reasons to read with such enthusiasm.

Girls' and Boys' Guides to Romantic Consumerism:
The Post-Literary as iPod in Novel Form

The notion of self that takes shape only through the exercise of taste distinctions, rather than as the repository of inner qualities or spiritual values has been widely attributed to life within consumer capitalism, but this chapter will complicate any such easy explanations. Acquiring and demonstrating taste is as essential to these novels as finding the right love relationship, but this particular taste crisis is in many ways unprecedented. Taste anxiety of one sort or another obviously has a long history in literary fiction, and one could argue that the novels of manners would not exist in either its traditional or its contemporary incarnations without a broad readership overwhelmed by such anxiety. The anxious American aristocrats who flocked to England in the nineteenth century, and the equally anxious British upper classes who felt the need to go on the Grand Tour through "the Continent" in search of the requisite taste, have been stable figures in literary fiction for well over a century. Bourdieu's often-invoked distinction between different forms of capital is especially useful in this regard, since, more often than not, the taste crisis boiled down to a conflict between financial and intellectual capital, and how the two could be traded with the greatest degree of sophistication, toward the greatest effect. That conflict between these two currencies of value remains solidly in place in the post-literary novel of manners, but the currency exchanges have become more complicated than ever before, due to the excess of advanced degrees and the wildly varying levels of disposable income. The books I discuss in this chapter are products of a pre-downturn consumer culture, but I read these novels not just as symptomatic of the excesses of a particular period. They are ultimately about the transactions between cultural and financial capital, not the giddy infatuation with brand names. They signal the need for a new kind of fiction that might serve as a guide for behavior when those exchanges are now, more than ever, in a constant state of flux. The price points then might be lower, but the appeal of fictions that address the complex interplay among love relationships, consumerism, and the value of reading fiction only continues to intensify.

The characters in these novels realize that a college education is a necessary, but insufficient, component of the contemporary self-cultivation project, because there is another kind of cultural knowledge out there that must be acquired as soon as possible. This is exemplified neatly by Amy Hawkins, the freshly minted dotcom millionaire who is the main character in Diane Johnson's *L'Affaire* (2003): "Eventually, she supposed, she would learn to be rich, but for now she hoped to grow from a corporate drone into being a better, more aware human being. . . . Above all, her resolutions concerned the acquisition of knowledge, or rather, culture, in its broadest sense, though she was under no illusion that she could do anything more than a crash course" (30). What causes this "sudden consciousness" is a remark she overhears in an antiques store about dotcommers like herself: "No one has taught them anything. If it weren't for Martha Stewart the whole culture would be down the drain. They don't know what they don't know, so they don't think of asking" (31). Amy, at least, seems to know what she needed to know:

> But it was interesting to wonder what these blue-haired ladies knew, or felt they knew, that she didn't, things about antique furniture, yes, but their tone, and the reference to housework guru Martha Stewart, implied a wider store of lore usually purveyed by mothers, equated with culture itself, endangered at that. And Amy didn't know any of it. From then on, daily, the world brought her new evidence of her lack of culture. (32)

> Despite herself, she knew about corporate buy-outs. What did she know about poetry, about meter and stanza form, music, tradition, masterpieces? The white wine glass, the red wine glass? . . . What is a *godet?* What was the line between despair and cynicism, between taste and vulgarity—a word she had so often heard used about the houses her friends were building? (71)

In certain ways, Hawkins's desire for the right sort of cultural knowledge is remarkably similar to the woman who wrote into the *Ladies Home Journal* in 1908 in search of good books (first mentioned in chapter 2). She is eager to self-improve and has even more disposable capital to accomplish her goals. But while the letter writer was convinced that the road to self-cultivation was paved with the right books, Hawkins knows that cultural knowledge also has to include vital information about a host of other associated tastes, in clothing, interior design, and what used to be called "domestic arts." As such, the reader of the *Ladies Home Journal* and Johnson's heroine are in inverse relationship to each other; the former can't afford to go to college and wants to read books, but appears to have no anxiety about her knowledge of more domestic tastes because that isn't cultural knowledge; the latter has gone to college, already knows more or less what the good books are, but is also fully aware of the fact that those books are insufficient for a thorough program in self-cultivation at the turn of the twenty-first century. The letter writer does not express any need for taste, just knowledge of the right books, which will automatically make her tasteful. For Johnson's heroine and her readers, no such automatic assumptions can be made. Yet perhaps the most significant difference between them is that the letter writer to the *Ladies*

Home Journal in 1908 couldn't walk into Barnes & Noble and find tables full of novels all about characters exactly like herself, characters whose pursuit of the right sort of cultural knowledge has acquired enormous entertainment value unto itself.

Making such taste distinctions, and demonstrating just how essential they are in developing a sense of identity and finding the appropriate love object is the central project of the post-literary novel of manners. One thing is certain—when Austen, James, Wharton, and Forster were sending their characters out in search of cultural knowledge, no one within those fictional universes was questioning the value of the contemporary literary novel as a key source of that knowledge. The post-literary novels of manners I will be focusing on in this chapter all position themselves in a popular literary culture of their own creation, solidly ensconced between the realms of vulgar bestsellers and irrelevant serious fiction. The dismissal of contemporary literary culture, combined with equally explicit affiliation with nineteenth- and early-twentieth-century novels of manners, was inaugurated by Fielding's *Bridget Jones's Diary* in 1996. The interdependency of this disaffiliation and reaffiliation, combined with an ambivalent invocation of self-help books, is set in motion before the story even begins. Bridget prefaces her diary with a list of resolutions designed to improve her behavior in the coming year. Under the heading "I Will Not," Bridget promises not to "waste money on: pasta-makers, ice-cream machines or other culinary devices which I will never use, books by unreadable literary authors to put impressively on shelves" (2). Literary authors may be impressive in some abstract sense within another taste culture, but they are unreadable, because they have no direct application in terms of offering advice about herself or her relationships. Like the pasta machine and the ice-cream maker, books by literary authors are specialty items that signal seriousness of intent on the part of those who buy them, but they don't have actual use value. They remain "objets" to be admired but since they just sit there, they are a waste of money. Bridget's new year's resolution acknowledges the residual prestige that unreadable literary books have for some people, somewhere, but at the same time, it devalues any cultural capital they might have by making their prestige factor a form of counterfeit currency.

But *Bridget Jones's Diary* is just as valueless without Jane Austen. It lays claim to being a contemporary novel of manners that is a cut above mere romance fiction and vapid self-help books, because it insists on a direct kinship with *Pride and Prejudice* consistently reiterated through an extended intertextual conceit. Fielding's novel incorporates the central plot of Austen's novel, most specifically in her search for a Mr. Right who will be *her* Mr. Darcy, her ideal love object, based on her repeated viewing of the BBC television adaptation of *Pride and Prejudice*. By naming the boyfriend Mark Darcy, Fielding could hardly have made the parallel more explicit, at least until the film adaptation of Bridget appeared and the Mr. Darcy of the BBC program actually became the Mr. Darcy of *Bridget Jones* through the casting of the same actor, Colin Firth. The use of Firth is emblematic of how completely the narrative universe of *Bridget Jones's Diary* depends on *Pride and Prejudice*: Firth functions as a character in one narrative universe, but he is simultaneously the living vestige of Austen's novel within it, without which the fictional universe collapses. But even when the intertextual meshing together is less overt, Austen's novel pervades *Bridget Jones* like Colin Firth's Darcy, because it functions as a free-floating pedigree. This is more than a self-help novel, because it takes so clearly for granted that all concerned — the novelist, filmmakers, characters, imagined readers, and viewers — have all at least seen the BBC adaptation even if they haven't read the novel. This is a shared cine-literary experience of a very particular variety that suggests a taste community that is both aware of the status of Austen's novels but delighted to see them undergo a radical makeover. Within this community of readers/viewers, Jane Austen is most assuredly *not* a pasta machine.

What follows Bridget's list of new year's resolutions may be an assemblage of newspaper columns deeply inflected by self-help books and women's magazines, but the consistent reiteration of Austen's presence in one form or another within this mix of authorities represents one of the chief distinguishing features of the post-literary novel of manners — the explicit self-positioning within a cultural landscape where forms of high and low culture, and visual and literary culture, are all omnipresent and completely intertwined. These novels envision narrative universes and a popular literary culture where they insist on fulfilling a function once performed by far more genteel authors now considered canonical. In his book *Trash Culture: Popular Culture and the Great Tradition* (1999), Richard Keller Simon argues that "if you watch television, go to the movies, read popular magazines, and look at advertisements, you are exposed to many of the same kinds of stories as someone who studies the great books of Western civilization. You have simply been encouraged to look at them differently" (1). As an example of what we might see, if we looked differently, he offers *Cosmopolitan* magazine as a contemporary female bildungsroman . . . a novel of manners, devoted to the translation of social gesture, dress, look, and public behavior into explicit meaning and concerned with the individual's relationship to social convention. . . . [T]he result is something akin to Jane Austen's *Sense and Sensibility* in the age of mechanical reproduction, a text now without any literary aura, repeated every month with minor variations, that takes the characters, issues, and plot of the Austen novel, and of related stories in the genres—Edith Wharton's *House of Mirth* and Gustave Flaubert's *Madame Bovary* are important precursors as well—and transforms them into Dadaist collage. . . . Appropriately the traditional author has disappeared into this modernist mass-cultural collage and in her place is the commercial marketplace, all the advertisers, editors, writers, and readers that make up a collective enterprise of completely inartistic intention. (117)

While this argument is convincing in regard to *Cosmopolitan*, post-literary novels of manners represent a more complicated phenomenon, because they don't depend on a literary critic to uncover their hidden connections to the traditional novel of manners; the last thing the author does is disappear into completely inartistic intention. Throughout the novels of Fielding, Banks, Johnson, and Fowler, traditional literary authors are repeatedly cited, and their novels incorporated through a variety of elaborate intertextual strategies in a concerted effort to make use of that literary aura, as the entire category of artistic intention is itself being redefined with the commercial marketplace of *books*. These novels insist on foregrounding their affiliations with Austen, Wharton, and Flaubert in no uncertain terms: they *are* the contemporary novel of manners. This is exactly the sort of novel Wharton would be writing about if she were describing the relationship between love and money in contemporary New York—just ask Candace Bushnell.

Or Emma McLaughlin and Nicola Kraus, who might insist that Charlotte Brontë is the more useful guide for life in that same New York. Establishing the differences between those with and without genuine taste, is the central project of their novel *The Nanny Diaries*. The book's post-literary credentials are presented before the action even commences: the opening quotation from *Jane Eyre* makes the reader well aware of its status as an inheritor of the governess novel. But here "Nanny" functions as taste arbiter in terms of what proper child care should be (she is writing a thesis at New York University on Jean Piaget's theory of egocentrism) and in terms of what constitutes a genuine education in tasteful living. The chief villain in the novel is the nouveau-riche mother, Mrs. X. She is not some glitz-loving monster from Long Island who whiles away her days reading Judith Krantz novels and ordering anything she wants from the Shopping Channel. Nanny zeros in on Mrs. X's obsession with acquiring cultural capital at all costs. Her coffee table features a massive book devoted to villas of Tuscany, and she labors mightily to get her child Grayer into kindergarten at the right private school. Rather than being deprived of it, Grayer is force-fed "culture" throughout the day; for example, "Mommy's exhausted Grayer. Get into bed and I'll read you one verse from your Shakespeare reader and then it's lights out" (220). All of this cultural information turns counterfeit, because it is so overtly instrumentalized — the Shakespeare reader is in the same library as guidebooks with titles such as *How to Package Your Child: The Preschool Interview* and *Make It or Break it: Navigating Preschool Admission.* The crassness of these transactions between cultural and financial capital becomes most apparent when Grayer is rejected by the school (aptly named Collegiate), and Nanny and Mrs. X meet with the "Long Term Development Consultant," who coaches parents and caregivers about enhancing their child's candidacy. After giving the wrong answers to too many questions (Nanny doesn't make him use an apparel chart when he gets dressed in the morning, and no, she doesn't have him translate the colors and sizes into Latin), the consultant tells her:

> "I have to question whether you're leveraging your assets to escalate Grayer's performance." Having let the cat out of the bag, she leans back and rests her hands in her lap. I sense that I should feel insulted. "Leverage my assets?" Hmm, anyone? "Nanny, I understand you are getting your degree in arts-in-education so frankly I'm surprised by the lack of depth surrounding your knowledge base here." (179)

This leveraging of the knowledge base that is predicated on direct exchange of cultural capital into financial capital renders Grayer's entire "education" invalid. Within the world of *The Nanny Diaries*, Shakespeare readers for children are as much a part of the new glitz as Chanel Bébé SPF 64 and signed first-edition *Babar* prints. While this scene obviously involves a certain degree of satirical exaggeration, the phrasing is especially deft, because this leveraging of the assets in one's knowledge base reveals one of the principal causes of this all-pervasive taste anxiety — the relationship between financial and cultural capital has never been more volatile, because so many different brokers of cultural value are setting such wildly varying exchange rates. What is the ultimate value of a college education in such matters? How *does* one cash it in? Or should it be cashed in at all? Does it remain most valuable as a kind of countervalue system that allows for instant superiority, at least in terms of self-image.

The Nanny Diaries offers at least a glimmer of an alternative world where genuine taste, and genuine sense of identity, may still be found. Nanny's grandmother's apartment is set in stark contrast to Mrs. X's mausoleum. Her grandmother functions as the resident paragon of taste, not because she presumes to be an authority on décor or clothing, but because she surrounds herself with her own choices, she inhabits her individual taste. On her first visit to her grandmother's home, Nanny is offered breakfast but declines because she's worried about missing her appointment with the financial aid office at the university. She says, seemingly in passing: "I glance up at the old Nelson clock. 'I wish I had time, but I've gotta get down town before the line at the Registrar is around the block'" (21). This may seem like a quick transitional moment in the novel, but Nanny's passing remark about her grandmother's kitchen clock reveals the complexity of taste cartography in the novel. Her grandmother's apartment, decorated in mid-century modernist classics like George Nelson wall clocks, punctuated with black-and-white family photos, and accompanied by the vintage Sinatra recording of "The Lady Is a Tramp" (another masterpiece from the mid-fifties), is an organic extension of who she is, because she has lived through that period and her sensibilities were forged during that golden age of sophisticated urbanity in New York. Her Nelson clock might be just the old clock in the kitchen, but in this novel, Nelson and Sinatra make Tuscany and Shakespeare seem like just so much Lavender Linen Water from L'Occitane, because they resonate as authentic expressions of intensely individual taste, which cannot be simply purchased. Mrs. X's apartment, on the other hand, is described by Nanny as a "hotel suite — immaculate, but impersonal. Even the lone finger painting I will later find taped to the fridge looks as if it were ordered from a catalogue. (Sub Zeros with a custom colored panels aren't magnetized.)" (2). The key distinction here is not old wealth versus new wealth, or mere wealth versus cultural capital. Nanny's ability to stand in judgment over the people who employ her as a servant depends on a hybridized value system consisting of equal measures of the intellectual capital she is acquiring via her degree at New York University, and a handed-down cultural heritage whose gold-standard status depends not on family estates or titled lineage but direct, lived connection to the lost age of genuine sophistication set in opposition to the vulgarity of contemporary New York.

There is, however, a taken-for-grantedness about the names of the right universities, designers, and brandnames—the reader already *knows* them, or is more than eager to acquire the knowledge, either from this novel, or shelter magazines, or catalogues. Granny's Nelson clock, or a version of it, actually is available for purchase, specifically from good-design catalogues like Design within Reach, which sells its own reproductions of the Nelson Spindle clock, the Noguchi coffeetable, and Eames chairs, thereby allowing customers (and readers of *The Nanny Diaries*) to recreate in their own homes the mid-century modernist mise-en-scène that is endlessly celebrated in shelter magazines such as *Dwell* and *Elle Décor* (which regularly feature articles about how to find modernist antiques that are deemed "timeless classics"). And for that audience, the real Nelson clock in the kitchen registers instantly as radioactively hip.

The Nanny Diaries offers a very particular kind of knowledge to its readers by insisting on its ability to deliver the vital ethnography along with narrative entertainment. This ethnographic dimension is visualized explicitly in the film version of *The Nanny Diaries* (2007). In the opening scene, we meet Scarlett Johansson as Nanny Annie Braddock, operating as a tour guide in the American Museum of Natural History. She identifies herself in the voice-over as a former anthropology major as the camera glides by the usual dioramas devoted to the world's peoples until it comes to rest on a display case devoted to the peoples of the Upper East Side of Manhattan, at which point her narration begins to detail their rituals as the camera takes us into "real" New York. From this point onward, the entire film functions as an extension of the tour guide's account. The viewer learns something about this tribe, but here the distinctions between the raw and the cooked, between the tasteless and tasteful, are no longer a matter of those who have knowledge (and a comfortable income) and those who have *just* money. The contemporary counterparts of the Schlegels and Wilcoxes have all been to college, and they have all acquired elite knowledge about taste, but not taste itself. In a culture where the acquisition of knowledge is placed at such a premium, and the dispensing of crucial information about making the right choices has become an industry unto itself, with taste mavens becoming media celebrities, knowledge about things tasteful is only a click away on the remote control or the keyboard. Consequently, the tasteless know as much as the tasteful about fine Bordeaux (if they've read their *Wine Advocate* or *Wine Spectator*), and the most vulgar-of-the-vulgar are as enthralled by Tuscany as the Honeychurches and Emersons. In Alex Wichel's novel *Me Times Three*, for example, the narrator describes "the guys in the Armani suits" who form the bulk of the eligible dates for the novel's heroine in the following way: "Their staggering bonuses had already purchased new duplexes with marble bathrooms and climate-controlled wine closets, where they could store their requisite cases of Chateau Margaux. One guy I knew liked to make a ceremony of opening a prize bottle, then chugging it as his friends cheered him on. You could just imagine what he'd be like in bed" (6). Within the ethnography of the contemporary novel of manners, it's all in how you use that knowledge, where you get it, and how you demonstrate it that really counts, and this requires a new taste cartography to get the lay of the land, especially since the expression of taste, and the expression of love, appear to be such thoroughly interdependent rituals.

In his masterful study *Literature and the Taste for Knowledge* (2005), Michael Wood argues eloquently about the different sorts of "knowledge" literature can provide. I will look closely at his analysis on Henry James in my next chapter, but in his introduction he makes a key point about the taste for knowledge that literary fiction offers: it can teach us certain things about the "complexity of the world" in terms of ambiguities and "obliquity" not available in other forms of discourse. The contemporary novels of manners shift the terms of this relationship through their insistence that they offer reliable knowledge about taste that is not available elsewhere. For Wood, Barthes's formulation is pivotal: "La science est grossière, la vie est subtile, et c'est pour corriger cette distance que la littérature nous importe — Knowledge is coarse, life is subtle, and literature matters to us because it corrects the difference" (35). Wood uses this as his point of departure to explore the intricacies of novels by James, Kafka, and others, but I think it may also be used to explain the phenomenal popularity of these post-literary novels, if we revise Barthes's formulation somewhat: knowledge in the form of guidebooks and Web sites is coarse, contemporary social life is too bafflingly subtle to be accounted for by mere guidebooks, and this novel corrects the difference by teaching you something those guidebooks can't deliver.

Melissa Bank's *Girls' Guide to Hunting and Fishing* (1999) is another post-literary novel that delivers a knowledge that can't just be leveraged or cashed in, but nonetheless depends on the discourse of the guidebook. The heroine, Jane Rosenthal, is a young writer-in-the-making trying to crack the literary scene in New York, only this time she is an Oberlin graduate, instead of a

Victoria's Secret model. Late in the novel she goes book shopping: "I don't want to admit to myself what I'm doing when I put my bike helmet on and head over to the Barnes & Noble a few blocks away. I pretend that maybe I'm just getting another Edith Wharton novel. But I by-pass Fiction and find Self-Help. . . . [T]here are stacks and stacks of *How to Marry Mr. Right*, the terrible book Donna told me about, terrible because it works. I take my copy up to the counter as furtively as I would a girdle or a vibrator" (240).

This is a complicated, but highly representative moment in terms of understanding the interplay between canonical fiction and self-help guides within this taste culture. Why would an Oberlin graduate, a would-be literary figure, even consider passing up Fiction for Self-Help? And at Barnes & Noble? But, conversely, why does Wharton even enter the picture here, if Self-Help is now the reading material of choice? That there has been a vast gulf between Serious Fiction and Self-Help books until quite recently hardly needs proving, since the latter have exemplified all that the former never could be. As easy-to-read, even easier-to-understand advice stated in thoroughly conversational prose that reduces emotional problems to a series of bulleted "tips" for improving behavior, nothing could be further from the Serious Fiction that has been predicated on sophisticated usages of language in pursuit of the complexities of human behavior. What is it about the nature of romance in consumer cultures that calls out for both self-help discourse and canonical literary masterpieces?

While working as a manuscript reader, Jane becomes involved with Archie Knox, an older, literary editor well established in the New York publishing world. Their love affair quickly becomes a master-apprentice relationship. They evaluate manuscripts together, and Archie takes her to literati receptions where they hobnob with other writers and editors. She tells him, "I feel like Helen Keller and you're Annie Sullivan." He reminds her regularly that her generation is "culturally bankrupt," and he undertakes her education, dispensing the much-needed cultural knowledge about classic Hollywood films and vintage jazz albums, and, of course, great novels. When they go to the country for the weekend, he reads her *Washington Square* by flashlight. As such, Archie represents traditional New York literary culture, the pre–Tina Brown *New Yorker* incarnate, ideally played by Jason Robards in his middle-aged prime. But the relationship collapses, due to one insurmountable problem, which speaks volumes about the use value of his kind of literary authority—Mr. New York Literary World is . . . *impotent*, a pasta machine without a crank, so to speak. Just as tellingly, the other voices of authority that Jane listens to are authors of the self-help book *How to Meet and Marry Mr. Right* that she buys when she stops by Barnes & Noble. Upon returning to her apartment with this vibrator of a book, the authors, Faith Kurtz-Abrowitz and Bonnie Merrill, move in with her, speaking to her directly in boldface self-helpese ("Don't Be Funny! Be Mysterious!"). She attempts to follow their advice, until she realizes it won't work if she wants to land her a Mr. Right from her own taste culture. Since the object of her affection is another Oberlin alum, their brand of self-help advice is as useless as Archie's—neither gives the cultural knowledge she needs to hook up successfully in a taste culture that is so explicitly post-literary, and at the same time, so overtly post-collegiate. She finds happiness when she learns to just be herself. So, even though the voices of traditional self-help are thoroughly discredited, the novel itself becomes a post-collegiate self-help novel, a point driven home by the book's dust jacket:

> *The Girls' Guide to Hunting and Fishing* reflects the quest of our time: how to love and understand one another better than we do and how to love in ways that allow us to be more fully ourselves. Its heroine, crackling with life, energy, and spirit, is a vivid and wise guide to these lessons. It's no wonder that a growing number of readers from the Midwest to midtown Manhattan, have come to Melissa Bank's work with a sense of instant recognition and gratitude for what she has given us all.

The discourse here is unashamedly therapeutic—the novel's value is measured in terms of self-actualization: reading it makes us more fully ourselves. No mention is made of any sort of stylistic achievement, nor is it even referred to at any point as a novel—its brilliance is in the lessons it gives to us, a reading community/target audience that knows its own tastes (and just as important, whom to trust). Archie gives no credibility to Jane's culturally bankrupt perspectives, but Faith and Bonnie fail to appreciate the game of love as played by graduates of the better liberal arts colleges and universities. Intellectual class distinctions are resoundingly reaffirmed by the end of the novel; just being yourself gets you the *right* Mr. Right if he comes from the alma mater, because when he's just being himself, his self looks an awfully lot like yours. The success of *Girls' Guide* was due in large measure to its ability to fill a vacuum in terms of cultural authority for this *us* of college-educated readers for whom mere self-help guides are guilty pleasures or simply beneath contempt, but who are no longer in thrall to traditional notions of what Serious Fiction should try to accomplish or what quality reading should be about.

That a shared taste culture (expressed in the shorthand of favorite books) is the bedrock for successful relationships is reiterated in Bank's next collection of linked stories, *The Wonder Spot* (2005). Its heroine, Sophie Applebaum, again works in publishing and has the same sort of literary/antiliterary conversations with various boyfriends. Her favorite novel comes, once again, from the Austen-Wharton-James-Forster stable—James's *Washington Square*, the same novel Archie read to Jane in *Girls' Guide*. And, once again, her search for Mr. Right has everything to do with identifying a shared taste in books; loving boyfriends and loving the same books go hand in hand:

> He'd just finished reading a new collection of short stories that he loved and I loved, and I told him about other collections I thought he might love. We loved the same dead writers, too—Hemingway and Fitzgerald but not Faulkner; neither of us had read *Ulysses*, and I said, "Let's never read it," and we swore that no matter what happened between us, we never would.
>
> After our dishes were cleared, he said, "I feel so great with you."
>
> After port, he leaned over and kissed me on the lips.
>
> After he'd paid the check, he led me out to the sidewalk and pulled me against him. (264)

After all that book talk, what else could have happened? (Mercifully, they did not move on to discuss their mutual admiration for *Washington Square*—spontaneous public sex acts would have been inevitable.) The therapeutic dimension of the "lessons" offered by this book depends on a knowledge base that cannot be leveraged in the same way that it was by the misguided nouveau-riche mother in *The Nanny Diaries*. Because there is no suggestion that the intellectual capital acquired in college needs to be cashed in as soon as possible for financial gain, the knowledge of books remains transcendent. Nothing can diminish its value. Yet there is another sort of transaction occurring in this scene between the economies of knowledge and love. Knowing certain authors, insisting on distinctions between them, and expounding on which ones you love passionately remains an essential process of self-definition and, therefore, a vital courtship ritual.

That the books these characters *buy* can be as much of an expression of innermost self as the books their favorite novelists *write* epitomizes what the sociologist Colin Campbell has referred to as "Romantic consumerism" (*The Romantic Ethic*, 1987). He argues compellingly that modern consumerism depends to a very great extent on the Romantic conception of artistic creation, expanded to include audience as well as artist. While he acknowledges the traditional wisdom—that it was the Romantics who laid the foundation for the modernist dismissal of consumer culture through their insistence on the singularity of artistic genius as prerequisite of *genuine* culture—he is also struck by the fact that this theory of artistic creation "places almost as much emphasis upon the 're-creative' abilities of the reader as upon the original creative faculties of the poet. . . . The reader is also, in that sense, assumed to be a creative artist, capable of conjuring up images which have the power to 'move' him. . . . Romanticism provided that philosophy of 'recreation' necessary for a dynamic consumerism: a philosophy that legitimates the search for pleasure as good in itself" (189).

The Romantic consumer as recreative artist, whose favorite medium of personal expression is selective acquisition, has recently become a central feature of the critical discourse devoted to the iPod. In his book *The Perfect Thing: How the iPod Shuffles Commerce, Culture, and Coolness* (2006), Steven Levy argues that the contents of one's iPod have come to embody the singularity of self: "Playlist is character. . . . It's not just what you like, it's *who you are*" (26). Just how ubiquitous this figure of the Romantic recreative consumer has become is thrown into sharp relief in his observation that "iTunes surfing is not merely a revelation of character but a means to a rich personal narrative, navigated by a click wheel. At one point the universal goal of the literate was to write the Great American Novel. Then it moved to the Great American Screenplay. And now, the Great American iTunes Library" (41).

When the Great American Author becomes the Great American Curator/Consumer, taste distinctions must be recorded time and time again, because they are, in effect, where the action is in terms of self-definition. In this regard, post-literary novels are more than just the contemporary version of the novel of manners—they are iPods in novelistic form. The relentless cataloguing of books read, movies watched, music listened to, and clothing purchased represents the articulation of the recreative self in a world where the value of any knowledge, particularly the knowledge furnished by a college education and literary fiction, is undergoing perpetual revaluation. There is no better example of this sort of iPod novel than Nick Hornby's *High Fidelity* (1995), since it celebrates a Romantic consumerism in which acquisition and display become the bedrock of identity formation.

When offering advice about finding the appropriate significant other, the narrator Rob insists that "what really matters is what you like, not what you *are* like." While he thinks that his friend Barry's suggestion, that one needs to hand out a questionnaire to prospective partners covering all the "music/film/TV/book bases," may be a bit extreme, he nevertheless concludes that there is "an essential truth contained within the idea, and the truth was that these things matter and there's no good pretending that any relationship has a future if your record collections disagree violently, or if your favorite films wouldn't even speak to each other if they met at a party" (17). The phrasing here is particularly revealing, because collections as expressions of taste appear to take on a life of their own, having conversations and going off to parties together. As taste-knowledge incarnate they become the tangible expression of self, a point made even more extensively when Rob talks about his record collection:

> Tuesday night I reorganize my record collection; I often do this at periods of emotional stress. There are some people who would find this a pretty dull way to spend an evening, but I'm not one of them. This is my life, and it's nice to be able to wade in, immerse yourself in it, touch it. When Laura was here I had the records arranged alphabetically; before that I had them filed in chronological order. Beginning with Robert Johnson, and ending with, I don't know somebody African, or whatever else I was listening to when Laura and I met. Tonight, though, I fancy something different, so I try to remember the order I bought them in; that way I hope to write my own autobiography, without having to pick up a pen. I pull the records off the shelves, put them in piles all over the sitting room floor, look for *Revolver* and go from there; and when I've finished, I'm flushed with a sense of self, because this, after all, is who I am. (55)

This might be a dull way to spend an evening, but not for anyone in a post-literary iPod novel, because one can just as easily imagine Jane Rosenthal or Sophie Applebaum getting the same thrill reorganizing their record or book libraries in the form of tangible autobiography. Two things are especially significant here. "All the music/film/TV/book bases" suggests that the connoisseurship that defines the self is no longer limited to just books. Autobiography, formerly done with a pen, is now a matter of constructing a sense of self out of diverse but thoroughly integrated libraries of popular culture, where there are no hard-and-fast distinctions between literary and nonliterary in terms of making the definitive taste distinctions that define who you really are. The model may still be literary—the library, the autobiography—but the exercise now involves more than just books. Just as important, this process is driven by emotional need. To paraphrase Levy, if playlist is character, then playlist is also self-help. The ultimate value of the library is not the accumulation of cultural knowledge for its own sake, because he engages in this archival work only during periods of emotional stress. For Rob, the library is most satisfying when it has therapeutic value, and it can perform that function only if he refuses to let contemporary literary fiction anywhere near that personal archive.

Make That Quality Fiction, Not Literary Fiction: Is Self-Help Such a Long Way Down?

In his recent novels and book reviews, Nick Hornby has continued to clear a space for the post-literary self-help novel, but the realization of its therapeutic potential appears to depend on the outright rejection of the officially literary. Once again, the battle lines are drawn not between literary fiction and entertaining fiction, as such, but between literary fiction and quality popular fiction that will "change your life and therefore deserves to be considered literary once we chuck antiquated notions of what it actually means to be literary." In other words, it is most decidedly not fueled by a "read anything you want" populism but by the desire to make distinctions between different types of quality reading. Celebrating reading while rejecting the self-consciously literary, in pursuit of a certain sort of underappreciated popular fiction, involves a complicated set of moves. Hornby pursues this project relentlessly, but most entertainingly, throughout *The Polysyllabic Spree* (2005), a collection of his book reviews that appeared in the literary magazine *The Believer*. He explains why he took the job as book reviewer:

> I assumed that the cultural highlight of my month would arrive in book form, and that's true, for probably eleven months out of the year. Books are, let's face it, better than everything else. If we played Cultural Fantasy Boxing League, and made books go fifteen rounds in the ring against the best that any other art form had to offer, then books would win pretty much every time. Go on, try it, "The Magic Flute" v. *Middlemarch*? *Middlemarch* in six. "The Last Supper" v. *Crime and Punishment*? Fyodor on points. See? I mean I don't know how scientific this is, but it feels like the novels are walking in. You might get the occasional exception, "Blonde

on Blonde" might mash up *The Old Curiosity Shop*, say, and I wouldn't give much for *Pale Fire*'s chances against *Citizen Kane*. And every now and then you'd get a shock because that happens in sport, so *Back to the Future III* might land a lucky punch on *Rabbit, Run*; but I'm still backing literature twenty-nine times out of thirty. Even if you love movies and music as much as you do books, it's still, in any given four-week period, way, *way* more likely you'll find a great book you haven't read than a great movie you haven't seen, or a great album you haven't heard. (58)

The conversational tone, the humor, and the sports analogy all clearly indicate that this is not your average literary criticism—even as it celebrates the joys of reading so exuberantly. Notice the choice of words in terms of characterizing those pleasures—it's a matter of books and literature, not anything literary. While the National Endowment for the Arts' *Report on Reading* may use one all-embracing category for what it calls literary reading, Hornby is determined to draw distinctions within that broad category. He distances himself ironically from the magazine's editorial board, whom he positions as card-carrying members of literary culture: "their idea of a good time is to book tickets to a literary event" (86). Throughout his monthly columns, Hornby draws comparisons between books he loves and the literary fiction he's supposed to be reading:

> Why hasn't anyone told me that *Mystic River* is right up there with *Presumed Innocent* and *Red Dragon*? Because I don't know the right kind of people, that's why. In the last three weeks, about five different people have told me that Alan Hollinghurst's *The Line of Beauty* is a work of genius, and I'm sure it is; I intend to read it soonest. I'm equally sure, however, that I won't walk into a lamp-post while reading it, like I did with *Presumed Innocent* all those years ago; you don't walk into lamp-posts when you're reading literary novels do you? . . . I'm happy to have friends who recommend Alan Hollinghurst, really I am. They're all nice, bright people. I just wish I had friends who recommended books like *Mystic River*, too. Are you that person? Do you have any vacancies for a pal? (106)

Hornby is most definitely that person in these columns, only he's the sort of friend who feels it's essential to trash the literary in order to champion the *really* good books. He is taken by *Mystic River* because it "seems like an encapsulation of the very best and most exciting kind of creative process and from the outside, the craft involved in the creation of *Mystic River* looks as if it involved the same stretch. . . . Lehane has ended up making it look so effortless that no one I've ever met seems to have noticed that he's done very much at all. But then, the lesson of literature over the last eighty years has been the old math teacher's admonishment: "SHOW YOUR WORKINGS!" Otherwise how is anyone to know that there are any?" (107). His attack on self-conscious craft as chief distinguisher of the truly literary becomes even more vehement in his appreciation of Chris Coake's short-story collection *We're in Trouble*:

> Sometimes, when you're reading these stories, you forget to breathe, which probably means that you're reading them with more speed than the writer intended. Are they literary? They're beautifully written, and they have bottom, but they're never dull. And they all contain striking and dramatic narrative ideas. And Coake never draws attention to his own art and language; he wants you to look at his people, not to listen to his voice. So they're literary in the sense that they're serious, and will probably be nominated for prizes, but they're unliterary in the sense that they could end up mattering to people. (116)

Interestingly, even though books punch-out movies and music on a regular basis, the model for the sort of novel Hornby thinks really matters to people is a cinematic one—namely the quality high-concept blockbuster in the hands of a someone like Lucas or Spielberg. He quotes Tom Shone's appreciation of Spielberg's *Jaws* in his book *Blockbuster: How Hollywood Stopped Worrying and Learned to Love the Summer* (2005). According to Shone, the golden age of American art cinema in the seventies (defined by the auteurist masterpieces produced by Scorsese, Brian De Palma, Francis Ford Coppola, and Peter Bogdanovich) was brought to a close not because of the drug-fueled hubris of those auteurs, combined with the move to conglomerate-driven film production for hyperactive teenagers (the central thesis of Peter Biskind's *Easy Riders, Raging Bulls* (1998), but because the films of Spielberg and Lucas represented a new era in quality, popular filmmaking. For Shone, this transitional period represents not the end of the halcyon days of American art cinema but a victory for common viewers, exemplified by himself and his friends in their youth:

> So if anyone killed the American film industry, let's be clear about this: it was me and Lethem, and millions of other kids just like us, who gathered together in the summer of 1977, seized our chance, and staged a coup

d'etat of our local movie theaters, thus launching Hollywood, in Biskind's words, on its course toward "infantalizing the audience, overwhelming him and her with sound and spectacle, obliterating irony, aesthetic self-consciousness, and critical reflection." Believe me, this took some work. Those suckers don't go down overnight. (Quoted by Hornby, *The Polysyllabic Spree*, 10)

This gleeful victory of popular film over aesthetic self-consciousness is the cinematic version of Hornby's dismissal of the literary, and here again one finds the celebration of a quality popular storytelling that, however roundly vilified as mere mass culture, still needs to be championed as a particular form of the popular that is superior to the literary or cinematic. When Hornby quotes Shone's appreciation of *Jaws*, the similarities between their respective positions could hardly be more explicit. According to Shone, what stays with you are less the big action sequences than small moments of characterization, like Brody's son copying his finger steepling at the dinner table.

> "To get anything like resembling such filets of improvised characterization, you normally had to watch something far more boring—some chamber piece about marital disintegration by John Castanets, say—and yet here were such things, popping up in a movie starring a scary rubber shark in the same movie. This seemed like important information. Why had no one told us before?"

Hornby comments:

> If this column has anything like an aesthetic, it's there: you can get finger steepling and sharks in the same book. And you really need the shark part, because a whole novel about finger steepling—and that's a fair synopsis of both the Abandoned Literary Novel and several thousand others like it—can be on the sleepy side. You don't have to have a shark, of course; the shark could be replaced by a plot, or, say, thirty decent jokes. (114)

Or to put it another way—in terms of the Cultural Fantasy Boxing League—when it comes to Hornby's own aesthetic, it's Hollywood Blockbuster vs. Literary Novel and the latter gets knocked out of the ring in the first round. This may, at first, seem difficult to reconcile with his "books are better twenty-nine times out of thirty" claim, but it's actually a thoroughly consistent argument, because for Hornby the best books are the ones that audiences actually enjoy—the sort of books that are closer to Hollywood films than literary novels. He drives this point home when he sums up how he feels about Shone's book: "This may be a strange thing to say about a book that embraces the evil empire of Hollywood so warmly, but *Blockbuster* is humane: it prizes entertainment over boredom, and audiences over critics, and yet it's a work of great critical intelligence. It wouldn't kill me, I suppose, to say I'm proud of the boy" (115).

This insistence that the pleasures "real" audiences experience while reading can be truly appreciated only by first knocking literary novels out of the ring ultimately boils down to what one is supposed to learn from reading fiction and what sort of intelligence comes into play. In his literary guidebook *How to Read a Novel: A User's Guide*, John Sutherland (chairman of the Man Booker Prize selection committee in 2005) argues: "A clever engagement with the novel is, in my opinion, one of the most noble functions of human intelligence. Reading novels is not a spectator sport but a participatory activity. Done well, a good reading is as creditable as a 10-scoring high dive. It is, I would maintain, almost as difficult to read a novel well as write one well" (12). Participating successfully in such a difficult sport, really "sticking" this reading business, depends on observing the protocols of close reading, which requires a certain kind of intelligence; even choosing the right title depends on "intelligent browsing." This would seem, on the face of it, to be a relatively uncontroversial assertion to make. But when Sutherland's book was reviewed in the *New York Times Book Review* (December 17, 2005), the reviewer was none other than the same Tom Shone that Hornby was so proud of, and Shone's flat-out attack on the book reveals just how completely the literary culture that Sutherland represents is being rejected. He zeros in on the just-quoted passage about novel reading and human intelligence:

> Does anyone go near the word "intelligent" without an armed escort these days? Until properly defined, it's a word of use only to those in the business of spreading fear, and indeed Sutherland's book is curiously fretful and anxious, rising to a ringing endorsement of actual novels only in its final pages. . . . Anyone interested in the way people really read novels ought to turn to Nick Hornby's "Stuff I've Been Reading" column for *The Believer* magazine: They're a real-time, on-the-ground accounts of one man's monthly battle to square the number of books he

buys with the books he actually reads, while fighting off the demands of TV, kids and soccer.

The one-two punch Shone employs here exemplifies the differences between traditional literary culture and this emergent quality fiction culture—intelligence, used the way that Sutherland wields it, as an unquestioned transcendent value, only forecloses the number of possible players. And since there are vast numbers of actual readers out there who are "really" reading and buying books compulsively without worrying at all about applying for club membership, Sutherland's reading as "clever engagement" can safely be dismissed as irrelevant, a vestige of a literary culture based on fear, rather than reading that is deeply immersed in the actuality of daily life, and all the more passionate because of that immersion.

But what sort of intelligence is asked for, and provided by, this quality fiction? The wildly divergent reviews of Hornby's novel *A Long Way Down* exemplify just how contested this question of "intelligence" has become, particularly in terms of how that intelligence relates to self-help discourse. The novel features four main characters, who all meet up on the top of a London building (Topper's House), planning to commit suicide the same night: Martin (a disgraced television celebrity), Maureen (a middle-aged single-mother caring for her invalid son), JJ (a failed American rock musician), and Jess (the alienated daughter of Labour minister of education). Upon meeting each other, and learning of each other's intentions, they form an ad hoc self-help group. There is no better example of how popular literary culture has been transformed into narrative universe, or how audience can become character, than in this novel, especially when this group decides to form their own book club. JJ, who is responsible for their "cultural program," because he is obsessed with reading, says: "I read the fuck out of every book I can get my hands on. I like Faulkner and Dickens and Vonnegut and Brendan Behan and Dylan Thomas" (29). He is the consummate self-cultivator, reading books to make up for the college education he missed. He is also what Shirley Brice Heath would call a social isolate reader:

> I've spent my entire life with people who don't read—my folks, my sister, most of the band, especially the rhythm section—and it really makes you really defensive after a while. How many times can you be called a fag before you snap . . .? Why does reading freak people out so much? Sure. I could be pretty anti-social when we were on the road, but if I was playing Game Boy hour after hour, no one would be on my case. In my

social circle, blowing up fucking space monsters is socially acceptable, in a way that *American Pastoral* isn't." (193)

His advocacy of reading meets with resistance within the group. Martin is skeptical because his ex-wife was a member of "one of those dreadful reading groups, where unhappy repressed middle-class lesbians talk for five minutes about some novel they don't understand and then spend the rest of the evening moaning about how dreadful men are" (93). Another one of the four, Jess, the hyperobnoxious teenager, completely rejects the reading group, as well as the literary self-help titles JJ has in mind for the group, particularly the ones that are supposed to have a therapeutic effect—namely, books by authors who have committed suicide.

> You should read the stuff by people who killed themselves! We started off with Virginia Woolf, and I only read like two pages of this book about a lighthouse, but I read enough to know why she killed herself: She killed herself because she couldn't make herself understood. You only have to read one sentence to see that. I sort of identify with her a bit, because I suffer from that sometimes, but her misfortune was to go public with it. And she had some bad luck too, if you think about it, because in the olden days anyone could get a book published because there wasn't so much competition. So you could walk into a publisher's office and they'd go, Oh, OK, then. Whereas now they'd go, No, dear, go away, no one will understand you. Try Pilates or salsa dancing instead.

While she is a less than perceptive reader of Woolf, she does zero in on why JJ is so drawn to books: "Is it because you didn't go to school? Is that why you think all books are great even when they're shit. Because some people are like that, aren't they? You're not allowed to say anything about books because they're books, and books are, you know, god" (189). As such, Jess incarnates the perfect antithesis of Michael Cunningham's Laura Brown in *The Hours*, the social isolate reader intending to commit suicide but who reads Woolf, and finds her such a kindred spirit that she has an out-of-the-body experience (on reading *Mrs. Dalloway*: "I am Virginia Woolf and I am not Virginia Woolf"). Jess wants none if it—she rejects not just Woolf, but reading as any kind of self-cultivation. There is no identification, and therefore no therapeutic rapport is possible. Woolf and Jess are anything *but* common readers.

At this point, where do we locate Hornby? In his "books win twenty-nine times out of thirty" mode, he sounds remarkably like JJ, the rock-obsessed passionate reader. But one can also hear echoes of his intense skepticism toward the literary channeling through Jess, particularly in her rejection of the sanctity of books and those readers who are taken in by an ideology of reading as pure transcendence. The answer, of course, is that both positions are endorsed and critiqued within the polyphonic spree that is *A Long Way Down*. Hornby creates a fascinating ambivalence about reading, alternately endorsing its potential to be truly transformative and rejecting the ideological baggage called literary culture that only appears to encumber it.

One finds exactly the same sort of structured ambivalence toward self-help discourse throughout *A Long Way Down*. Just as Bank incorporates the self-help book within *The Girls' Guide to Hunting and Fishing*, only to reject it in its pure form and then reinvent it on her own terms, Hornby as master ironist creates a remarkably similar hybrid, using that polyphonic narrative structure and an ever-shifting ironic voice to create a space for his own version of the quality self-help novel. Two of the four characters (Jess and Martin) express contempt for self-help anything, but JJ and Maureen are convinced that therapeutic exchanges can indeed help ease their pain. Late in the novel, Jess organizes an "intervention" for the families of the four central characters in her role as agent provocateur, and the resulting disaster is a brilliant burlesque of touchy-feely, self-help discourse.

> Jess clapped her hands together and stepped into the center of the room. "I read about this on the Internet," she said. "It's called an intervention. They do it all the time in America."
>
> "All the time," JJ shouted. "It's all we do."
>
> "See if someone is fucked . . . messed up on drugs or drink or whatever, then the, like, friends and family and whatever all gather together and confront him and go, you know, Fucking pack it in . . . This one's sort of different. In America they have a skilled . . . Oh shit, I've forgotten the name. On the web site he was called Steve."
>
> She fumbled in the pocket of her jacket and pulled out a piece of paper.
>
> "A facilitator. You're supposed to have a skilled facilitator and we haven't got one. I didn't know how to ask. I don't know anyone with skills." (268)

Martin is appalled by the prospect: "I rubbed my hands together, as if I were relishing the prospect of all the delicious and nutritious self-knowledge I was about to tuck into" (271). But JJ refuses an offer of a plane ticket home in order to get a band together. "I got one here." He wants to stay, "just until everyone's okay." Maureen's last speech in the novel is even more unequivocal about the benefits of the self-help experience she's had with the other three: "Do you remember Psalm 50? Call upon me in the day of trouble: I will deliver you, and you shall glorify me. I went to Topper's House because I had called and called and called and there was no delivery and my days of trouble seemed to have lasted too long, and showed no signs of ending. But then He did hear me, in the end, and He sent me Martin and JJ and Jess" (312). Most tellingly, Martin's last sentence in the novel reveals a far less dismissive attitude toward self-knowledge: "Hard is trying to rebuild yourself, piece by piece, with no instruction book and no clue as to where all the important bits are supposed to go" (322). By the end of the novel, Hornby is clearly engaged in two parallel rescue operations that are completely intertwined—saving reading from literary culture, and saving self-understanding from the self-help industry.

The critical reception of *A Long Way Down* and Bank's *The Wonder Spot*, which hit bookstores within a week of each other in the summer of 2005, provoked a kind of national referendum among book reviewers on the post-literary self-help novel. Hornby's novel was hailed either as a triumph, or practically unreadable, depending on the individual critic's perspective on the self-help potential of fiction. In his *Publisher's Weekly* review, reprinted as the main review of the book at its Amazon homepage, Tom Perrotta could hardly be more enthusiastic about the novel. He is particularly appreciative of Hornby's desire to hybridize the subject matter of the literary novel with narrative machinery drawn from high-concept filmmaking, the sort of films that Shone praises and Hornby refers to as his aesthetic (or, to put it another way, what I've been referring to as post-literary fiction, or what Hornby might refer to as the Finger-Steepling, High-Concept, Quality Popular novel):

If Camus had written a grown-up version of *The Breakfast Club*, the result might have had more than a little in common with Hornby's grimly comic, oddly moving fourth novel. . . . It's a bold set-up and perilously high-concept, but Hornby pulls it off with understated ease. . . . Hornby takes a Dickensian risk in creating a character as saintly and pathetic as Maureen, but it pays off. In her quiet way, she's an unforgettable figure, the moral and emotional center of the novel. This is a brave and absorbing book. It's a thrill to watch a writer as talented as Hornby take on the grimmest of subjects without flinching and somehow make it funny and surprising at the same time. And if the characters occasionally seem a little more eloquent or self-aware than they really have a right to be, or if the novel turns the tiniest bit sentimental at the end, all you can really fault Hornby for is an act of excessive generosity, an authorial embrace bestowed upon some characters who are sorely in need of a hug.

Here Perrotta is as supportive of the novel's self-help ambitions as he is of the hybridizing of literary fiction and Hollywood film. Michiko Kakutani, on the other hand, in her review of *A Long Way Down* in the *New York Times*, has only contempt for both ambitions. She dismisses the book as a "maudlin bit of tripe" but reserves special scorn for its post-literary and self-help dimensions. Where Perrotta saw real possibilities in the coupling of Albert Camus and John Hughes, and found these characters huggable, Kakutani rejects both:

> The premise of *A Long Way Down* feels like a formulaic idea for a cheesy made-for-television movie. . . . But as the book progresses, even the pretense of trying to write idiosyncratic characters falls away, as each member of the "Quitters Club" begins to spouting the same brand of inane platitudes and self-help truisms. Needless to say, *A Long Way Down* ends—and this is hardly giving away the book's conclusion, as the reader can see coming from several miles away—with each of the characters undergoing a personal transformation of sorts and rediscovering his or her will to live. A sappy and utterly predictable ending to a sappy and utterly predictable novel.

Perrotta's and Kakutani's reviews, taken together with Hornby's monthly columns for *The Believer*, exemplify the ongoing turf battle over what constitutes literary fiction. Where Perrotta and Hornby contend that the quality fiction that matters to real readers can occur only when it moves away from the literary, Kakutani believes that certain distinctions need to remain in force, and the move to television genres and self-help discourse trigger the trip wires that mark the literary off from the nonliterary at the most fundamental level. For Kakutani, this is, finally, "a cringe-making excuse for a novel."

I don't want to suggest any kind of easy bifurcation of literary cultures here, that is, Populist Amazon vs. Elitist *New York Times*, because their respective arenas overlap far too extensively. Perrotta himself reviews for the *Times*, and his novels regularly receive glowing reviews there. That being said, Perrotta's endorsement of Hornby's novel undoubtedly has a great deal to do with the comparability of their respective projects. Perrotta has written a post-literary novel of manners of his own, *Little Children* (2004), in which his transposition of Flaubert's *Madame Bovary* is as overt as Fielding's appropriation of Austen or Bushnell's invocation of Wharton. The main story arc concerning infidelity in the suburbs and the character of Sarah, the bored housewife married to a dolt, but determined to find passion one way or another, make the parallels between the novels apparent, but the transposition becomes overt when Sarah is invited to join a book club and the selection that night happens to be, you guessed it, *Madame Bovary*. Perrotta, however, gives a great deal of integrity to the group, which consists of women who are insightful, informed readers, a point made vividly clear when Sarah is told to make sure she reads the "Steegmuller translation." For Perrotta, this club apparently represents all that is good about amateur readers and popular literary culture. For these characters, it represents an oasis within their suburban existence, a point that is spelled out explicitly when Sarah experiences a kind of revelation during their discussion of the novel:

> All at once, it came to Sarah. It was like being back at the Women's Center. For the first time since she graduated from college, she'd managed to find her way into a community of smart, independent, supportive women who enjoyed each other's company and didn't need to compete with one another or define themselves in relation to the men in their lives. It was precisely what she'd been missing, the oasis she'd been unable to find in graduate school, at work, or even at the playground. She'd searched for it so long that she'd even come to suspect that it hadn't actually existed in the first place, at least not the way she remembered it, that it was more than the product of her romantic undergraduate imagination than anything real in the word. But it had been real. It felt like this, and it was a huge relief to be back inside the circle again. (191)

Perrotta values that community of women reading together, but the reviews of Bank's *The Wonder Spot*, which appeared within a week of *A Long Way Down*, were similarly polarized, only in this case, the evaluation of Bank's novel was tied to a larger referendum on the fate of "chick-lit" as something that might have had a degree of literary credibility at some point but had since plummeted to the realms of mere genre fiction. One finds a remarkably similar split between the critics who are themselves practitioners of the popular literary, and those who labor to distance themselves from it, even if they are perceived to be fellow travelers. As for the former, Jennifer Weiner, author of *Good in Bed* (2001) and *In Her Shoes* (2003), gave Bank's novel a rave review while serving as guest critic for *Entertainment Weekly*:

> Melissa Bank is one lucky lady. Her first book, *The Girls' Guide to Hunting and Fishing*, was published in 1999, when a girl could turn a witty, rueful tale about a single girl looking for love without being instantly cast into the pale pink purgatory known as "chick lit." Back in those heady days, just after Bridget Jones and prior to the explosion of sexy, sassy tales packaged in Easter egg pastels, you could be a young, urban female writer exploring the life and times of a young urban heroine and still have the critics take you seriously. You didn't have to gild your manuscript with McSweeney's-esque footnotes or name check your Grandpa's shtetl: nor did you have to invite autobiographical comparisons by touting your time working for Anna Wintour. (88)

Weiner makes a crucial point about the evolution of chick-lit—as it has grown in popularity it has been rejected by critics as subliterary genre fiction. She doesn't pin this all on the critics, since her comment about the "Easter egg pastels" acknowledges the role that the publishing industry has played in diminishing its legitimacy as quality fiction, as the industry has turned what might have been considered Women's Fiction into mass-market chick-lit. Her choice of words reveals a host of interdependent presuppositions about the relationship between the poplar literary and the officially literary. Writing chick-lit is a kind of "purgatory" because, while it sells, it gets no respect from "the critics," and getting critical respect is still something she obviously believes it deserves, because this is not mere genre fiction but a form of quality fiction written by women, about women, for women. Her reference to "McSweeney's-esque footnotes" is significant here, because the category of literary fiction is apparently still in the hands of literary magazines, a realm where literary taste depends on ironic erudition, not identification with character, which for Weiner distinguishes the fiction that really matters to readers. Weiner's privileging of this identification sounds a lot like Hornby's rejection of the literary as self-conscious craft. And like Hornby, while she rejects the literary establishment, she still insists on making critical distinctions that install popular literary novels above both the merely popular and the irrelevant literary: "So *The Wonder Spot* isn't just a great read. It's a wake-up call, alerting the literary establishment that stories about young women coming of age can still be enthralling, engaging and deserving of notice. . . . Sophie Applebaum's story might end while she's still groping toward her place in the world. Lucky for fans of smart, identifiable heroines who feel like our best friends, only better, Melissa Bank has definitely found hers" (88).

In her review of *The Wonder Spot* in the *New York Times*, Curtis Sittenfeld also uses the novel as an occasion to weigh in on the fate of chick-lit, but she is as fiercely critical of the novel as Weiner is laudatory, and for many of the same reasons. Her diatribe against the book is in some ways surprising, since her own novel, *Prep* (2005), was circulated within the same orbit and read by the same audiences; the homepage for Bank's novel at Amazon, for example, lists *Prep* along with *A Long Way Down* under the heading "Customers Who Bought This Book Also Bought." The only critical blurb on the cover of *Prep* comes from none other than Tom Perrotta ("One of the most impressive debuts novels in recent memory"). And when asked by *Entertainment Weekly* what she was reading now, Bank responded: "Curtis Sittenfeld's *Prep*." Yet in her review in the *Times*, Sittenfeld distances herself from both Bank and the entire category of chick-lit.

> To suggest that another woman's ostensibly literary novel is chick-lit feels catty, not unlike calling another woman a slut—doesn't the term basically bring down all of us? And yet, with *The Wonder Spot*, it's hard to resist. A chronicle of the search for personal equilibrium and Mr. Right, Melissa Bank's novel is highly readable, sometimes funny and entirely unchallenging: you're not a lot smarter after finishing it. I'm as resistant as anyone else to the assumption that because a book's author is female and because that book's protagonist is a woman who actually cares about her romantic future, the book must fall into the chick-lit genre. So it's not that Bank's topic is lightweight; it's that she writes about it in a lightweight way. (9)

By beginning with "ostensibly literary" this critique makes it quite clear that Sittenfeld knows full well that there is a category of fiction out there that makes claims for literary status but she doesn't think it's warranted. She shares certain premises with Weiner: that there is indeed a vast difference between what is considered truly literary and mere chick-lit, and that to assume that women writing about women in love automatically puts a novel in the latter category is offensive, but critics keep doing it anyway. But Sittenfeld parts company with Weiner and Bank by saying, in effect, that this disdain is merited because most chick-lit is just bad writing; so, ultimately, the fault is with the people who write it, not the people who review it. Craft is reasserted here as the key distinguisher of literary fiction, and Bank is on the other side of the divide because her writing is lightweight. The key difference between Weiner and Sittenfeld, then, is a matter of evaluative criteria. Where Weiner makes identification the all-important factor in her argument for its status as quality fiction, Sittenfeld sees that identification factor as the principal reason it remains chick-lit:

> Undeniably, there were times when I laughed or winced in recognition as I read; I understood exactly what Sophie meant, and that's when I liked the book best. But this, ultimately, is the reason I know *The Wonder Spot* is chick-lit: because its appeal relies so much on how closely readers relate to its protagonist. Good novels allow us to feel what the characters feel, no matter how dissimilar their circumstances and ours. *The Wonder Spot* contains real meaning only if we identify with Sophie enough to infuse it with meaning of our own. (9)

The fact that Sittenfeld doesn't learn much from this novel, that the reader is not a lot smarter after having read it, suggests that she is also determined to reassert the value of self-cultivation as a process distinct from self-help, because the latter is just empathetic reading. Here Sittenfeld, high school English teacher sworn to initiating AP English students into the mysteries of great literature, comes shining through—self-improvement occurs by appreciating good writing, not by merely identifying with the main character. Good books give us knowledge, not just emotional connection. What she means by "real meaning" we will allow her to sort out with her students, but it probably has something to do with her reaffirmation of the most traditional notions of aesthetic value.

These oppositions between craft and identification, between reading as knowledge acquisition and reading as quality self-actualization, are at the center of the turf war over literary fiction, and the battle lines drawn by these novelists are remarkably similar to the debates about Oprah Winfrey's Book Club detailed earlier in this book. Sittenfeld's dismissal of *The Wonder Spot* on the grounds of craft are not that different from my students' reservations about Oprah's presentation of *Anna Karenina*—sure it's great to identify with Anna, but what about Tolstoy's writing? Of course, it's a great tragic romance, but in formal terms, it ain't exactly a made-for-television movie, so there should be some consideration of the differences, right? Yet the passionate reading that fuels the popular literary and allegedly sets it apart from the professionalized reading of academics and literary critics depends on more than the savoring of distinctive prose styles. That being said, passionate reading of the wrong books (only "ostensibly literary" books, for example) disqualifies all that passionate reading. But when is that passion not misspent? When does a popular literary novel become acceptable reading material according to the taste ideology mobilized by Sittenfeld?

In order to answer that question, I want to introduce another novel here as a kind of test case for these conflicting accounts of what really makes for a literary reading experience—Diane Johnson's *Le Divorce* (1997). In many ways, this novel fits the post-literary formula perfectly. It very self-consciously invokes both Jane Austen and Henry James as it tells the story of two sisters: Roxey, who is too romantic, and Isabel, who is too analytical. The novel begins when Isabel, the naïve American, comes to Paris in search of cultural information, hoping, in her words, "to get some of my rough edges buffed off that the University of Southern California failed to efface" (5). Just in case the reader has missed the parallels to *Sense and Sensibility* and *The Portrait of a Lady*, the novel is larded with literary quotations, and each chapter begins with an epigraph drawn from James, Emerson, Constant, or Voltaire. An American expatriate writer is a major character, and passages like this one sprinkled throughout make the connections hard to miss: "There are, also, certain ghosts of Hemingway, and Gertrude Stein, Janet Flanner, Fitzgerald, Edith Wharton, James Baldwin, James Jones—all of them here for something they could not find back home, possessed of an idea about culture and their intellectual heritage, conscious of a connection to Europe. Europe, repository of something they wish to know, and feel they are entitled to by ancestry to know" (3).

The redundancy of this literariness, the endless guarantees of guarantees that this is a genuinely literary experience, obviously works, at least for some critics. In his review of the novel in the *New York Times*, Malcolm Bradbury says, "Johnson treads—very consciously and cleverly—across the ancient and hallowed turf of the international novel." But this is a "postmodern rendering" for Bradbury, because "the Isabel Archer character is our lively first-person narrator Isabel Walker, who has just dropped out of film school." He concludes, "*Le Divorce* is a refreshing and critical variant on the old myth, as well as being, in its best passages, that much rarer thing: a genuinely wise and humane novel, by a very good writer." The literariness of all this good writing is also attested to repeatedly in the critical blurbs printed in the opening pages of the paperback edition of the novel: "One savors each page. . . . If one were to cross Jane Austen and Henry James, the result would be Diane Johnson" (*San Francisco Chronicle*); "Wickedly skillful. An adventurous work of art, and one that makes the delicate point that a novel (like the French food it gently mocks) can be delicious and serious at the same time" (*Philadelphia Inquirer*).

But what sort of delicious literary experience does one find in this adventurous work of art? What makes for the good writing? As for the status of the narrator Isabel Walker as film school dropout, *Le Divorce* begins with a promising prologue: "I suppose because I went to film school, I think of my story as a sort of film. In a film, this part would be under the credits, opening with an establishing shot from a high angle, perhaps the Eiffel Tower, panning tiny scenes below" (1). All sorts of intriguing premises are established in the opening pages, which suggest that Johnson may indeed be updating the novel of manners by situating it in a world where literary and visual cultures have become thoroughly intertwined—Isabel is a product of the University of Southern California film school, and her sister Roxey a product of the University of Iowa's Writers Workshop. In this coupling of graduate school pedigrees, one might expect a sophisticated interplay between the literary and the cinematic. Unfortunately, this does not come to fruition, because Isabel as first-person narrator is saddled with an arch-literary narrative voice, given to saying such things about film as:

> I think of life as being like film because of what I learned at the film school at USC. Film, with its fluid changefulness, its arbitrary notions of coherence, contrasting with the static solemnity of painting, might also be a more appropriate medium for rendering what seems to be happening, and emblematic too perhaps of our natures, Roxey's and mine, and the nature of the two societies, American and French. The New World and the Old, however, is too facile a juxtaposition, and I do not draw the conclusions I began with. If you can begin with conclusions. But I suppose we all do.

Now if one considers good writing—genuinely literary writing—to be a matter of witty phrasing and a relatively complicated prose style, then this would be indeed a pure delight. This, most assuredly, does not sound like Bridget Jones or Jane Rosenthal out on a shopping spree. Yet if one conceives of genuinely good writing as the skillful articulation of character through the subtle variations in narrative voice, cut to the measure of that character's psychology, then Isabel's reflections on film are something else—stunningly bad writing. This is not the voice of a twenty-something film student just off the plane from L.A. Speaking as a former film graduate student, who used to live in Paris, no less, who knew and worked with other film grad students from places like USC, the University of Iowa, the University of California, Los Angeles, and New York University, I can say with utmost certainty: Isabel Walker, you're no film graduate student. The only way this voice could be emanating from this character is if the ghost of a demonic Henry James, desperate to return to the land of the living, decided to take possession of a beautiful young woman's body but, *hélas*, nothing that *intéressant* is gonna happen in this book, *chérie*. The narrative voice in this passage is not a contemporary film student but the Austen-Wharton-James third-person narrator at its most precious. Isabel didn't learn any of this at USC film school, but Johnson learned how to write like this from reading James. She can, of course, channel those voices all she wants, but when she presumes to push it through Isabel's consciousness, the end result is a kind of literary theme-park, the novelistic equivalent of the Great Authors mural at the Starbucks café at my local Barnes & Noble. Or another analogy may be even more appropriate. In its presentation of a hermetically sealed world where the action takes place in locations used in James novels, rendered in the voices of literary icons past, *Le Divorce* is the literary equivalent of Jack Rabbit Slim's, the retro diner in *Pulp Fiction*—a world where everything, from the décor, to the waiters, to the names of the items on the menu, are all invocations and citations of a lost but still fetishized textual universe. At Jack Rabbit Henry's, this literary wax museum with a pulse, Isabel Archer-Walker replaces Buddy Holly as your server, and one can only imagine the menu: "Do you want that 5-Dollar Chai, *Daisy Miller*, or *Fleda Vetch*?"

A genuinely literary experience in this case—one that may be recognized as such by critics and passionate readers—depends on time travel to the appropriate era, but not necessarily in terms of historical setting. Johnson's novels focus on what is ostensibly contemporary transatlantic society, yet that rendering of the contemporary depends on a historical literariness in which good writing depends on more tone and art direction than stylistic refinement. In other words, the good writing that separates the literary wheat from the chick-lit chaff is a matter of confirming shared sensibilities. The book as best friend is every bit as essential for the Devoutly Literary novel and its readership as it is for chick-lit and its devoted readers. *Le Divorce* is an especially useful novel in terms of understanding the continuum between the two, because it is all about finding the appropriate significant other in stylish locations, and the interplay between romantic love and literary love is all over the map. But this channeling of James and Austen is given greater critical respect than the appropriation of canonical novels of manners by Fielding, Bushnell, Bank, and company because it so relentlessly celebrates the best-friend factor for another taste culture. *Le Divorce* was, not surprisingly, nominated for the National Book Award. Nor is it coincidental that Johnson's novel was the only contemporary novel of manners that was adapted by Merchant and Ivory—it was always already a Merchant and Ivory project waiting to be filmed. The brief description of the film at the Amazon home page for the DVD begins by asserting that Merchant and Ivory have "left the corsets behind" in this adaptation, but only in terms of actual costumes—the sensibility that underwrites the entire narrative is resolutely of another era, where the spirit of literariness still somehow hovers, waiting to be recalled.

That which is called literary, then, is "ostensibly" a matter of good writing, but also really dependent upon the promise of certain pleasures, the right cultural mise-en scène, formed by a relatively stable set of recurring locations and characters animated by the same desires, as well as a remarkably similar set of sensibilities shared by novelists, characters, and avid readers—in other words, a kind of category fiction called Lit-lit, which is the subject of chapter 6.

6

THE DEVOUTLY LITERARY
BESTSELLER

A true book lover's book . . . A testament to resilience and to the power of words.
—blurb on the back cover of *Balzac and the Little Chinese Seamstress* (2002)

Wondrous . . . masterful . . . *The Shadow of the Wind* is ultimately a love letter to literature intended for readers as passionate about storytelling as its young hero.
—blurb from *Entertainment Weekly* on the back cover of *The Shadow of the Wind* (2005)

The Thirteenth Tale is a love letter to reading, a book for the feral reader in all of us. Diane Setterfield will keep you guessing, make you wonder, move you to tears and laughter and, in the end, deposit you breathless yet satisfied back upon the shore of your everyday life.
—Dustjacket copy for *The Thirteenth Tale* (2006)

I have this fantasy book club in my mind where other people feel as passionately as I do about reading. As if it were a really good kiss. The sheer pleasure and intimacy of having a relationship with a novelist and all of the characters is transcendent—even sensual. Certain passages keep resonating in my head long after I've closed the book, and I often can't wait to get back to the story, as if it were a secret lover.
—*Literacy and Longing in L.A.* (2006)

I begin this chapter with these passages because they epitomize one of the most distinctive developments within popular literary culture—the feverish celebration of literary reading as an experience so overpowering that it can only be described in erotic terms. While the novels by Fielding, Bushnell, Bank, and Hornby that I discussed in the previous chapter all make extensive use of literary intertexts and are filled with characters who make the choice of reading material a key determinant in selecting the proper love object, none of those novels identifies the act of reading as erotic. Literary fiction, if given the right sort of radical makeover, can offer vital lessons in finding the right partner with whom erotic pleasure may be inevitable, but reading, as an end in itself, gets you nowhere but home alone on a Saturday night. Not so surprisingly, none of those post-literary novels has been circulated as a literary bestseller and none has won any prestigious literary prizes.

Judging by the winners and short-list nominees for the most prestigious literary prizes awarded between 2004 and 2008, the best way to ensure that a novel will be deemed a literary bestseller, and make a big splash in the awards game, is to feature a highly self-conscious celebration of the transformative power of the written word and equally impassioned advocacy of the need for aesthetic beauty. The most obvious examples of just how explicit these imperatives have become, and how they have been critically acknowledged accordingly, are Alan Hollinghurst's *The Line of Beauty* (winner of the Man Booker Prize and one of the top ten Notable Books in the *New York Times* in 2004) and Zadie Smith's *On Beauty* (one of the top five novels short-listed for the Man Booker and one of the top five Notable Books in fiction in the *Times* in 2005). You also need more than just the invocation of canonical novels by Austen, Wharton, James, and company—you need to make the man himself, Henry James, your main character and make the trials and tribulations of writing literary fiction the central action of the novel, which is the case with both David Lodge's *Author, Author* and Colm Toibin's *The Master* (short-listed for the Booker and among the *Times'* top ten Notable Books in 2004). Or you need to have a main character repeatedly denying that literary writing can transform your life in substantial ways, only to have him undergo a traumatic conversion experience that convinces him that literary beauty can indeed save your life, as is the case in McEwan's *Saturday* (one of the *Times'* top five Notable Books in fiction in 2005, long-listed for the Booker). Or you can feature a character who reads voraciously and insists on detailing her close encounters with important literary novels, as in Marisha Pessl's *Special Topics in Calamity Physics* (among the *Times'* top five Notable Books in fiction in 2006), in which the narrator, a maniacally well-read Harvard undergraduate, presents her table of contents as an English class syllabus—"Core Curriculum (Required Reading)," with each chapter bearing the name of a relevant classic (chapter 18, *A Room with a View*; chapter 25, *Bleak House*, etc.). Or you can just go whole hog and make all of your characters New York intellectuals, each defined by the books they're either in the process of writing, or by the books they're currently reading, as in Claire Messud's *The Emperor's Children* (another of the *Times'* top five Notable Books in fiction, 2006). Or in the case of Kate Christensen's *The Great Man* (winner of the PEN Faulkner Award in 2008), you can focus more specifically on the New York art world and fill your fictional universe with painters, might-have-been novelists, and two biographers, and then conclude the action with what appears to be a reprint of a review of those biographies in the *New York Times Book Review*. Or, in the case of Junot Diaz's *The Brief Wondrous Life of Oscar Wao*, which won the Pulitzer Prize in 2008, you can ostensibly avoid that world entirely by concentrating on a working-class family from the Dominican Republic now living in New Jersey, but still nevertheless subscribe to all things bookish by making the title character a helpless book nerd: "You really want to know what being an X Man feels like? Just be a smart bookish boy of color in contemporary U.S. ghetto" (22).

That's obviously a whole lot of intertexuality going on, only in these novels it's not a matter of one author just invoking another—it's a kind of *lived* intertextuality, since these characters—whether they be Henry James, New York intellectuals, or a sci-fi-reading nerd like Oscar—can't really function without the books they read, and they apparently can't exist as characters unless they're situated within the universe of literary fiction. All of these novels promise to deliver bona fide aesthetic experiences and are advertised accordingly. These are, most assuredly, not the sort of literary novels that Bridget Jones puts in the same category as pasta machines, the impressive books designed with serious intent but that have no practical use in the actual world.

In these Devoutly Literary novels the act of reading becomes an all-sustaining pleasure that is available only between the covers of a book. While I have argued throughout the previous chapters that the popular literary is a prime example of media convergence, these novels which are hailed by book reviewers as love letters to the power of literary reading reject any such convergence by celebrating the absolute singularity of literary reading the way it used to be—a solitary, exclusively print-based pleasure far removed from the realm of adaptations, television book clubs, Web sites, and superstores. Consider the opening scene in *The Shadow of the Wind*, where the main character, Daniel, is taken by his father to the Cemetery of Forgotten Books:

> This is a place of mystery, Daniel, a sanctuary. Every book, every volume you see here, has a soul. The soul of the person who wrote it and of those who read it and lived and dreamed with it. Every time a book changes hands, every time someone runs his eyes down its pages, its spirit grows and strengthens. When a library disappears, or a bookshop closes down, when a book is consigned to oblivion, those of us who know this place, its guardians, make sure that it gets here. In this place books no longer remembered by anyone, books that are lost in time, live forever, waiting for the day when they will reach a new reader's hands. Every book you see here has been somebody's best friend. In the shop we buy and sell them, but in truth books have no owner. Now they have only us, Daniel. Do you think you'll be able to keep such a secret?

Here books have achieved the status of sacred relics, still filled with intrinsic, transformative power but in need of a cult of readers to serve as their guardians, the people of the book who know their secrets. Yet I first encountered *The Shadow of the Wind* on the "Zafon table" at Barnes & Noble, where it sat alongside his new novel *Angel's Game*, the publishing industry's equivalent of a summer blockbuster release. Barnes & Noble isn't exactly a cemetery, nor is Borders, which made it a featured selection of the Borders Book Club, nor is Amazon, which included video interviews with the author at the homepage for the novel. While the novel presents reading as an imperiled activity kept alive only through the intervention of a small but devoted cult, the critical blurbs on the front and back covers attest to its vast mass-market potential—"One gorgeous read" (Stephen King). This apparently paradoxical situation epitomizes the current state of the literary bestseller. A novel that revolves around a cemetery of forgotten books is marketed aggressively by superstores and Amazon as an "international phenomenon," driven by a testimonial about how it is a love letter to literature from none other than *Entertainment Weekly* (the preeminent mass-market entertainment magazine in North America) and by praise from Stephen King (the author synonymous with bestselling genre fiction for the previous three decades). In other words, literary reading now comes with its own self-legitimating mythology that sanctifies the singularity of reading novels as an aesthetic experience, the way they *used* to be read, yet these same novels become global bestsellers only through the intervention of popular literary culture.

But how do these Devoutly Literary novels create this value for themselves? Just what sort of aesthetic experience is being offered and why is it so *transformative*? Who are these people of the book? And how have these self-consciously literary novels, which insist so strenuously on the singular therapeutic power of the literary, become a kind of *category fiction*, what I'm referring to as *Lit-lit*?

Answering these questions requires an approach that integrates the concerns of traditional aesthetics and cultural studies in unprecedented ways, primarily because each has tended to either discredit or simply ignore the other in wholesale fashion. The former will be of very little help in answering those questions, since it insists so steadfastly that genuine aesthetic experiences take place only in far more rarefied circumstances. Denis Donoghue's *Speaking of Beauty* (2003) exemplifies this refusal to even consider the possibility that some sort of aesthetic experience might actually occur within the realm of popular culture. He is delighted that academics are now interested in talking about aesthetic issues, once again, but forecloses the possibility that anyone other than the professional devotees of fine art can really have such experiences: "The most immediate reason to talk about beauty is the hope of saving it from the mercenary embrace of TV and advertisements. The hope is a frail one, since the owners of these instruments make their money by effecting strong links between health, beauty, high spirits, and sex" (26). If the discussion of the aesthetic experience must, as Donoghue insists, distance itself unilaterally from such a world because "the commercialization of art has removed its intrinsic or useless quality and turned the beautiful object into common processes of exchange," then the return to aesthetics signals only the return of a kind of guilt-free polo playing for academics—fun for the club members, but completely irrelevant to just about everyone else.

Cultural studies has rightly argued that this insistence on the intrinsic value of the genuine aesthetic object is the worst sort of theoretical mystification, because it isolates aesthetic texts so completely from the circumstances of their circulation and evaluation by a wide variety of different audiences. That being said, the determination to demystify aesthetic texts has precluded much discussion of how aesthetic texts are, nevertheless, a very particular type of cultural production, one that involves experiences not offered by other consumer products. Not so surprisingly, then, the sort of novels and films that have been avoided at all costs are those that have insisted on their own transcendent power. But the Devoutly Literary novels I will be focusing on in this chapter do exactly that. They are determined to prove their apartness through their ability to offer profoundly transformative aesthetic experiences—but they are also literary bestsellers. In other words, they are a form of popular culture that claims to provide a grand alternative to "all that"—distinguished, prize-winning novels, whose aestheticism has become their main selling point. As such, they cannot be fully appreciated either by traditional aesthetics or by the traditional forms of cultural studies. It is one thing to ponder whether watching Oprah's Book Club is an aesthetic experience, but quite another when we take up novels that insist, in no uncertain terms, that reading them will be a firsthand encounter with *beauty*. How are these aesthetic experiences marked off as such? And why have they become so marketable?

I want to pursue these questions by looking first at how the novels by Colm Toibin, David Lodge, and Alan Hollinghurst all imagine the relationship between the type of beauty offered by reading literary fiction and other sorts of aesthetic beauty, specifically those offered by material culture. Literary critics have theorized about the pleasure of the text for the past three decades, and we now know a fair amount about the various libidinal energies that are involved in the act of reading. In much the same way, the pleasures furnished by material objects have also been theorized about just as relentlessly by sociologists eager to identify the underlying desires that animate consumer culture. Yet I know of no attempt to situate the two in reference to each other. Throughout these novels, the experience of aesthetic beauty is alternately set apart from the realm of material pleasures, and at other points, just as tightly intertwined within those material pleasures. If we hope to gain better understanding of the literary bestseller and its readership at the turn of the twenty-first century, I think it is vitally important to understand the ways in which certain kinds of "beauty" now circulate within this taste culture, in and around and through those books. Just what sort of "literacy" do these novels take for granted as the basis for appreciating that beauty?

Karen Jay Fowler's *The Jane Austen Book Club* reveals a great deal about that literacy, particularly in regard to the relationship between literary and material pleasures. The members of a reading group meet monthly in each other's homes to discuss a different Austen novel, and the first line of Fowler's novel attests to the importance of books in terms of defining their self-image: "Each of us has a private Austen." So intimate is the relationship between self-image and choice of reading material that they are dubious about Grigg (the only male member of the group), not just as reader, but also as a person, because his favorite Austen novel is *Northanger Abbey*, and "This was not a position we could imagine anyone taking" (120). That this reading takes place within a landscape of quality consumerism, in which selection of reading material is one of a number of interdependent, all-defining taste choices, is exemplified by another moment in Fowler's novel. When the group visits Grigg's home for the first time, the other members are expecting the worst: "We had been curious about Grigg's housekeeping. Most of us hadn't seen a bachelor pad since the seventies. We were picturing mirror balls and Andy Warhol." He scores points with the other members because he serves "a lovely white from the Bonny Doon vineyard" alongside the buffet he prepares for them, but they are relieved when they discover "a rug by the couch that many of us recognized from the Sundance catalogue as something we ourselves had wanted, the one with the poppies on the edges. The sun glanced off a row of copper pots in the kitchen window" (121).

Each of us may have our own Austen, but apparently, each of us also has our own Sundance catalogue that is another form of required reading within this taste culture. The choice of books, like the choice of wine, rugs, and cooking utensils, attests to a set of shared values and rituals. They share the same novels in their discussions, but those discussions work only if their homes share the same quality mise-en-scène for all that book talk. This is fiction that comes with its own art direction. Here Sundance needs no introduction because the upscale home décor and clothing catalogue is as much a part of this world as Jane Austen. Identification between the characters, and between these characters and the readers of Fowler's novel, is secured by a shared taste for quality literature and quality décor, both of which can be referred to with equal specificity because the novel assumes a thorough familiarity with both, at which point, consumer objects lusted after by the club members can be cited, like a favorite literary passage.

And well they should, since the Sundance catalogue is just as determined to combine literary and material pleasures into a thoroughly integrated aesthetic experience that includes this same Jane Austen, as well as Virginia Woolf, and Jhumpa Lahiri, and Gabriel García Márquez. The winter 2006 catalogue featured a home library ensemble entitled "Winter Wanderlust? Escape with a Good Book," which furnishes exactly the right sort of mise-en-scène for Fowler's book clubbers, including a leather club chair, tripod library lamp, Cornell bookcase, serape rug, and "Great Winter Reading"—which offers books by Wallace Stegner, William Kittredge, and Terry Tempest Williams to complete the experience. And in the Sundance summer catalogue of 2006 a seasonal selection of books is again offered to customers, but in this case the "Summer Reading Set of 8" is presented as a mini-library:

> We've gathered the collective experience of some pretty smart people and come up with a pre-packaged mini library of Sundance staff favorites—eight eclectic classics that span hemispheres, genres, and eras—for an armful of armchair adventure and beach-blanket travel. Included are *Mrs. Dalloway* by Virginia Woolf (197 pp.); *Crossing to Safety* by Wallace Stegner (335 pp.); *The Namesake* by Jhumpa Lahiri (291 pp.); *Charing Cross Road* by Helen Hanff (97 pp.); *Love in the Time of Cholera* by Gabriel García Márquez (348 pp.); *Chronicles Volume One* by Bob Dylan (293 pp.); *Pride and Prejudice* by Jane Austen (435 pp.); and *Tracks* by Robyn Davidson (256 pp.). All paperback. See sundancecatalog.com for more info.

Quality readers obviously want quality fiction for their pleasure reading, only here it's the clothing and décor catalogue, not the online bookstore or television book club that is hooking them up with the appropriate titles. Notice too that the staff recommendations—a fixture at independent bookstores and now also at most superstores—are offered as the reason why we should have faith in this particular armful of books. We should trust these "pretty smart people" to choose our books for us, but here the expertise has everything to do with quality reading as an expression of taste rather than indicator of abstract knowledge. If customers trust this staff enough to choose from their selection of clothing, jewelry, and décor items, then they can certainly be trusted to choose the reading material to complete the ensemble. I say "ensemble," because the facing page in the catalogue is a full-page photograph of a model reading a book, with the text that urges us to read, because it's "fundamental."

The model looks directly out at the catalogue reader, dressed simply in unspecified jeans, the "Poplin Boyfriend Shirt" ($50) and "Zen Thong Sandals" ($160). Here the only accessory is not the Native American–style jewelry featured throughout the rest of the catalog but the book she holds

RECHARGE,
REJUVENATE... READ
(IT'S FUNDAMENTAL)

19. "Read": model with book, from the summer
2006 Sundance catalogue

in her hands. Except for the barely discernable capital letters that identify
the catalog items in the picture, the image appears to be a public service announcement for reading, yet it also functions as an effective visualization of
the place of literary reading within the broader taste culture that Sundance
cultivates so brilliantly, a world where books are transcendently important
enough to deserve this kind of philanthropic endorsement, but also eminently stylish, as much as expression of one's tasteful self as the Zen thong
sandals, or the "Field of Poppies" rug, or all of the Arts and Crafts–style
furniture.

So what did Henry James know about furniture?

The Literary Bestseller, Neo-Aestheticism, and Quality Consumerism at Different Price Points, or Henry James at Target

Resurrecting Henry James in order to demonstrate anew the value of literary fiction is, at first glance, a somewhat perplexing move, since James
may indeed be a literary god, but his notoriously complicated prose style
would hardly make for the most effective hook to win converts to the cause.
His emotional detachment poses yet another obstacle: Shakespeare in love,

maybe, but reimagining James's writing as elegant transcription of carnal lust is, well . . . more of a stretch. Yet James is a central figure in the Devoutly Literary novel—proving that literary fiction provides a transcendent aesthetic pleasure that makes mere sex pale by comparison to the ecstasies available between the covers of the right book. In other words, according to these novels, Lady Viola was right the first time—there is nothing better than a play, or in this case, the right sort of literary novel.

In his compelling essay "What Henry Knew" (2005), Michael Wood argues that James's novels give us certain types of knowledge and that he focuses on the "strong and multiple valences of the word *know*" throughout his novels. Wood delineates seven different types of knowledge in *The Wings of the Dove*, and this overt complication of what anyone can know with certainty is what I used to think Henry knew and what I tried to convey to my students when I taught his novels (although not nearly as elegantly as Wood does in his essay). But according to the Jamesian novels that appeared in 2004, Henry knew with utmost certainty about other matters—he knew about royalties, and he knew that furniture is important, . . . very, very important.

This invocation of James is not a matter of summoning back the Master of literary style as the embodiment of all that the literary marketplace no longer values. When I first heard that Toibin, in *The Master*, and Lodge, in *Author, Author*, had turned James into a fictional character, I imagined the worst—novels that would transport the reader back to the halcyon days of American literary culture when stylistic refinement was valued for its own sake and the publishing industry had not abandoned quality in pursuit of pure profit. But instead of a willful amnesia about the current state of the literary marketplace, both Toibin and Lodge concentrate on James as a stylist in pursuit of literary success measured in terms of financial gain as well as artistic refinement. Both making teasing references to the later 1890s, when James wrote what are widely acknowledged to be his masterpieces (*The Ambassadors*, *The Wings of the Dove*, and *The Golden Bowl*), but they situate the action in the late 1880s and early 1890s, concentrating on James's ill-fated attempt to go for box office success with his play *Guy Domville*. In *Author, Author*, Lodge makes James's desperate attempts to become a popular author, on his own terms, the central arc of the novel. These novels may be set in the 1890s, but James's plight is clearly intended to resonate powerfully in the present—how does one write literary fiction that will be widely read in a world where badly written bestsellers dominate and publishers appear to want only those books that will sell? According to Lodge's novel, James had always

> secretly hoped that he might become wealthy as well as famous by his writing. It was not because he lusted for gold as such, or for the luxuries that it might buy—yachts, carriages, and diamond cravat pins had no attraction for him. It was because to make significant amounts of money and to advance the art of fiction—to transfix this double target with a single arrow—was the only way for a novelist to impress the materialistic nineteenth century. Dickens and George Eliot had managed it. Why not HJ?. . . To reverse this decline by the work of his pen, to count royalties in tens of thousands, while maintaining the highest artistic standards, was Henry's dream. But as the years passed, the prospects of realizing it appeared fainter and fainter. Not that it was getting more difficult for novelists to become rich—quite the contrary—but they were the wrong ones. There was Rider Haggard, for instance who's bloody and preposterous. She sold 40,000 copies in 1887. (95)

That James was bedeviled by the desire to be both artistically and financially successful is not a revelation to James scholars, because such concerns do indeed figure in his letters. But for nonspecialist readers familiar with James only as the stylist supreme, the father of the modernist novel, this is indeed a different perspective on the Master. As a high school student working through *The Turn of the Screw* and *Daisy Miller*, and then as an undergraduate savoring the mysteries of *The Ambassadors* and *The Wings of a Dove*, I never even heard mention of James's despair over his failure to write bestsellers. But then my English education in the seventies was shaped entirely by the modernist master narrative that could not allow for anything other than the great divide between the art and mere commodity. By situating James in a world where he is seemingly surrounded by examples of mediocre novels becoming bestsellers while his artistry goes underappreciated (his closest friends, George du Maurier and Constance Fennimore Woolson, both write runaway bestsellers: respectively, *Trilby* and *Anne*), Lodge presents the reader with a James who is never so lost in his sacred art that he isn't above comparing the size of the ads for *Guy Domville* to those of rival plays in the West End as he reads the theater listings in the *London Times*. In his hands, the Master may despair about not being more widely read, but we are lead inexorably to one relatively simple conclusion—James shouldn't have tortured himself with such concerns, because the bestselling authors have become the stuff of footnotes, while his devotion to his sacred art has rendered him immortal. The traditional dichotomy between genuine art and the marketplace is triumphantly reaffirmed because, after all, we all already knew who won in the long run, so we regard Henry's concerns about his marketability as sadly misguided, right from the opening anxiety attack.

Yet the relationship between aestheticism and consumerism was far more complicated during the 1880s. Jonathan Freedman, in his masterful study of this period, *Professions of Taste: Henry James, British Aestheticism, and Commodity Culture* (1990), demolishes exactly this dichotomy.

> James was able to complete the professionalization of the high-culture artist that the aesthetic movement began but failed to accomplish; he was enabled to institutionalize himself in the competitive literary marketplace of Edwardian London as the great Master of the new Art of Fiction, and thus to create a career model for the writers and artists who were to follow in his wake. . . . And this move, born equally of the commodification of art and the artistic career, and the resistance to such commodification, helped accomplish the full delineation of a zone of "high culture," the creation of a separate niche amidst a complex market economy for the earnest production and avid consumption of austere, self-regarding art. (xxvi)

Because the ultimate goal of Lodge's novel is to reaffirm the separation between aesthetic refinement and the marketplace, it doesn't acknowledge the massive expansion of that niche within the popular literary culture of the past decade. Within the world of *Author, Author* there are only two categories, literary novels and bestsellers, yet within the literary culture that Lodge's own novel circulates in, the twain that could not meet have become a thriving category of quality fiction called literary bestsellers, cultivated most energetically by authors, publishers, book superstores, and television book clubs. At the end of *Author, Author*, Lodge, as the voice of the author, breaks into the fictional universe of his novel:

> *It's tempting, therefore to indulge in a fantasy of somehow time-traveling back to that afternoon of late February 1916, creeping into the master bedroom of flat 21, Carlyle Mansions, casting a spell on the little group of weary watchers at the bedside, pulling up a chair oneself, and saying a few reassuring words to HJ, before he departs this world, about his literary future. How pleasing to tell him that after a few decades of relative*

obscurity he would become an established classic, essential reading for anyone interested in modern English and American literature and the aesthetics of the novel. That all of his major works and most of his minor ones would be constantly in print, scrupulously edited, annotated, and studied in schools, colleges, and universities around the world, the subject of innumerable postgraduate theses and scholarly articles and books . . . and what fun to tell him that millions of people all over the world would encounter his stories in theatrical and cinematic and television adaptations . . . and that film and TV tie-in editions of these books would sell in large quantities. (375)

Perhaps it would be fun to tell HJ how important he has become to AP English students, college professors, and Harvey Weinstein, but I think it would be even more fun, and even more satisfying to the Master, to tell him something else: that in the future his life would become the subject of not one, but two literary bestsellers in the same year and that another book (*The Line of Beauty*), which would attempt to update him—in the form of a "Jamesian novel" about the fin de siècle of the twentieth century—would win a prize designating it the best novel written in a year in the early twenty-first century . . . and it would sell like hotcakes. While James may indeed be pleased to hear about his academic canonization and the royalties he could expect from all the movie and television rights, I think he would be delighted to learn about the robust flourishing of what he himself had always longed to write—a literary bestseller.

In *The Master*, Toibin breaks down the traditional dichotomy between literary culture and consumer culture by suggesting that James may well have been devoted to his sacred art, but he also had a taste for up-market material goods. Lodge assures the reader in his novel that HJ's anxiety about his books' not selling was not fueled by a desire for luxury items; in Toibin's novel, Henry likes to shop, and his dissatisfaction with his royalties has everything to do with his taste for the right sorts of material objects:

It was easy to feel that he was destined to write for the few, perhaps for the future, yet never to reap the rewards that he would relish now, such as his own house, and a beautiful garden, and no anxiety about what was to come. He retained pride in decisions taken, the fact that he had never compromised, that his back ached and his eyes hurt solely because he continued to labor all day at an art that was pure and unconstrained by mere mercenary ambitions. For his father and his brother, and for many in London too, a failure in the market was a kind of success, and success in the market a matter not to be discussed. He did not ever in his life actively seek the hard doom of general popularity. Nonetheless, he wanted his books to sell, he wanted to shine in the marketplace and pocket the proceeds without comprising his sacred art in any way. It mattered to him how he was seen; and being seen not to lift a finger to make his work popular pleased him; being seen to devote himself to solitude and selfless application to a noble art gave him satisfaction. He recognized, however, that lack of success was one thing, but abject failure was another. (20)

In this novel, a taste for literary books and a taste for interior design items are completely intertwined—both reflect a singular, discriminating sensibility. When he acquires Lamb House, he begins to develop a sense of self articulated in terms of the décor that he surrounds himself with: "For so many years now he had had no country, no family, no establishment of his own, merely a flat in London where he worked. He did not have the necessary shell.... [I]t was as though he lived a life without a façade, a stretch of frontage to protect him from the world. He dreamed of now being a host, having friends, and family to stay; he dreamed of decorating an old house, buying his own furniture and having continuity and certainty in his days" (123). In these dreams decorating is as much an expression of his singular aesthetic sensibility as his writing. It is most decidedly not a matter of merely acquiring material goods versus the creation of genuine art. James is taken around London in search of the proper décor items by Lady Wolseley, a woman of immense taste who has read his novel *The Spoils of Poynton* and is convinced that the widowed Mrs. Gareth, ready to die for her carefully collected treasures of Poynton, was based on her: "'Not the greed,' she said, 'and not the foolishness and not the widowhood, I have never gone in for widowhood. But the eye, the eye that misses nothing, can see how a Queen Anne chair can be restored, or a faded tapestry hung in the shadows, or a painting bought for the frame'" (125). Her ultracultivated eye for décor reveals the density of meaning hidden in those surfaces, a talent that we normally associate only with James as literary master: "Lady Wolseley provided him with a secret guide to London, to the hidden places from which he could fill and furnish Lamb House; she offered him also a version of London at its most densely packed, most resolutely inhabited. Each object he fingered and handled possessed a wondrous history that would never be known, suggesting England to him in all its old wealth and purpose" (127). James becomes so enamored of his acquisitions that Constance Fennimore Woolson, his "most intelligent reader," teases him about his "addiction to refinements."

These dual addictions, to writing as sacred art and to interior decoration as an equally exacting form of self-expression, may seem like contradictory impulses to readers whose impressions of James have been shaped so thoroughly by modernist critics, which celebrate the former but can only dismiss the latter as commodity fetishism. But within the British and American aesthetic movement of James's time, those addictions were tightly intertwined, mutually reaffirming expressions of *the eye* responsible for both sorts of critical judgment. Freedman makes the essential point:

> The aestheticist project of the beautification of everyday life, its privileging of sense experience its evocation of a redemptive world elsewhere where such experiences could be ceaselessly realized—all these intersected with the dynamics of late-nineteenth and early-twentieth-century American culture so as to exert a significant pressure on its social and ideological configurations. For example, the concerns of British aestheticism coincided with those of mid-century American domestic ideology in such a way as to make palatable, even desirable, new, more luxurious tastes in household decoration and ornamentation; under the guidance of Morris, and even more powerfully, his popularizers, Americans were led to supplant the ideal of the "American home" with that of the "House Beautiful." (82)

This notion of a "redemptive world" formed by a series of associated, interconnected tastes unified by the power of the eye privileges the experience of beauty as an end in itself, wherever that eye might find it. But that ideology of taste requires another essential component—the transformation of buying into a form of self-expression that so diminishes the taint of cold hard cash that the experience of beauty remains somehow transcendently elsewhere. Freedman argues that this aestheticism involved more than just a celebration of interior design. "What we witness is the emergence of a rhetoric of that deployed 'cultural' and the 'aesthetic' as advertising slogans, as part of a naive, but nevertheless effective strategy for advertising commodities that would at once glorify and efface the act of consumption itself by grounding the most mundane acquisitive choices in the nonmaterial realm of transcendent value designated by the aesthetic" (109).

I have pursued this point at some length because I think it has enormous relevance for understanding the literary bestsellers that emerged in the late 1990s. This sort of effaced consumerism that makes the pursuit of aesthetic experience something that may be explicitly advertised as such, without invalidating the experience, had to be solidly in place for the literary best-seller to thrive as a superior form of quality reading within the past decade. Just as important, our understanding of the place and function of literary bestsellers, especially the Devoutly Literary, neo-aesthetic novels, depends on our coming to terms with another integral feature of contemporary taste formations—that a taste for things literary and things of a more material nature (furniture, houses, clothing) are no longer mutually exclusive but wholly interdependent pleasures. When the authors of the National Endowment for the Arts report *Reading at Risk* tried to delineate the profile of the serious reader in terms of other leisure-time activities, they identified museum going and attendance at classical music concerts as the definitive "associated tastes." While there is no reason to dispute the fact that museum going is an important associated taste, I think it is just as productive to trace the activities that form another associated taste that has everything to do with the pursuit of aesthetic pleasure—shopping at good-design chain-stores, reading shelter magazines and décor catalogues such as Sundance, or watching décor-porn programming on cable television. The relationship between reading literary fiction and this particular range of associated tastes needs to be explored more fully, because both are predicated on the search for self-defining aesthetic pleasures that are themselves dependent on quality consumerism, outside the sanctified spaces of the academy and the museum.

This convergence of tastes for things literary and things material was accelerated by a publishing industry increasingly determined to place books in consumer destinations that are anything but bookstores, at least in the traditional sense of the term. This trend was covered by a front-page story in the *New York Times*, entitled "Selling a Little Literature to Go with your Lifestyle" (November 2, 2006). According to its author, Julie Bosman, the appearance of literary titles in stores such as Anthropologie, Urban Outfitters, and Restoration Hardware was part of a new marketing strategy:

> With book sales sagging—down 2.6 percent as of August over the same period last year, according to the Association of American Publishers—publishers are pushing their books into butcher shops, car washes, cookware stores, cheese shops, even chi-chi clothing boutiques where high-end literary titles are used to amplify the elegant lifestyle they are attempting to project. . . . "You walk into Restoration Hardware and you want the couch, and the vase and the nightstand, and then you want the

two books that are on the nightstand," said Andrea Rosen (vice president for special markets at HarperCollins). "The books complete the story."

And, one could argue just as easily, the décor completes the books, or more precisely, it completes the quality literary reading experience, since it provides the right mise-en-scène—the furniture and the books are both a matter of *interior* décor. Rosen's choice of words here is especially apt. In order for the furniture ensemble to become a compelling purchase, it has to have a "story" that places the consumer-reader into a narrative fashioned out of a host of interdependent choices that form a total taste environment, the books completing the décor, the décor completing the books.

This is not to suggest that quality reading used to take place in some sort of clean, well-lighted minimalist place where nothing was supposed to get in the way of the transcendent reading experience. An appreciation of the finer things in life was clearly not banished from the premises, in fact one could argue that it was simply taken for granted—readers of quality fiction obviously had good taste, just as they obviously had an interest in museum exhibitions and classical music concerts. That went without saying. The omnipresence of gorgeous set decoration in practically every corner of the Merchant and Ivory universe exemplifies this casual taken-for-granted quality. That visual sumptuousness is the result of meticulous art direction, but we don't see the characters doing much to actually transform their domestic space into a fully personalized total design aesthetic. The decor is already just there, along with the appropriate reading material. In the Devoutly Literary universe, the relentless quest for the self-defining purchase, whether it be a décor item or a literary novel, forms the central action of the novel because the taste for those finer things in life needs to be catalogued, relentlessly. Writing and reading literary fiction is not just foregrounded as one of the finer things in life—it is woven into an entire web of interdependent aesthetic pleasures that form both the action and stage set for the quality literary experience, both within the novels and in the domestic space of the reading of those books. Henry James longs to make Lamb House as much of an expression of his artistic sensibility as any of his novels; Toibin's novel sits on the Restoration Hardware night table.

I have been using the term "neo-aestheticism" to describe this phenomenon not just because so many novels and adaptation films have been set in the golden age of British and American aestheticism at the turn of the twentieth century. One of the cornerstones of that aestheticism was, after all, exactly this sort of cultivation of tastes for all of the finer things in life as part of an all-encompassing celebration of aesthetic pleasure in which appreciation of décor was deemed as essential as an appreciation of fine art. This fusion of artistic and material tastes that is so much part of the impassioned advocacy of beauty in Devoutly Literary novels of the early twenty-first century was omnipresent in the Arts and Crafts movement of the late nineteenth century and the early twentieth, a movement that, not so surprisingly, has been enjoying a phenomenal resurgence in both museum exhibitions and consumer culture. During the same three-year period (2004–6) in which *L'Affaire*, *The Master*, *The Line of Beauty*, *On Beauty*, and *Author, Author* were published, three museum retrospectives devoted to the Arts and Crafts movement were launched by major museums—"The Arts and Crafts Movement in Europe and America" (organized by the Los Angeles County Museum), "International Arts and Crafts" (which originated at the Victoria and Albert Museum, London), and "Louis Comfort Tiffany at Laurelton Hall: An Artist's Country Estate" (the Metropolitan Museum of Art in New York). The title of this last exhibition sums up the neo-aesthetic agenda in epigrammatic form—private domestic space is the ultimate form of artistic expression. This is articulated in no uncertain terms in the exhibition statement:

> Laurelton Hall, Louis Comfort Tiffany's extraordinary country estate in Oyster Bay, New York, completed in 1905, was the epitome of the designer's achievement and in many ways defined the multifaceted artist. Tiffany designed every aspect of the project inside and out, creating a total aesthetic environment. The exhibition is a window into Tiffany's most personal art, bringing into focus this remarkable artist who lavished as much care and creativity on the design and furnishing of his home and gardens as he did in all of the wide-ranging media in which he worked.

The emphasis here on the "total aesthetic environment" is significant, because the museum show demonstrates how the cultivation of domestic space could become a kind of home-grown *Gesamtkunstwerk* in which all taste distinctions are outward manifestations of a unified personal aesthetic, a taste ideology that has expanded exponentially in terms of who feels capable of trying to achieve that total design environment by the popularization of a certain way of talking the talk of aesthetic pleasure and a concomitant revolution in terms of marketing high design for mass audiences.

The resurgence of the Arts and Crafts movement, then, is not just a matter of taking delight in a certain style—that resurgence is also attributable to the ways that it now provides for talking the talk of aesthetic appreciation in which pure aesthetic pleasure is deemed redemptive for everyone, rather than a trivial pleasure reserved for the elite. The Web site exhibition statement for the "International Arts and Crafts" exhibition stresses the same sort of total design aesthetic as the "Tiffany at Laurelton Hall" show, but the chief goal here is to focus on the ways that redemptive beauty infused all aspects of domestic life: "Led by theorists John Ruskin and William Morris, the movement promoted the ideals of craftsmanship and individualism along with the integration of art into everyday life. Arts and Crafts principles changed the way people looked at the things they lived with—from teacups and spoons to tapestries and stained-glass windows—and resulted in a new respect for the work of individual craftsmen." This integration was made possible in terms of placing exemplars of such works on display in meticulously curated shows, but also through the gift shops that accompany them. When I attended "The Arts and Crafts Movement in Europe and America" during its time at the Milwaukee Art Museum, the last "gallery" of the exhibition was an elaborate display of Arts and Crafts–style pottery, lamps, rugs, and wall hangings, all available for purchase. One could quite literally take the beautiful into one's home in the form of museum reproductions produced by the Frank Lloyd Wright Foundation, or other décor items executed by contemporary individual craftsmen working within the form vocabulary of the Arts and Crafts movement (Pewabic pottery, Motawi tile, etc.). Here were beautiful objects directly inspired by the work of James's contemporaries, the sort of exquisitely crafted objects that the Master himself may have lusted after and contemplated taking back home, just as I did as I wandered through the galleries.

This celebration of the redemptive power of pure aesthetic beauty in the form of return to Arts and Crafts is not limited to museum shops. When I began my research for this book I happened to be looking for a couch for my living room, and I visited Crate and Barrel, a good-design chain store on Michigan Avenue in Chicago, one of the most superheated consumer environments in the United States. I encountered there an entire ensemble of furniture named the "Morris Collection," complete with a copy of Barbara Myer's *In the Arts and Crafts Style* placed judiciously on the coffee table as the book accessory that "completed the story" of this ensemble. The mass production of Morris may indeed seem like a perversion of his craft-based aesthetic, but the Arts and Crafts movement celebrated exactly this sort of taking the beautiful into domestic space, making the average family home into the house beautiful. In her review in the *New York Times* (July 26, 2005) of "The Arts and Crafts Movement in Europe and America" exhibition at the Milwaukee Art Museum, Roberta Smith stresses exactly this connection. She describes the Arts and Crafts movement as one of those "great switching stations of thought during the Victorian Era and commensurate in its way with Darwinism, Marxism, and photography." She details the inbound tracks: medieval art, English Gothic revival, the writings of Ruskin and Morris, and the rage against the industrial revolution. Her list of outbound tracks includes the styles and figures one would expect (art nouveau, art deco, de Stijl, Bauhaus, and Frank Lloyd Wright) but also good-design chain stores and catalogues such as those by Ikea, Pottery Barn, and Design within Reach. Making the beautiful accessible to a broad audience, specifically in terms of how such objects may form the fabric of everyday life in middle-class homes, dorm rooms, and elsewhere may indeed be seen as an extension of that aestheticism of the late nineteenth century, but the ability to realize that goal on a massive scale depends on delivery systems that provide both the aesthetic objects and the way to talk about their redemptive beauty as a process of self-definition, at which point any domestic space is potentially as much of a total aesthetic environment as Tiffany's Laurelton Hall or the Sundance catalogue reading room.

The convergence of that Arts and Crafts aestheticism and the contemporary literary bestseller reached its zenith in the late summer of 2007, when Nancy Horan's novel *Loving Frank* was at the top of the bestseller lists, and readers began to encounter stacks of copies on the front tables at Borders and Barnes & Noble superstores across the country. According to Horan's account of their scandalous love affair, Frank Lloyd Wright and Mamah Cheney were drawn inexorably to each other because of the aesthetic sensibility they shared and could find nowhere else in their stolid Midwestern world. The end result reads like a cross between *Shakespeare in Love* and *The Girl with the Pearl Earring*: we learn the source of Wright's creative genius and, at the same time, see how an unassuming young woman, possessed of a genuine aesthetic spirit, could captivate the master: "It frightened her to feel so out of control. But any thoughts of ending the affair floated away the minute he set foot in the same room. Frank Lloyd Wright was a life force. He seemed to fill whatever space he occupied with a pulsing energy that was spiritual, sexual, and intellectual all at once. And the wonder of it was, he wanted her" (28). Reading together becomes a kind of aesthetic foreplay for Frank and Mamah, as their mutual admiration for the same works of literature, art, and architecture enflames their passion for one another. As a bookish woman who initially feels a world apart from the flamboyant aestheticism of Frank but then blossoms when she begins to open herself up to the power of aesthetic pleasure, this Mamah Cheney could be the Laura Brown of Oak Park, the Girl with the Ginko Leaf Earring. Transcendent aesthetic experience is not restricted to the Frank Lloyd Wrights, Vermeers, and Virginia Woolfs of this world, but neither is it available to absolutely everyone—it becomes available to a select type of seemingly average individuals who, despite all appearances, nonetheless possess a heightened sensitivity to all things artistic.

The widespread popularity of Arts and Crafts aestheticism in museum shows, good-design stores, and literary bestsellers represents the complicated, often contradictory dimensions of the movement and it is only by appreciating those tensions that we can fine-tune our understanding of the popularized neo-aestheticism that is so all-pervasive within the Devoutly Literary. Freedman makes the critical point that there were two dominant, yet thoroughly antithetical impulses in conflict at the end of the nineteenth century—the overtly democratizing side of aestheticism, particularly in the works of Morris and Ruskin, whose criticism can be easily read as a kind of "aesthetic Reform Act, an extension of the franchise of art appreciation from exclusively elite circles to any patient and attentive reader of his work," and the anti-egalitarian side, represented by Pater and Wilde, in which the aesthete proclaims himself a "rare and superior being, capable of special perception and appreciation," the dandy who insists that the proper appreciation of the beautiful is anything but a universal or communal experience. The literary bestseller, like the good-design chain store, represents a neat synthesis of these two impulses by extending the franchise to a mass audience of connoisseurs—people who know that the proper appreciation of the aesthetic is not universal but is certainly downloadable from any of a variety of authorities who function not as dandies but as popular connoisseurs, devoted to bringing the aesthetic pleasure to anyone attentive enough to watch television design makeover programs or read shelter magazines.

One of the most vivid examples of this popularized aestheticism is the motto of Target discount stores, "Design for All"—the same discount chain that sponsors Project Literacy, a philanthropic enterprise that underwrites a number of literary events around New York (regularly advertised in full-page ads in the *New York Times*), as well as sponsoring exhibitions such as "Massive Change: The Future of Global Design" (curated by Bruce Mau) and "Free Tuesdays" at art museums throughout America. Design for All involves more than just bringing good design at an affordable price to mass audiences; what makes it an especially clear-cut reaffirmation of the democratization of aesthetic appreciation that was central to the Arts and Crafts movement is the language used to describe the use value of beauty.

I'll offer just one example of how all-pervasive this neo-aestheticism has become. While I was writing this chapter, I was in my local Target store one afternoon and I decided to pick up a pizza cutter because the wheel had fallen off my old one. I opted for one in the Michael Graves Collection because I liked the chunky handle, and for five dollars, it seemed like a good buy. The cardboard packaging informed me, however, that I had made this decision without realizing what was really at stake, because there, in addition to a photo of the man himself, and his hand-written signature, was this product description: "The Michael Graves product line is an inspired balance of form and function. At once it is sensible and sublime, practical and whimsical, utilitarian and aesthetically pleasing. Michael Graves creates useful objects, which not only carry their own weight, but simultaneously lift our spirits." By imbuing this kitchen utensil with the power to "lift our spirits" because it is "aesthetically pleasing," the beautiful has a use value unto itself; is not just useful and beautiful, it is useful *because it is* beautiful — without it, our spirits will not be lifted.

While Target stores provide abundant evidence of the popularization of aesthetic appreciation, they are even more significant as epicenters of a new cluster of associated tastes that surround and inform the literary bestseller. Judging by this "Ode on a Pizza Cutter," which sounds as if it was authored by a contemporary aesthete channeling the ghost of William Morris as determinedly as Lodge and Toibin channel Henry James, the mission statement for Design for All could well be "Redemptive Aesthetic Experience for Everyone (at a remarkably affordable level)." The extension of the franchise for aesthetic appreciation moves in a number of directions simultaneously. The same Target store where I bought my pizza cutter features not only design collections by Graves, Todd Oldham, and Thomas O'Brien; it also features, just as prominently, literary bestsellers on face-out displays in their Recommended Reading section, right next to another display for the Target Book Club, Bookmarked.com. Last but not least, when I stopped to get my daughter a treat at the café, the plastic cup that held her drink was emblazoned with the following message: "All for books, and books for all—Join Book Club today! Target.com/readysitread."

My point here is not to prove that we need to talk about décor in order to get a handle on literary bestsellers but rather that we need to pay far closer attention to the ways in which décor and books are given redemptive use value within a discourse of popular connoisseurship found on dust jackets as well as pizza cutter packaging, a discourse that valorizes the beautiful for its own sake and makes its appreciation something that all can experience within the heart of consumer culture. While the British and American aestheticism of the late nineteenth century and the early twentieth generated two conflicting narratives regarding aesthetic experience—one that expanded the franchise of aesthetic appreciation to the middle class, and one that restricted it to a professionalized elite—it was the latter that become dominant at the beginning of the twentieth century within the academy and the museum, and it held sway for decades to come. But at the beginning of the twenty-first century, that other narrative, the one that advocated the democratization of aesthetic pleasure, has made a triumphant return. One could, of course, argue that consumer culture has always been all about selling beauty in the form of fashion, cosmetics, luxury automobiles, and so on, and that the appreciation of beauty has hardly gone unremarked. But what is at play here is the massification of elite tastes made possible by the mass production of goods and the mass dissemination of a new way of talking the talk of aesthetic appreciation, in which the aesthetic experience becomes explicitly designated as such, on pizza cutter packaging at Target and by bestselling Booker Prize finalists and books on the *Times'* Top Ten Notables list.

Hollinghurst's novel *The Line of Beauty* exemplifies how this updated neo-aestheticism works in the literary bestseller of the early twenty-first century. The main character is Nick Guest, a young man who was "out as an aesthete" at Oxford (but not yet out as homosexual). The novel opens in 1983, shortly after Nick has moved into the home of his school chum/wicked crush, whose family has a majestic home in London. The first thing we are told about Nick is how much he relishes the house and its décor. A long paragraph detailing his enjoyment of its many luxurious features ends with: "Above the drawing-room fireplace there was a painting by Guardi, a capriccio of Venice in a gilt frame; on the facing wall were two large gilt-framed mirrors. Like his hero Henry James, Nick felt he could 'stand a great deal of gilt'" (6). He is intending to write a doctoral thesis on James, and his devotion to the Master has everything to do with his obsession with style. When the family brings him along to a wedding at a stately home, Hawkeswood, Nick wanders through the magnificent library. The host, Lord Kessler, sees that he's taken down a copy of *The Way We Live Now*, and asks him if he's a Trollope man, and he responds disdainfully, "What was it Henry James said, about Trollope and his 'great heavy shovelfuls of testimony to constituted English manners'?" (52). Later in the conversation, when Lord Kessler asks him about his chosen field of study, he replies that he wants to have a look at "style":

> "Style *tout court*?"
>
> "Well, style at the turn of the century—Conrad, and Meredith and Henry James, of course." . . .
>
> "Ah," said Lord Kessler intelligently, "Style as an obstacle."
>
> Nick smiled. "Exactly. . . . Or perhaps style that hides things and reveals things at the same time." For some reason this seemed rather near the knuckle, as though he were suggesting Lord Kessler had a secret. "James is a great interest of mine, I must say."
>
> "Yes, you're a James man I see now."
>
> "Oh, absolutely!" and Nick grinned with pleasure and defiance, it was like coming out, which revealed rather belatedly why he wasn't and never would be married to Trollope.
>
> "Henry James stayed here, of course, I'm afraid he found us rather vulgar," Lord Kessler said, as if it had only been last week. (54)

This exchange is significant for a number of reasons. In foregrounding its affiliations so pointedly, *The Line of Beauty* engages in the same kind of literary self-positioning as *Bridget Jones's Diary* or *Trading Up*. As in those novels, there is unvarnished fascination with style as expressed in terms of material objects—in addition to writing a dissertation about James, Nick wants to do a film adaptation of James's novel *The Spoils of Poynton*: "I think it *could* be rather marvelous, don't you. You know Ezra Pound said it was just a novel about furniture, meaning to dismiss it of course, but that was really what made me like the sound of it!" (213). And as with these novels, the relevance of those canonical novels of manners to contemporary society is taken for granted, as if Austen, Wharton, or James really had been there last week. Hollinghurst goes further out of his way to make the parallels as exact as possible—during his stay at Hawkeswood, Nick goes through the family photo albums and finds that the Master was indeed a guest there too, and he now sits in the library just as the Master once did. James was here last week, Hollinghurst is here this week.

Yet one of the main reasons that Hollinghurst's novel won the Man Booker Prize, and was roundly promoted as a literary bestseller, is that Nick, unlike the heroines of Fielding, Banks, and company, is a self-professed aesthete, and the novel strives to update the Jamesian novel in all of its self-conscious aestheticism. In response to a friend's question about whether James's motto was "Art makes life," Nick tells a friend in the words of the Master, "It is art that *makes* life, makes interest, makes importance, for our consideration and application of these things, and I know of no substitute whatever for the force and beauty of its process" (139). Hollinghurst reiterates the primacy of the aesthetic even as he attempts to update James by taking him headlong into the decadence of twentieth-century London. This highly self-conscious aestheticism functions as social critique within the novel in a variety of different forms. Nick is appalled by the nouveau riche, who have enormous amounts of capital but are devoid of taste. The conspicuous consumption of luxury décor made possible by the boom economy of the mid-eighties is unguided by the proper *eye*, resulting in chaotic consumerism—only the intensely cultivated, intensely personalized eye of the aesthete can transform commodity into collection. What distinguishes Hollinghurst's version of neo-aestheticism from James's is the way in which it becomes an articulation of gay identity in a homophobic culture. Through the invocations of James, as quotable aesthete hero, or in the form of actual copies of his books that keep popping up throughout *The Line of Beauty*, Nick invokes James dozens of times and ponders how the Master would articulate that which was unimaginable in his fiction: "Nick wondered for a moment how Henry would have got round it. If he had fingered so archly at beards and baldness, the fine pared saliences of his own appearance, what flirtings and flutterings might he not have performed to conjure up Rickey's solid eight inches?" (209).

Nick, like Henry, can stand a "great deal of gilt" in the various forms it takes at the end of the twentieth century, but so, apparently, can the readers who form the potential audience for this novel. I bought my copy of *The Line of Beauty* because it won the Booker Prize, just as thousands of other readers did. It came to all of us already humming with significance, a book to be read as the Important Literary Novel whose aesthetic qualities are emphasized as a selling point on the back cover just as explicitly as they were on the packaging for Graves's pizza cutter at Target: "In an era of endless possibility, Nick finds himself able to pursue his own private obsession with beauty—a prize as compelling to him as power and riches are to his friends . . . Richly textured, emotionally charged, disarmingly funny, it is a major work by one of the finest writers in the English language."

Whether this "obsession with beauty" is a critique of "riches" unguided by taste, or simply the poetry of the high-end consumer sales pitch is, of course, debatable, but one thing is certain—the aesthetic pleasure that enjoys transcendent power within this fiction is also what makes it highly marketable for readers in search of such pleasures when they come with the guarantee of genuine culture, a prize-winning novel by one of the finest writers in the English language.

From Chick-lit to Lit-lit, Longing for Which Sort of Literacy?

Given the interplay between aestheticism and its marketability, it is not surprising that literary fiction has become a form of category fiction. This transformation is, in part, attributable to the ways in which publishers now target quality audiences and present certain novels as books to be read for exactly those readers. But it is also attributable to a remarkable consistency in the fictional worlds created and the pleasures that are offered there. I want to turn to McEwan's *Saturday*, because it is a paradigmatic example of a literary novel that is a critically esteemed "notable book" that also works like genre fiction for its devoted audience.

In his review of *Saturday* in his column in *The Believer* (April 2005), Nick Hornby praises it as a "very good novel, . . . humane and wise and gripping," but he lambastes what it suggests about the state of literary reading in the United Kingdom and United States. After quoting statistics regarding the decline of reading, he says:

> And meanwhile, the world of books seems to be getting more bookish. Anita Brookner's new novel is about a novelist. David Lodge and Colm Toibin wrote novels about Henry James. Alan Hollinghurst wrote about a guy writing a thesis on Henry James. And in Ian McEwan's *Saturday*, the central character's father-in-law and daughter are both serious published poets and past winners of Oxford University's Newdigate Prize for undergraduate poetry. . . . Sort it out, guys! You can't all write literature about literature! One book a year, maybe, between you—but all of the above titles were published in the last six months. There are, I think,

two reasons to be a little bit queasy about this trend. The first is quite simply, it excludes readers. I don't want people who haven't got a degree in literature to give up on the contemporary novel. . . .Taken as a group, these novels seem to raise the white flag: we give in! It's hopeless! we don't know what those people out there want! Pull up the drawbridge!

But they are a group, and novelists and their publishers know exactly what those readers out there want—novels about passionate readers just like themselves, who have a taste for the finer things in life. Rather than a retreat, it represents a headlong charge into the marketplace in search of the quality readership for which this fiction can be identified as books to be read and loved passionately by exactly the right audience. They have indeed sorted it all out already; this readership wants to read about people just like themselves, only that much more literary. Hornby is concerned about this exclusive focus on characters who are "highly articulate people. Henry Perowne, the father and son-in-law of the poets, is a neurosurgeon, and his wife is a corporate lawyer; like many highly educated middle-class people, they have access to and a facility with language, a facility that enables them to speak very directly and lucidly about their lives. . . . [T]here's a sense in which McEwan is wasted on them" (83). He argues that the success of Roddy Doyle with infrequent readers is attributable to his ability to be "smart about people who don't have the resources to describe their own emotional states. . . . It seems to me to be a more remarkable gift than the ability to let extremely articulate people say extremely literate things."

While this is undoubtedly an important distinction, I think there's another way to regard this insularity. The readership of the Devoutly Literary novel doesn't *need* McEwan in the way that readers might need Roddy Doyle. It's not a matter of needing instruction as much as of finding a kindred spirit who shares your sensibilities and believes in the power of reading. To return to Bridget Jones's analogy, *Saturday* isn't a literary novel that functions like a pasta machine or an ice-cream maker, because it has an important use value—it affirms the·superiority of your taste culture. Chick-lit was condemned by Curtis Sittenfeld for the best-friend coziness between characters and readership founded on their mutual tastes and sensibilities. The lead blurb on the back of my paperback copy of *In Her Shoes* exemplifies this perfectly, since, according to *People* magazine, "This book is like spending time with an understanding friend who has the knack for always being great company. Bottom line: wonderful fit." The popularity of the Devoutly Literary novel depends on exactly the same sort of cozy fit between characters and readership, the same sense that they're "just like us." Consider the blurb for another Lit-lit book, Hellenga's *The Fall of the Sparrow* (1998): "Here's the new Robert Hellenga novel, as richly detailed and absorbing as *The Sixteen Pleasures*. You know what you need to do: boil the tea water, get into bed, tell your family to go away for a few days and begin the journey." What sort of journey do these novels offer, and who's supposed to sign up for the trip?

McEwan's novel, then, details the life of Henry Perowne, neurosurgeon. As a narrative of a day in the life of a wealthy contemporary Londoner, the novel bears more than a passing resemblance to *Mrs. Dalloway*, and there are a number of references to literary authors throughout the book, even though Perowne himself is skeptical about the power of literary fiction. His daughter, Daisy, studied English at Oxford, and her first book of poetry has just been published. She is responsible for Perowne's literary education, but throughout most of the novel, the narrator details only his failure to be affected by her recommended readings, because they lack the clarity of scientific prose. He admires *William* James, for example, because

> James had the knack of fixing on the surprising commonplace—and in Perowne's humble view, wrote a better-honed prose than his fussy brother, who would rather run round a thing a dozen different ways than call it by its name. Daisy, the arbiter of his literary education, would never agree. She wrote a long undergraduate thesis essay on Henry James's late novels and can quote a passage from *The Golden Bowl*. . . . At her prompting, he tried the one about the little girl suffering from her parents' vile divorce. A promising subject but poor Maisie soon vanished behind a cloud of words, and at page forty-eight Perowne, who can be on his feet seven hours for a difficult procedure, who has run the London marathon, fell away exhausted. Even the tale of his daughter's namesake baffled him. What's an adult to conclude about Daisy Miller's predictable decline? That the world can be unkind? It's not enough. . . . Perowne is counting on Daisy to refine his sensibilities. (64)

> He thinks it would be no bad thing to understand what's meant, what Daisy means, by literary genius. He's not sure he's ever experienced it at first hand, despite various attempts. He even half doubts its existence. . . . In fact, under Daisy's direction, Henry has read the whole of *Anna Karenina* and *Madame Bovary*, two acknowledged masterpieces. . . . If, as Daisy said, the genius was in the details, then he was unmoved. . . .

Work that you cannot begin to imagine achieving yourself, that displays a ruthless nearly inhuman element of self-enclosed perfection—this is his idea of genius. This notion of Daisy's, that people can't live without stories, is simply not true. He is living proof. (67)

Now, what's going to happen to poor Henry Perowne before this novel can come to an end? Will he realize the error of his ways, and finally allow his Henry James–loving daughter to refine his appreciation for literature? Will he finally have a firsthand experience of literary genius? Will he realize just how transformative the written word can really be? Dear reader, we all know by now that this man has a date with fate, a redemptive literary experience is just waiting for him like a bullet with his name on it. The man doesn't get *Henry James*?! That's like stomping on a crucifix in one of these neo-aesthetic novels. And that means he needs killin' . . . or redeemin', and by God, McEwan pulls out all the stops on his transformation. Daisy refines his sensibilities the hard way—she recites a Matthew Arnold poem to thugs who are about to rape her while her family looks on, but since they enjoy a firsthand experience with literary genius for the first time, they relent. Perowne tries to do a quick interpretation of the poem as it's being read, but he's baffled at first, because he's a doctor, after all, who doesn't really believe in literary genius, remember? The thugs, Baxter and Nigel, have given Daisy a copy of her own book of poetry to read as part of the spectacle of cruelty they are about to inflict, but then Daisy decides to recite "Dover Beach" instead—as a poet, she knows about metrical heavy ordinance and decides to go with a poem that will drop Baxter where he stands. When she finishes reciting, Baxter is at first dumbstruck, and then says excitedly,

> "You wrote that. You *wrote* that."
> It's a statement, not a question. Daisy stares at him, waiting.
> He says again, "You wrote that." And then hurriedly, "It's beautiful. You know that, don't you. It's beautiful. And you wrote it."
> "Oi, Baxter." Nigel cocks his head at Daisy and smirks.
> "Nah, I've changed my mind."
> "What? Don't be a cunt."
> "Why don't you get dressed," Baxter says to Daisy, as if her nakedness were her own strange idea. (231)

Baxter knows literary beauty when he hears it, and he is transformed by mere exposure, literary language possessing a nearly radioactive power. It comes from out of nowhere and immediately transports all who hear it into another realm of transcendent understanding, more or less like the Papageno's bells in *The Magic Flute*. The bad guys dance with delight at the sound of genuine beauty—they just can't help themselves.

Saturday, like *The Line of Beauty*, *The Master*, *Le Divorce*, *The Jane Austen Book Club*, *The Sixteen Pleasures*, *The Archivist*, *The Dante Club*, *Literacy and Longing in L.A.*, *Balzac and the Little Chinese Seamstress*, *Heyday*, *The Thirteenth Tale*, *The Guernsey Literary and Potato Peel Pie Society*, *The People of the Book*, *The Shadow of the Wind*, and *Author, Author*, is literary genre fiction, what I'm calling "Lit-lit" for short, which is category fiction every bit as much as Westerns or bodice-ripper romances, but for a far more cultivated readership (who would be appalled by the very idea that all these quality literary books were mere genre fiction). If a genre depends on a relatively stable, instantly recognizable narrative universe consisting of recurring locations, iconography, dialect, conflicts, and an overarching logic that justifies all the characters' actions, no matter how baffling they would be to a nonfan, then Lit-lit certainly fits the bill. In terms of spatial locations, instead of dance floors, deep space, or desert landscapes, one finds a remarkable number of scenes taking place in libraries, classrooms, private studies, theaters, and galleries. In terms of temporal locations, just as the action in a Western has to take place between the 1860s and 1914, the action in the Lit-lit novel transpires either between the 1880s and the 1920s, or in a hybridized phantom universe composed of equal parts of the early twenty-first century and the late nineteenth. In terms of character occupations, the uniformity here makes detective fiction seem wildly diverse; in these novels you can't throw a rock without hitting a novelist, professor, or a graduate student in literature or art history and, most important, everyone reads, with a vengeance. That sameness in occupation produces a consistent iconography. The objects invested with intense significance aren't six guns and light sabers—books, manuscripts, and paintings get the big close-ups and the dadada-*dum* music. And as far as specialized generic dialect is concerned, the language they all speak is as uniform as any hard-boiled detective novel. Instead of gats and gams and kissers in short, choppy sentences, it's frightfully articulate speech, accessorized with endless references to books, travel, classical music, décor, and haute cuisine.

More pointedly, one finds a generic logic in these novels that gives purpose and explanation to all character action. The transformation of McEwan's hoodlums into poetry hounds can transpire only within a fictional universe where the power of reading is a given, one of the taken-for-granteds that form the bedrock logic of that narrative. Watching a Western, the viewer knows why "a man's gotta do what a man's gotta do." At the end of *The Wild Bunch*, for example, Pike and company decide to march into certain death to try to rescue a newcomer to the band who is being held captive by the evil generalissimo, who has just paid them handsomely for the stolen rifles they've delivered. They have their money and are free to go anywhere they choose, yet they opt for certain death without any discussion whatsoever. After a night of drunken revelry in the whorehouse, they get up the next morning, look at each other, laugh, load their guns, and then go get shot to pieces in the final bloodbath. Any discussion would be superfluous, because both the characters, and the fans of the genre, know this is how this world works—everything depends on a shared, unquestioned sense of just what a man's gotta do. This sort of shared logic is the foundation of all popular genres. Stella Dallas stands outside in the rain watching her daughter marry the rich kid and his mother opens the drapes so she can see, because within the logic of the maternal melodrama, a woman's gotta do what a woman's gotta do—character action is always already automatically justified. In musicals, characters spontaneously burst into song, not because they happen to be talented—their otherwise bizarre behavior is considered completely natural, because, as Gene Kelly tells us in *Singin' in the Rain*, these people, "*Gotta* dance! *Gotta* dance! *Gotta* dance!"

I offer these examples because within the fictional universe of Lit-lit, we find characters that spontaneously "Gotta read ! Gotta quote! Gotta recite!" for audiences who are just as automatically enthusiastic in their response to all that aesthetic razzmatazz. Of course the ruffians are transformed by hearing all those literary words—it goes without saying that they could only respond in this way. Perowne may initially be skeptical about the power of literary genius, but he gets redeemed in the end, and in the meantime, he just goes on and on about books and why they don't work for him the way they do for everyone else in the family. In any world other than a "Lit-lit" universe, someone like Henry just wouldn't give that much thought to literary fiction at all.

These self-consciously literary novels about the writing and reading of literary texts, however, do not "show their workings" (to use the phrase Hornby employs to characterize literary fiction), because they involve none of the self-reflexive play of the metafictional texts one finds in William Gass's *In the Heart of the Heart of the Country* (1968), John Barth's *Lost in the Funhouse*

(1969), Italo Calvino's *If on a Winter's Night a Traveler* (1981), or Julian Barnes's *Flaubert's Parrot* (1984). Those narratives were perpetually in the process of undermining the status of a fictional universe by drawing the reader's attention to the words on the page, insisting that any kind of fictional reality was finally just a matter of print on paper. The problematics of literary composition were, in effect, what these stories were *about*, and that self-reflexivity came with a high degree of ambivalence, which was expressed by the authors themselves within those fictions, exemplified by this passage from Barth's "Life Story":

> You, dogged, uninsutable, print-oriented bastard, it's you I'm addressing, who else, from inside this monstrous fiction. You've read me this far then? Even this far? For what discreditable motive? How is it you don't even go to a movie, watch TV, stare at a wall, play tennis with a friend, maybe make amorous advances to the person who comes to your mind when I speak of amorous advances? Can nothing surfeit, saturate you, turn you off? Where's your shame? (12)

This is never a move on the board in the Lit-lit novels, which endlessly celebrate the joys of the literary experience, where readers aren't print-oriented bastards but print-loving brethren—there is simply no room for ambivalence in a world that imagines literary reading to be so imperiled. The exchange between the Lit-lit novel and its passionate readership depends on a different kind of wonderful *fit*, and might go something like this:

> You lover of books, it's you I'm addressing from inside this wonderful fiction. You've read me thus far, of course, because we both know what's really *special* about the *magic of reading* in all of its transformative power. Some might prefer to watch TV or play video games but we know that Jane and Henry offer something just a *little* more enriching, don't we? So why don't you come over, I'm making my bouillabaisse, and I'll open that new Rhone clone from Boony Doon that Parker went nuts over. And I've got to show you the rug I'm lusting after in the new Sundance catalogue.

This exchange between novel and readership in Lit-lit depends on a host of shared tastes and reading pleasures of a familiar, dependable sort. In other words, the reading pleasures normally associated with genre fiction. My goal in demonstrating how these contemporary self-conscious literary novels resemble genre fiction more than metafiction is not to diminish either the quality of the writing or the quality of the pleasures they generate. But reading pleasure here is not some all-purpose pleasure of the text, or hymn to the joys of solitary reading; the exchange between this particular sort of literary novel and its readers is all about the celebration of an imagined reading community, and the novels by McEwan, Lodge, Toibin, Fowler, and their kind all consolidate and consecrate that community as much as television book clubs, Vintage Press chat rooms, or Amazon list makers.

In this regard, Lit-lit fiction more closely resembles the "white glove" detective fiction written between the world wars by Dorothy Sayers, Michael Innes, and others than it does the metafiction of the sixties. In novels such as *Clouds of Witness* (1926), *Gaudy Night* (1935), and *The Long Farewell* (1956), the story may revolve around the central mystery, but the locations and characters are uniformly genteel and the majority of those characters read books and won't let you forget it—literary allusions are tossed about casually like so many decorative throw pillows, alongside references to vintage port and first editions. The Lord Peter Wimsey novels offer a smorgasbord of refined tastes, and readers aren't there because he can ratiocinate like no other genius detective—they're there for the lifestyle, every bit as much as Merchant and Ivory fans are there for the décor and the costuming. Lit-lit novels are remarkably similar in terms of the all-pervasive bookishness and the intertwining of literary taste with comparable sophisticated tastes in gastronomy, décor, and clothing. But in Lit-lit novels, the central question is not who done it, but when will X have his/her transformative aesthetic experience? The world of the white-glove detective novel became so formalized that it was transformed smoothly into the ever-popular board game *Clue*. In that game, the player takes the role of detective solving the crime in the country house, posing questions to crack the case: Was it Colonel Mustard in the Drawing Room with the lead pipe? Was it Miss Scarlet in the Billiard Room with the revolver? Given the generic nature of Lit-lit, it's easy to imagine a comparable board game, in which players try to determine who will have the aesthetic epiphany: Will it be the Physician in the Drawing Room with the Matthew Arnold poem? Or the Aesthete in the Billiard Room with the Henry James novel? Or the Jane Austen Reader in the Living Room with the Sundance poppies rug?

The staging of the aesthetic experience, the demonstration of the power of culture to lift us up, is crucially important, because the aesthetic pleasures afforded by these novels is primarily a matter of describing how characters undergo such experiences. In other words, one of the most significant differences between the aesthetic writing of a century ago and contemporary neo-aesthetic novels is that the former was determined to make the reading of the text an intense aesthetic experience unto itself through flamboyantly "artful" stylistic strategies, where the latter depicts characters having such experiences, in prose styles that feature anything but such stylistic virtuosity. Bushnell, Johnson, Hollinghurst, and company may want to rewrite the novel of manners, but, in terms of their prose style, they resemble one another far more than their literary forbears—well-tailored, genteel realism will do very nicely, thank you. The mise-en-scène, here as it is in all such scenes in Lit-lit fiction, revolves around the staging of the literary experience in which epiphany is the reading transformation scene that the reader is expected to take on faith. As such, these transformation scenes resemble the paintings incorporated in my daughter's *The Reading Woman* calendar that she got last Christmas from her grandmother. Here, paintings such as Kerr-Lawson's *Caterina Reading a Book* (1888), Wiles's *Woman Reading on a Beach* (1899), Waltrous's *Just a Couple of Girls* (1915), and Fantin-Latour's *La Liseuse* (1861) provide beautiful images of the act of reading, featuring attractive, earnest-looking young women reading passionately in very pretty, tasteful surroundings.

The reading transformation scenes in Lit-lit fiction work in much the same way. They depict the act of reading as an exquisite aesthetic experience, but the aesthetic quality is largely picturesque. We are shown people enjoying the pleasures of reading, but the book we hold in our hand offers little more than the literary equivalent of these paintings—the words only depict aesthetic pleasure felt by others, resulting in a bizarre pornography of reading in which pleasure comes from watching others lost in the pleasure of reading really great novels or looking at really great paintings. In making the reading scenes so pivotal, these novels produce the literary equivalent of the Miramax "author's hand" close-ups discussed in chapter 4, only here the hand that holds the book is every bit as important as the hand that holds the pen, provided that hand is simply throbbing with the pleasures of reading.

Just how far the resulting book talk is from metafictional "book talk," is thrown into sharp relief in Dai Sijie's *Balzac and the Little Chinese Seamstress* (2002). Here, virtually all of the features of Lit-lit are solidly in place, and advertised accordingly. The cover of the American paperback edition has "National Bestseller" emblazoned across the top and on the back cover, and the lead blurb from the *Washington Post Book World* insists that this is "a funny, touching, sly and altogether delightful novel . . . about the power of art to enlarge our imagination." One of the featured blurbs on the first page is from the *Boston Herald*, which identifies its intended audience: "A true book lover's book. . . . A testament to resilience and to the power of words." That this transformative power of reading is being used as the primary selling point is made even more abundantly clear in the back cover copy: "In this enchanting tale about the magic of reading and the wonder of romantic awakening . . . ." The narrator also attests to this magical power when he describes his first encounter with the Balzac novel *Ursule Moiret*: "The messy affair over the inheritance and money that befell her made the story all the more convincing, thereby enhancing the power of the words" (57).

This power fuels another standard feature of the Devoutly Literary—the virtual erasure of the differences between writing and reading passionately. ("Readers are artists too, you know.") The narrator doesn't want to just read *Ursule Moiret*; he transcribes it onto the lining of his coat. Once transcribed, and transformed into a form of oral storytelling by the narrator and his friend Luo, it has the power to mesmerize the noble savage, instantaneously. When Luo reads from this coat to the little seamstress, she takes it from him and rereads it herself:

> When she'd finished reading she sat there quite still, open-mouthed. Your coat was resting on the flat of her hands, the way a sacred object lies in the palm of the pious. "This fellow Balzac is a wizard," he went on. "He touched the head of this mountain girl with an invisible finger, and she was transformed, carried away in a dream. It took a while for her to come down to earth. She ended up putting your wretched coat on. She said having Balzac's words next to her skin made her feel good, and also more intelligent." (62)

Because of this power to transform listeners into passionate readers on contact, there are no differences between popular storytelling and literary prose, or between readers and authors within Sijie's novel. Before they acquire their trove of literary classics, Luo and the narrator tell stories based on the films they've seen to entertain their audiences of simple country peasants, but the stories they draw from their reading of Balzac and Dumas novels prove even more mesmerizing. The narrator strings the village tailor along à la Scheherazade, with nightly installments of *The Count of Monte Cristo*:

The artistry of the great Dumas was so compelling that I forgot all about our guest, and the words poured from me. My sentences became more precise, more concrete, more compact as I went along . . . I lost all sense of time . . . How long had I been talking? An hour? Two? We had arrived at the point of the story where our hero, the French sailor, was locked up in a cell for the next twenty years. I felt drowsy, and I had to stop.

"Right now," Luo whispered to me, "you're doing better than me. You should have been a writer." Intoxicated by this compliment, coming as it did from a master storyteller, I drifted off to sleep. Suddenly I heard the old tailor's voice rumbling in the dark.

"Why did you stop?"

The difference between the celebratory hymn to the glory of reading of Lit-lit and the self-reflexivity of metafiction becomes especially clear-cut if we compare Dai Sijie's use of Dumas to Italo Calvino's "transcription" of the same novel in his story "The Count of Monte Cristo." Calvino constructs an elaborate imaginary universe of possible texts out of the fictional universe constructed by Dumas, but Sijie describes the narrator's retelling of Dumas. As such, it is heartfelt testimony to the master's storytelling powers, a *depiction* of the telling and reading and listening. The mise-en-scène focalizes, as it does in all such scenes in Lit-lit fiction, on the reading transformation scene in which the reader is expected to take the epiphany on faith. But no great leap of faith is required here, since the readership in attendance is already firmly convinced that such power exists and relishes the reaffirmation.

Jennifer Kaufman's and Karen Black's novel, *Literacy and Longing in L.A.* (2006) is another *Portrait of a Reading Woman* in novel form, which reveals how much more aggressively authors and publishers began, between 2002 and 2006, to identify an intended audience as a specific type of reading community. The main character, Dora, is a passionate reader, longing for the next right book and the next Mr. Right to come into her life, more or less in that order. She is surrounded by a bookish mise-en-scène that extends throughout her adventures. We learn right from the start that her mother named her after Eudora Welty and that her sister, Virginia, was named after, well, you know who. When they were children, their mother would take them on literary field trips in search of the homes and haunts of famous writers. After Dora finishes her degree at Columbia University (duly noted), she moves to L.A., where she eventually marries Palmer, who eventually gets "the top job at Sony Pictures." As an avid reader who also happens to be a very attractive woman living in glitzy surroundings with a husband who is a major player in Hollywood, Dora obviously bears a strong resemblance to Janey Wilcox in Candace Bushnell's *Trading Up*. The resemblance is stronger yet if one considers Dora's insider observations about L.A. Instead of "In the Hamptons, everyone . . ." we get, "In Bel Air, everyone . . . ." And in both novels the name-dropping of designer labels is ubiquitous, from Prada bags to "my *Dolce*." But what makes this novel a devoutly Lit-lit novel, instead of a post-literary novel of manners, is Dora's relentless reading and incessant book talk. She insists, "I collect books the way my girlfriends buy designer handbags," but it's actually more accurate to say she does both. That's a "scholarly biography of Henry James" in that Prada bag, *buddy*! Like Janey, she has a healthy respect for one-night stands, but for Dora the ultimate ecstasy is reading. As the title suggests, the longing for both a literary good read and a literary good lay are interdependent—a point made quite clearly when she falls for Fred, the hunky guy with a doctorate in Comparative Literature who works at her favorite independent bookstore. She has great sex with Fred, after what is referred to as "esoteric foreplay" (e.g., he quotes Edward Lear, and Dora responds, "Oh shit, I'm thinking, He's at it again. I melt every time. 'Let's forget the movie,' I whisper"; 164). But no matter how wonderful this esoteric sex might be, or how graphically it is described, the most erotic scenes in the novel are clearly meant to be the bathtub scenes, where Dora enjoys the ecstasy of reading whatever she wants, on her own terms.

> I have a whole mantra for my book binges. First of all, I open a bottle of really good wine. Then I turn off my cell phone, turn on my answering machine, and gather all of the books I've been meaning to read or reread or haven't. Finally, I fill up the tub with thirty-dollar bubble bath, fold a little towel at the end of the tub so it just fits the crook of my neck and turn off the music. . . . Within my bathroom walls is a self-contained field of dreams, and I am in total control, the master of my own elegantly devised universe. The outside world disappears, and here, there is only peace and a profound sense of well-being. (8)

This kind of passion clearly depends on the right partner, and Dora also details her dance card in an extended description of her library, which is arranged according to her own emotional logic, exactly as Rob's record library is organized in Hornby's *High Fidelity*. Vestiges of some earlier academic training in reading appear throughout the novel (she went to *Columbia*, okay?), but ultimately it is the intensely personal nature of her reading that gives her the greatest pleasure. Fred turns out to be an utterly self-absorbed bastard, but the insightful reader knew this affair never would go so well after Dora tells us, "He has a degree in comparative literature and he did his thesis on heterogeneous space in post-modern literature. What does that mean?" (18). She also provides her own portrait gallery of Readers Reading, arranged as an "unspoken hierarchy of readers"—Purists, Academics, Book Worshippers, people who just want an old-fashioned story, bottom-feeders who do their reading via audio tapes, and so on. But *Literacy and Longing in L.A.* adds something else to the portrait gallery—a list of suggested readings, as in Nancy Pearl's *Book Lust*. Dora might refer to favorite books and authors repeatedly, but the authors Kaufman and Mack provide a list of these very books at the end of the novel:

> *Book List*
> Authors, artists, and works that are discussed or mentioned in this
>   novel, listed in order of their first appearance.
> Ted Kooser, poet
> Jorge Luis Borges, author
> John Gardner, author

And this list continues, for the next ten pages, until it concludes with "Emily Dickenson, poet." This list is obviously a handy thing to have around, and it also reveals a great deal about the sort of reading community this book celebrates. The book talk rarely stops for very long, and everything is thoroughly marinated in bookish pleasures—but the reflections on reading are unilaterally celebratory, containing none of the ambivalence found in metafictional texts that are determined to *show their workings*. The citation of Julian Barnes provides a particularly telling example of this difference. Dora tells Palmer:

> "I think the only time I'm really happy is when I'm reading. 'Books make sense of life,'*—Somebody said that. Anyway, that's how I feel."

---

* Julian Barnes, *Flaubert's Parrot*

Even though Dora doesn't remember the source of the reference, the authors provide it anyway in a footnote at the bottom of the page, a gesture which, in and of itself, suggests a great deal about the particular brand of bibliophilia at play. Apparently, the readers of this novel aren't expected to know the source of the reference either, but it's taken for granted that they want to be told so they can track the book down if they care to. Even more revealing, however, is the invocation of Barnes's book as confirmation of Dora's passionate book addiction, since that phrase, when it appears within the flamboyantly metafictional *Flaubert's Parrot*, expresses a profound ambivalence about the transformative power of literary reading. Barnes's narrator, Geoffrey Braithwaite, may be obsessed with books by and about Flaubert, but as the novel progresses it becomes increasingly apparent that this obsession insulates him from the heartbreak of his wife's adultery and death: "Ellen. My wife: someone I feel I understand less well than a foreign writer dead for a hundred years. Is this an aberration, or is it normal? Books say: She did this because. Life says: She did this. Books are where things are explained to you; life is where things aren't. I'm not surprised that some people prefer books. Books make sense of life. The only problem is that the lives they make sense of are other people's lives, never your own" (168). The citation of *Flaubert's Parrot* in *Living and Longing in L.A.* suggests none of this ambivalence—when I read the passage "books make sense of life," complete with informative footnote, I felt as if I was supposed to write "How true!" in the margin. In Barnes's novel, the "book talk" never stops, but what literary reading fails to accomplish is detailed as extensively as what it might deliver in the best of circumstances. In a Lit-lit novel like *Literacy and Longing in L.A.* there is only unequivocal celebration of literary reading, in which book talk becomes endless recommendation. The passionate readers in these fictions aren't really bibliophiles, in the truest sense of the term, because the details of book collecting are relevant only in terms of arranging one's library as an extension of one's self—details concerning which editions, or the state of individual copies of books as collectible objects, rarely become important. The activity of reading is what's addictive, not the hunt for the books themselves. And academic readers in a Lit-lit book are generally disqualified as people who have lost their amateur status, and inevitably their ability to read for pure pleasure, unless they undergo a reverse transformation process and return to pure reading. As passionate readers who also act as experts on reading, the readers in Lit-lit fiction come closest to the figure of the librarian, the master reader whose expertise is measured not in terms of critical reading but of enthusiastic recommendation, at which point these characters resemble national librarians/list makers like Nancy Pearl or Sara Nelson, author of *So Many Books, So Little Time* (2004), rather than the book-obsessed characters of metafictional texts. Not surprisingly, *Literacy and Longing* includes an appreciative blurb from Nelson on its back cover: "The book is sharp, seamless, and very, very funny. I wish I had written it." In effect, Nelson already has written the nonfiction guide to reading it, since Kaufman's and Mack's novel reads more like the fictionalization of *So Many Books, So Little Time* than *Flaubert's Parrot*.

The convergence of the Lit-lit novel and the Guide to Reading book, complete with a list for further reading at the back, depends on a form of book talk that is nowhere to be found in *Flaubert's Parrot*, even though Barnes's narrator is a self-professed amateur reader who is even more dismissive of academic critics. The book talk that circulates through that novel is not the unalloyed celebration that it is endlessly recommending, but then the absence of that sort of discourse is understandable. When Barnes's novel first appeared in 1980, there was no popular literary culture held together by a set of interlocking delivery systems with its own way of talking the talk of literary appreciation, all unified by an ideology of reading as personal transformation, advocated with varying degrees of explicitness by Oprah Winfrey, the list makers at Amazon, the Target Kids Book Club, prize-winning Lit-lit novels, and the Sundance catalogue. It is precisely this ideology of reading that mandates the celebration of reading, as a sophisticated form of self-help therapy and as an even more sophisticated means of demonstrating personal taste, that provides the thrill factor for the pornography of reading that is so inescapable in Lit-lit fiction.

Just how overtly that pornography of reading has been transformed into a thriving form of genre fiction intended for an expanding target audience is exemplified by both the conception and the promotion of Diane Setterfield's novel *The Thirteenth Tale* (2006). The main character, Margaret Lea, works in her father's antiquarian bookshop, where she devotes most of her day to reading books and is given to saying things like, "I did not simply read them. I devoured them. Though my appetite for food grew frail, my hunger for books was constant. It was the beginning of my vocation." Here too we find the alternation between the languages of spiritual and sexual ecstasy to describe the reading experience. Although Margaret's vocation may lead her to devote herself to nineteenth-century novels and reject contemporary fiction, she is captivated by the tales of the "most popular living novelist," Vera Winter (who writes about people in stories with beginnings, middles, and ends where they're supposed to be): "I remember the *Thirteen Tales* that took possession of me with its first words and held me captive all night. I wanted to be held hostage again. . . . Miss Winter restored to me

the virginal qualities of the novice reader, and then with her stories she ravished me" (31). Reading the right sort of literary books may indeed get Margaret's reading spectacles all steamed up, but the cohesiveness of this genre
is secured by more than a generic logic that justifies all character behavior and the trumpeting of erotically charged reading experiences that lead
them to recommend books compulsively while they circulate through the
stable iconographic locations found on the Lit-lit game board—libraries,
bookshops, and bathtubs, and so on. The identification of a "literary good
read" as a new form of category fiction also depends on how those titles are
connected to a reading community that will know that this book is indeed
intended "just for them." Genres depend on the stability of conventions and
shared values but also the transformation of individual fans into communities that can be identified as target audiences. As the "Inaugural Selection"
of a new program, Barnes & Noble Recommends, *The Thirteenth Tale* was
the featured selection on its own table in the rotunda of my local store.
This display was addressed to a very particular readership identified by
the pamphlets introducing this new series, which included reading group
discussion questions, an author bio, advance reviews, and this mission
statement:

Unputdownable
This word is not in every dictionary but it is one that booksellers often
use. Nothing gives us more pleasure than recommending books that we
have read and loved. And finding unputdownable books gives us the
greatest pleasure of all. The number of books that are hand-sold in our
stores everyday is staggering: every day, our booksellers lead readers
to hundreds of books—new and old—across every category and topic
imaginable. Even more staggering is the number of new titles being published. From among these we often find works of exceptional merit that
go on to become both popular and critically acclaimed. Barnes & Noble
Recommends provides us with the opportunity to share such books with
you. From the thousands of titles published each season we select one
book we love. Each selection will be a book that that we know is a rivet-
ing read and a work of extraordinary quality worthy of stimulating discussion. Each Barnes & Noble Recommends selection will be chosen by
our discriminating and independent-minded booksellers from across the
country. Each selection will be a book we are sure you will recommend
to another reader.

Within this discourse of reading as emphatic recommendation shared by characters, readers, and booksellers of Lit-lit, the selling of books is merely the excuse for entering into a conversation about loving books. In Setterfield's novel, Margaret tells the reader that the quaint book shop that she and her father operate "makes next to no money," but it is "a place to read. . . . [T]he shop was both my home and my job. It was a better school for me than school ever was and afterward it was my own private university. It was my life" (14). (Whether Margaret has taken any courses at Barnes & Noble University is never specified, but the author who created her was there on the faculty at www.bn.com/bookclubs throughout November 2006.) This is pure fan talk, but here the fans all sound like overstimulated librarians. The use value of reading literary fiction at this point transcends the search for the appropriate significant other. The pleasures of reading culminate in the relentless articulation of personal taste as an end in itself—the erotics of reading depending equally on private, masturbatory delights and the exhibitionist thrill of enthralled recommendation in the most public arenas. As such, Lit-lit represents the perfect convergence of all of the interdependent components of popular literary culture—literary *category* fiction that observes all of the already formalized conventions that guarantee entertainment value for passionate amateur readers, catered to enthusiastically by superstore and Web site bookstores, with all of the players speaking the same language of popular connoisseurship with utmost confidence. The language of the novel, its appreciation, and its marketing are all blended seamlessly into the same book talk, which recommends a shared sensibility as much as any favorite title.

What I've been describing as the Lit-lit genre of literary fiction represents a complicated development that cannot be judged unilaterally positive or negative. The Lit-lit phenomenon certainly provides ample evidence that a there is a stable, thriving market for literary reading of a most sophisticated variety, and it should continue to flourish as long as it is cultivated so lovingly by segments of the publishing, film, and television industries. One could argue that this is an extremely positive development, since it represents what allegedly isn't supposed to happen—a form of literary reading has emerged within the heart of electronic culture via that electronic culture, even if it holds itself apart as an alternative to all that noise. The best-friend clubbiness gives the solitary pleasures of reading literary fiction a social dimension that it previously lacked, except for a rarefied audience of professionalized readers. That celebration of shared sensibilities provides a degree of cohesiveness, a sense of belonging to a reading community, actual or virtual, which obviously only intensifies the pleasures of reading for thousands of readers. As such, Lit-lit represents a thorough-going incorporation of reading into the textures of day-to-day life, a world where reading has indeed become part of the furniture. And as such, it may well represent the best chance for literary reading to become the sort of lifelong activity that teachers and professors of English can only hope to inspire.

So that's all to the good, right? Indeed it is, but there are also things about the Lit-lit phenomenon that are just as disturbing in regard to the future of reading literary fiction. Is it really so wrong to want to sit in a swell leather club chair while reading one of this year's Notable Books? Of course not, provided that the book isn't the print equivalent of that leather club chair, all richly textured and evocative of another, more tasteful age, when reading was truly valued. That Margaret Atwood appears in *Bon Appetit* as a celebrity foodie (March 2006), for example, exemplifies just how thoroughly intertwined the pleasures of reading have become with those other formerly elite pleasures that are now offered throughout popular culture. On the other hand, this issue is entitled "WARM and COZY," a title that could also apply to most Lit-lit novels, since their celebration of shared pleasures rarely leads to anything that might be a challenge to its readers' core values. Azar Nafisi, author of *Reading Lolita in Tehran*, was featured in advertisements for Audi automobiles in a series entitled "Never Follow," along with celebrities such as David Bowie, Daniel Libeskind, K. D. Laing, and John Malkovich. The publicist, Rod Brown (management supervisor for the Audi of America account at McKinney & Silver), explained why Nafisi was chosen: "We want to make Audi distinct from BMW or Mercedes by associating it with these people. We wanted people who weren't just famous or rich but who are doing something really cool. A light bulb went off, Azar is to literature what Audi is to cars" (quoted in Julie Salamon's article in the *New York Times*, 2004). For a writer best known as a book club leader to acquire that kind of celebrity status reveals a great deal about the very different sort of conversation now being conducted about books and how audible it has become. That Nafisi's name is associated with a luxury car also suggests a fair amount about this audience, which believes in the transformative power of literary fiction so absolutely that it works as a sales pitch, of the most discreet variety.

Reading within the Lit-lit taste community relies on certain "production values." As such, Lit-lit novels have a great deal in common with Miramax adaptation films, since "the words are the special effects," to echo Harvey

Weinstein—but only if they're given the right mise-en-scène, and only if they're all about people just like us, only maybe more attractive and with a lot more time on their hands to read. I've used the term "Miramaxing" to describe a type of adaptation film, but it can also be just as descriptive of a particular form of literary fiction with the right sort of art direction and sensitive attractive characters, identified as a text-to-be-read for a particular quality audience. The conception and promotion of *The Thirteenth Tale* is pure Miramax, long before it ever becomes an adaptation film.

The best-friend coziness factor becomes especially pernicious when it is built on an ideology of reading that insists that the transformative power of words is available to all, but is really appreciated only by we few, we happy, tasteful few, who already know that power. At that point, the "we few" dimension of Lit-lit becomes a double-edged sword, frightening away as much as it safeguards. It undoubtedly provides a high degree of cohesiveness and a deep sense of belonging for those who affiliate with it, since that community of book lovers is imagined as such an imperiled group, clinging to genuine aesthetic values while the electronic culture that surrounds it threatens annihilation at any moment. This sort of us-versus-them opposition is all-pervasive throughout the NEA's *Reading at Risk* report, but the sanctification of this community of book lovers under siege, this ideology of the faithful remnant struggling to survive, is nowhere more obvious than in one of the novels chosen by the NEA for its community-wide Big Read projects in the spring of 2006—Ray Bradbury's *Fahrenheit 451* (1953). No other novel in the history of literature presents in more pristine form this scenario of the "we few, we happy few" readers imperiled by mass culture but all the happier for it. This is indeed a brilliant choice of reading material, if you're looking for converts to a cult of readers. They can identify with Montag, the brave, sensitive fireman who, though surrounded by electronic media when not otherwise burning books, eventually sees the light when he gets a load of what reading really involves, after he meets the wonderfully sensitive book people, at which point he's just "*Gotta* read, *gotta* read . . ." (Cut to Wide Shot of Montag dancing with his copy of Dickens and surrounded by banks of television monitors. Bring up music. Cue flames.) This conversion to the imperiled cult approach may indeed be a powerful rhetorical strategy for enlisting potential readers. In Althusserian terms, this is very skillful form of interpellation, since the Fireman as Noble Savage in the Electronic Jungle answers the call once he hears all those words. But is this 1950s fable about the evils of mass culture really the most effective way to convince people that reading books is facing certain extinction when they are surrounded by television book clubs, literary adaptations at the multiplex, and super-store bookshops in practically every mall in America? When the Sundance catalogue, as well as posters in school libraries feature Orlando Bloom and company urge us to READ! at all costs, and the kids' drink cup at another chain store tells youthful customers to sign up now for the Target Kids Book Club—a message surrounded by a cluster of pandas, ducks, monkeys, and crocodiles, all avidly reading books? To employ the old "if-visitors-from-another-planet-suddenly-arrived-they'd-think . . ." conceit, those newly arrived aliens would surmise that this society was one run by a tribe of Book People, hell-bent on eradicating all forms of electronic media (while a guerilla underground traded DVD copies of *The Sopranos* and *Mad Men* and walked through the woods, committing them to memory). And those aliens better be ready to read their Bradbury, or there's going to be trouble, . . . big trouble.

The imperiled clubbiness of the Devoutly Literary may consolidate a community of readers by validating their shared sensibilities, but it comes with an enormous risk—that potential readers may not answer the call be-cause they don't want to affiliate with a club that gives no validity to any as-pect of their cultural life other than literary reading. The noble savages will simply go elsewhere. Popular literary culture represents a powerful counter-argument to the *Fahrenheit 451* scenario, since it is built, from the ground up, on the interdependency of the print and visual culture, not a world of books versus wall screens, which persists only within an ideology of reading that can accept just one form of literacy and, therefore, must demonize all electronic culture.

In order to visualize that interdependency, I want to return to the Au-thors Mural at my local Barnes & Noble café, which I discussed in the open-ing pages of this book, but update it so that it captures the current state of literary culture, not the retro diner version of all things literary. Imag-ine that mural as a wraparound diorama, complete with moving pictures and soundtrack. It would include many of the same figures but redeployed among a new cast of characters. Jane Austen would still be there, of course, but at a table with Helen Fielding, Colin Firth, and Kiera Knightly, all locked in conversation while Jane reads her copy of *The Jane Austen Book Club* on her Kindle and Kiera leafs through an issue of *Vogue* (December 2005), where she's featured in a photo retelling of *The Wizard of Oz*, costarring the likes of Jasper Johns as the Cowardly Lion, Brice Marsdan as the Scarecrow, and Chuck Close as the Wizard. At the next table, Harvey Weinstein is in animated conversation about the art and business of adaptation with Nicole Woolf and Gwyneth Plath, right alongside Oprah's table where William Faulkner and Leo Tolstoy (wearing his "I Wasn't Scared" T-shirt) delight a cluster of Book Clubbers by imploring them to help them complete the creative process. And Henry James would no longer be lost in thought, trying to evade Oscar Wilde's gaze—he'd be holding court, talking about his celebrity profile in *Vanity Fair* with Alan Hollinghurst, Colm Toibin, Ian McEwan, and Helena Bonham Carter, saying wickedly amusing things about Harvey. And on the walls behind them, images from *The Hours* and *Shakespeare in Love* and *The English Patient* and *Atonement* and *No Country for Old Men* would run perpetually, interspersed with Amazon pages clicking back and forth endlessly between "Listmania" lists, "So You Want to Be . . ." guides and "Better Together" package deals. At a table below, I sit with my own daughters, whose conversation, on a given Saturday afternoon, ricochets from Harry Potter to Alfonso Cuaron to E. L. Konigsburg to Wes Anderson to William Joyce to *Family Guy* to YouTube to *The Invention of Hugo Cabret* to Baz Luhrmann and the enormous aesthetic pleasure they get from them all. I could be concerned that the special apartness of literary reading will be diminished by its place in that mix, or that as readers they will be addressed primarily as quality consumers. They will indeed encounter that omnipresent consumerism, but they will also encounter other readers in the realm of popular literary culture who will be just as passionate about defining themselves in terms of their aesthetic choices. I'm delighted that literary fiction forms part of the cultural mixes they assemble with such gusto to articulate who they are, and what is crucially important to them. I could, as a curator of the written word, long for a time when literary reading transcended that mix, but I have no desire to engage in time travel to an imaginary past where reading was *really* transformative. We sit in Barnes & Noble at the beginning of the twenty-first century, not the end of the nineteenth, and given the access to the excess of cultural information, we're all curators now, of words *and* images.

BIBLIOGRAPHY

Allen, Brooke. "Two—Make that Three—Cheers for the Chain Bookstores." *Atlantic Monthly* 286, no. 12 (July–August 2001).

Andrew, Dudley. *Concepts in Film Theory*. New York: Oxford University Press, 1984.

Angel, Karen. "Shakespeare & Co. Exits NYC'S Upper West Side Stage." *Publisher's Weekly* 243, no. 25 (June 17, 1996).

Appadurai, Arjun. "Introduction: Politics and the Commodities of Value." In *The Social Life of Things*. Cambridge: Cambridge University Press, 1986.

Bank, Melissa. *The Girls' Guide to Hunting and Fishing*. New York: Viking, 1999.

———. *The Wonder Spot*. New York: Viking, 2005.

Barnes, Julian. *Flaubert's Parrot*. New York: Vintage Books, 1984.

Barth, John. "Life Story." In *Lost in the Funhouse*. New York: Doubleday, 1968.

———. "The Literature of Replenishment." 1980. Reprint in *The Friday Book*. New York: Putnam, 1984.

Barthes, Roland. *The Pleasure of the Text*. New York: Hill and Wang, 1975.

Bennett, Tony. "Texts in History: The Determinations of Readings and Their Texts." *Journal of the Midwest Modern Language Association* 18, no. 1 (fall 1985).

Biskind, Peter. *Down and Dirty Pictures*. New York: Simon and Schuster, 2004.

———. *Easy Riders, Raging Bulls: How the Sex-Drugs-and-Rock 'n' Roll Generation Saved Hollywood*. New York: Simon and Schuster, 1998.

Bloom, Harold. *How to Read and Why*. New York: Scribner, 2000.

Bourdieu, Pierre. *The Field of Cultural Production*. New York: University of Columbia Press, 1993.

Bradbury, Malcolm. "The Customs of the Country." Review of *Le Divorce*, by Diane Johnson. *New York Times Book Review*, February 2, 1997.

Bradbury, Ray. *Fahrenheit 451*. New York: Simon and Schuster, 1953.

Browning, Dominique. "Anything but the Eighties." *House and Garden*, May 2000.

Bushnell, Candace. *Trading Up*. New York: Hyperion, 2002.

Byatt, A. S. *Possession*. New York: Vintage Books, 1990.

Calvino, Italo. *Why Read the Classics?* New York: Pantheon Books, 1999.

Campbell, Colin. *The Romantic Ethic and the Spirit of Modern Consumerism*. New York: Blackwell, 1987.

Carvajal, Doreen. "Reading to the Bottom Line." *New York Times Magazine*, February 19, 1999.

Christensen, Kate. *In the Drink*. New York: Doubleday, 1999.

Christie, Ian. "Talks with Martin Scorsese." In *Film, Literature, Heritage: A Sight and Sound Reader*, ed. Ginette Vincendeau. London: BFI Publishing, 2001.

Corrigan, Tim. *Film and Literature: An Introduction and Reader's Guide*. New York: Prentice Hall, 1998.

———. "Which Shakespeare to Love? Film, Fidelity, and the Performance of Literature." In *High-Pop: Making Culture into Popular Entertainment*, ed. Jim Collins. Malden, Mass.: Blackwell, 2002.

Cunningham, Michael. *The Hours: A Novel*. New York: Farrar, Straus, Giroux, 1998.

———. "The Novel, the Movie: My Baby Reborn." *New York Times*, January 19, 2003.

Cusk, Rachel. *The Country Life*. New York: Picador, 1997.

Daldrey, Stephen, dir. *The Hours*. Miramax-Paramount, 2002.

DeBona, Geurric. "Dickens, the Depression, and MGM's *David Copperfield*." In *Film Adaptation*, ed. James Naremore. Rutgers, N.J.: Rutgers University Press, 2000.

Deer, Patrick. "Defusing *The English Patient*." In *Literature and Film: A Guide to the Theory and Practice of Film Adaptation*, ed. Robert Stam and Alessandra Raengo. Malden, Mass.: Blackwell, 2004.

Delany, Paul. "Who Paid for Modernism?" 1993. Reprinted in *New Economic Criticism*, ed. Martha Woodmansee and Mark Osteen. New York: Routledge, 1995.

Dettemar, Kevin, and Stephen Watt. *Marketing Modernisms*. Ann Arbor: University of Michigan Press, 1996.

Dimaggio, Paul. "Cultural Entrepreneurship in Nineteenth-Century Boston." In *Rethinking Popular Culture*, ed. Chandra Mukerji and Michael Schudson. Berkeley: University of California Press, 1991.

Donoghue, Denis. *Speaking of Beauty*. New Haven, Conn.: Yale University Press, 2003.

Dorris, Michael. *The Most Wonderful Books: Writers on Discovering the Pleasures of Reading*. New York: Milkweed, 1997.

Duncan, Carol. *Civilizing Rituals: Inside Public Art Museums*. New York: Routledge, 1995.

Dyer, Richard. "Nice Young Men Who Sell Antiques and Gay Men in Heritage Cinema." In *Film/Literature/Heritage: A Sight and Sound Reader*. London: British Film Institute, 2001.

Eagleton, Terry. *Literary Theory*. Cambridge, Mass.: Blackwell, 1996.

Fadiman, Anne. *Ex Libris: Confessions of Common Reader*. New York: Farrar, Straus, Giroux, 1998.

Farr, Cecilia Konchar. *Reading Oprah: How Oprah's Book Club Changed the Way America Reads*. Albany: State University of New York Press, 2005.

Feinberg, Rene. "B&N: The New College Library?" *Library Journal*, February 1, 1998.

Fialkoff, Francine. "Franzen: Too Highbrow for Oprah?" *Library Journal*, November 15, 2001.

Fielding, Helen. *Bridget Jones's Diary*. New York: Viking, 1996.

Finnamore, Suzanne. *Otherwise Engaged*. New York: Vintage Contemporaries, 1999.

Fitzpatrick, Kathleen. *The Anxiety of Obsolescence: The American Novel in the Age of Television*. Nashville, Tenn.: Vanderbilt University Press, 2006.

Fowler, Karen Jay. *The Jane Austen Book Club*. New York: Putnam, 2004.

Franzen, Jonathan. *The Corrections*. New York: Farrar, Straus, Giroux, 2001.

———. "The Reader in Exile." In *How to Be Alone: Essays*. New York: Farrar, Straus, Giroux, 2002.

———. "Why Bother?" 1996. Reprinted in *How to Be Alone: Essays*. New York: Farrar, Straus, Giroux, 2002.

Freedman, Jonathan. *Professions of Taste: Henry James, British Aestheticism, and Commodity Culture*. Stanford, Calif.: Stanford University Press, 1990.

Freeman, Hadley. "Words Smith." *Vogue* (Britain), October 2005.

Gans, Herbert. *Popular Culture and High Culture*. New York: Basic Books, 1984.

Gilbar, Steven. *Reading in Bed: Personal Essays on the Glories of Reading*. New York: David R. Godine, 1999.

Graffagnino, Kevin. *Only in Books: Writers, Readers and Bibliophiles on Their Passion*. Madison, Wisc.: Madison House Publishers, 1996.

Guillory, John. *Cultural Capital: The Problem of Literary Canon Formation*. Chicago: University of Chicago Press, 1993.

Gunning, Tom. "The Cinema of Attraction: Early Film, Its Spectator, and the Avant-garde." In *Film and Theory: An Anthology*, ed. Robert Stam and Toby Miller. Malden, Mass.: Blackwell, 2000.

Hare, David. *The Hours: A Screenplay*. London: Penguin Faber, 2002.

Hartley, Jenny. *Reading Groups*. New York: Oxford University Press, 2001.

Haskell, Molly. "When Oscar Is Bad, He's Very Very . . . ." *New York Times*, March 24, 2002.

Higson, Andrew. "The Heritage Film and British Cinema." In *Dissolving Views: Key Writings on British Cinema*, ed. Andrew Higson. London: Cassell, 1996.

Hill, John. *British Cinema in the 1980s: Issues and Themes*. Oxford: Clarendon Press, 1999.

Hipsky, Martin. "Anglophil(m)ia: Why Does America Watch Merchant-Ivory Movies?" *Journal of Popular Film and Television* 22, no. 3 (1994).

Hollinghurst, Alan. *The Line of Beauty*. London: Picador, 2004.

Hornby, Nick. *About a Boy*. New York: Riverhead Books, 1997.

———. *High Fidelity*. New York: Riverhead Books, 1995.

———. *A Long Way Down*. New York: Riverhead Books, 2005.

———. *The Polysyllabic Spree*. New York: McSweeney's, 2004.

———. Review of *Saturday*, by Ian McEwan. *The Believer*, April 2005.

Howe, Nicholas. 1999. "The Cultural Construction of Reading in Anglo-Saxon England." In *Old English Literature*, ed. R. M. Liuzza. New Haven: Yale University Press, 2002.

Hughes, Robert J. "Summer Reading." *Wall Street Journal*, May 14, 2004.

Hutcheon, Linda. *The Canadian Postmodern*. Toronto: Oxford University Press, 1988.

Huyssens, Andreas. *After the Great Divide: Modernism, Mass Culture, and Postmodernism*. Bloomington: Indiana University Press, 1986.

Hynes, Arleen, and Mary Hynes-Berry. *Bibliotherapy, the Interactive Process: A Handbook*. Boulder, Colo.: Westview Press, 1986.

Jacobs, Lea. "Reformers and Spectators: The Film Education Movement in the 30s." *Camera Obscura*, January 22, 1990.

Jenkins, Henry. *Convergence Culture: How Old and New Media Collide*. New York: New York University Press, 2006.

Johnson, Diane. *L'Affaire*. New York: Dutton, 2003.

———. *Le Divorce*. New York: Dutton, 1997.

———. *Le Marriage*. New York: Plume, 2000.

Johnson, Steven. "Curatorial Culture." *New York Times*, December 27, 2003.

———. *Everything Bad Is Good for You*. New York: Riverhead Books, 2005.

Kakutani, Michiko. Review of *A Long Way Down*, by Nick Hornby. *New York Times*, June 20, 2005.

Kaplan, Rob. *Speaking of Books: The Best Things Ever Said about Books and Book Collecting*. New York: Crown, 2001.

Katz, Lillian. "The Disposition to Write and Read." *The Project Approach Catalogue 4*. Available at www.ceep.crc.uluc.edu.

Kaufman, Jennifer, and Karen Black, *Literacy and Longing in L.A.* New York: Delacorte Press, 2006.

Kelly, Kevin. "Scan This Book!" *New York Times Magazine*, May 14, 2006.

Latham, Sean. *Am I a Snob? Modernism and the Novel*. Ithaca, N.Y.: Cornell University Press, 2003.

Levy, Steven. *The Perfect Thing: How the iPod Shuffles Commerce, Culture, and Coolness*. New York: Simon and Schuster, 2007.

Lodge, David. *Author, Author*. New York: Viking, 2004.

Long, Elizabeth. "The Book as Mass Commodity: The Audience Perspective." *Publishing Research Quarterly* 3, no. 1 (1987): 9–30.

———. "Textual Interpretation as Collective Action." In *The Ethnography of Reading*, ed. Jonathan Boyarin. Berkeley: University of California Press, 1992.

Lyotard, Jean-François. *The Postmodern Condition*. Minneapolis: University of Minnesota Press, 1984.

Madden, John, dir. *Shakespeare in Love*. Miramax-Universal, 1999.

Maidman Joshua, Janice, and Donna Di Menna. *Read Two Books and Let's Talk Next Week: Using Bibliotherapy in Clinical Practice*. New York: Wiley, 2000.

Marcus, James. *Amazonia: Five Years at the Epicenter of the Dot.com Juggernaut*. New York: New Press, 2004.

Marcus, Laura. "Virginia Woolf and the Hogarth Press." In *Modernist Writers and the Marketplace*, ed. Ian Willison, Warwick Gould, and Warren Chernaik. New York: St. Martin's Press, 1996.

McEwan, Ian. *Saturday*. New York: Doubleday, 2005.

McLaughlin, Emma, and Nicola Kraus. *The Nanny Diaries*. New York: Penguin, 2002.

Mendelson, Edward. *The Things That Matter: What Seven Classic Novels Have to Say about the Stages of Life*. New York: Random House, 2006.

Merchant, Ismail. *Ismail Merchant's Florence: Filming and Feasting in Tuscany*. New York: Harry N. Abrams, 1994.

Merchant, Ismail, prod., and James Ivory, dir. *A Room with a View*. Merchant-Ivory Productions, 1985.

Miller, Laura. "Book Lovers' Quarrel." *Salon.com*, October 26, 2001.

———. *Reluctant Capitalists: Bookselling and the Culture of Consumption*. Chicago: University of Chicago Press, 2007.

Minghella, Anthony, dir. *The English Patient*. Miramax, 1997.

Modleski, Tania. *Loving with a Vengeance: Mass-Produced Fantasies for Women*. Hamden, Conn.: Archon Books, 1982.

Monk, Claire. "The British Heritage Film and Its Critics." *Critical Survey* 7, no. 2 (1995).

———. "Sexuality and Heritage." In *Film, Literature, Heritage: A Sight and Sound Reader*, ed. Ginette Vincendeau. London: BFI Publishing, 2001.

Moore, Charles. *You Have to Pay for the Public Life: Selected Essays*, ed. Kevin Keim. Cambridge: MIT Press, 2004.

Morrison, Toni. "The Reader as Artist." *O: The Oprah Magazine*, July 2006.

Mullen, John. *How Novels Work*. Oxford University Press, 2006.

Munsterberg, Hugo. "The Means of the Photoplay." In *Film Theory and Criticism*, ed. Gerald Mast, Marshall Chen, and Leo Braudy. New York: Oxford University Press, 1992.

Nafisi, Azar. *Reading Lolita in Tehran: A Memoir in Books*. New York: Random House, 2003.

Naremore, James, ed. *Film Adaptation*. Rutgers, N.J.: Rutgers University Press, 2000.

National Endowment for the Arts. *Reading at Risk: A Survey of Literary Reading in America*. Research Division Report 46. Washington: NEA, 2004.

———. *Reading on the Rise: A New Chapter in American Literacy*. Washington: NEA, 2009.

Nelson, Sara. *So Many Books, So Little Time*. New York: Dutton, 2004.

Noble, Elizabeth. *The Reading Group*. New York: Perennial, 2004.

O: The Oprah Magazine. "Our First Ever Summer Reading Issue." July 2006.

Ohmann, Richard. *Selling Culture: Magazines, Markets and Class at the Turn of the Century*. Middletown, Conn.: Wesleyan University Press, 1996.

Ondaatje, Michael. *The English Patient*. New York: Vintage, 1992.

Pearl, Nancy. *Book Lust: Recommended Reading for Every Mood, Moment, and Reason*. Seattle, Wash.: Sasquatch Press, 2003.

Perren, Alisa. "Sex, Lies, and Marketing: Miramax and the Development of the Quality Indie Blockbuster." *Film Quarterly* 55, no. 2 (winter 2001).

Perrotta, Tom. *Little Children*. New York: St. Martin's Press, 2004.

———. Review of *Long Way Down*, by Nick Hornby. *Publisher's Weekly*, May 21, 2007.

Petro, Patrice. *Joyless Streets: Women and Representation in Weimar Germany*. Princeton, N.J.: Princeton University Press, 1989.

Pevsner, Nicholas. *A History of Building Types*. Princeton, N.J.: Princeton University Press, 1976.

Powers, Richard. *Galatea 2.2*. New York: Farrar, Straus, Giroux, 1995.

Quindlen, Anna. *How Reading Changed My Life*. New York: Ballantine Books, 1998.

Radway, Janice. *A Feeling for Books*. Chapel Hill: University of North Carolina Press, 1997.

———. "Interpretive Communities and Variable Literacies." In *Rethinking Popular Culture*, ed. Chandra Mukerji and Michael Schudson. Berkeley: University of California Press, 1991.

Rainey, Lawrence. *The Institutions of Modernism: Literary Elites and Public Culture*. New Haven, Conn.: Yale University Press, 1998.

Ratliff, Ben. "The Amicable Kidnapping of *The English Patient*." *New York Times*, March 24, 1997.

Rooney, Kathleen. *Reading with Oprah: The Book Club That Changed America*. Fayetteville: University of Arkansas Press, 2005.

Roth, Philip. *The Human Stain*. Boston: Houghton Mifflin, 2000.

Rubin, Joan Shelley. *The Making of Middlebrow Culture*. Chapel Hill: University of North Carolina Press, 1992.

Rushdie, Salman. *Midnight's Children*. New York: Knopf, 1981.

Sadashige, Jacqui. "Sweeping the Sands: Geographies of Desire in *The English Patient*." *Literature and Film Quarterly* 26, no. 4 (1998).

Salamon, Julie. "Author Finds That with Fame Comes Image Management." *New York Times*, June 8, 2004.

Schatz, Thomas. *The Genius of the System*. New York: Pantheon, 1988.

Schiffrin, André. *The Business of Books*. New York: Verso, 2000.

Schine, Cathleen. *She Is Me*. Boston: Little, Brown, 2003.

Schwartz, Lynne Sharon. *Ruined by Reading: A Life in Books*. New York: Beacon Press, 1997.

Schwarzbaum, Lisa. "The Crusader." *Entertainment Weekly*, March 21, 1997.

Scott, A. O. Review of *Cold Mountain*, by Charles Frazier. *New York Times*, December 25, 2004.

Setterfield, Diane. *The Thirteenth Tale*. New York: Washington Square Press, 2006.

Shaffer, Mary Ann, and Annie Barrow. *The Guernsey Literary and Potato Peel Pie Society*. New York: Dial Press, 2008.

Shakespeare, William. *Shakespeare in Love: The Love Poetry of William Shakespeare*. Miramax Hyperion, 1998.

Shapiro, James. Review of *Pieces of My Mind*, by Frank Kermode. *New York Times Book Review*, September 21, 2003.

Shone, Tom. *Blockbuster: How Hollywood Stopped Worrying and Learned to Love the Summer*. New York: Free Press, 2005.

———. "Criticism for Beginners." Review of *How to Read a Novel: A User's Guide*, by John Sutherland. *New York Times Book Review*, December 17, 2006.

Sijie, Dai. *Balzac and the Little Chinese Seamstress*. New York: Knopf, 2001.

Simon, Richard Keller. *Trash Culture: Popular Culture and the Great Tradition*. Los Angeles: University of California Press, 1999.

Sittenfeld, Curtis. *Prep*. New York: Random House, 2005.

———. "Sophie's Choices." Review of *The Wonder Spot*, by Melissa Bank. *New York Times Book Review*, June 5, 2005.

Smith, Roberta. Review of "*The Arts and Crafts Movement in Europe and America*" exhibition, Milwaukee Art Museum. *New York Times*, July 26, 2005.

Smith, Zadie. *On Beauty*. New York: Penguin, 2005.

Sontag, Susan. "The Decay of Cinema." *New York Times Magazine*, February 25, 1996.

Stam, Robert. "Beyond Fidelity: The Dialogics of Adaptation." In *Film Adaptation*, ed. James Naremore. Rutgers, N.J.: Rutgers University Press, 2000.

————. *Literature through Film: Realism, Magic, and the Art of Adaptation*. Malden, Mass.: Blackwell, 2004.

Stam, Robert, and Alessandra Raengo. *A Companion to Literature and Film*. Malden, Mass.: Blackwell, 2004.

————. *Literature and Film: A Guide to the Theory and Practice of Film Adaptation*. Malden, Mass.: Blackwell, 2004.

Stock, Brian. *The Implications of Literacy*. Princeton: Princeton University Press, 1987.

Sutherland, John. *How to Read a Novel: A User's Guide*. New York: St. Martin's Press, 2006.

Swift, Graham. *Waterland*. New York: Poseidon Press, 1983.

Tannock, Stuart. "Nostalgia Critique." *Cultural Studies* 9, no. 3 (1995).

Thorpe, Helen. "The Assault of the Salonistas." *New York Times Book Review*, February 20, 2000.

Todd, Richard. *Consuming Fictions*. London: Bloomsbury, 1996.

Toibin, Colm. *The Master*. New York: Scribner, 2004.

Updike, John. "The End of Authorship." *New York Times Book Review*, June 25, 2006.

Urrichio, William, and Roberta Pearson. *Reframing Culture*. Princeton, N.J.: Princeton University Press, 1993.

Vincendeau, Ginette. "Introduction" to *Film, Literature, Heritage: A Sight and Sound Reader*, ed. Ginette Vincendeau. London: BFI Publishing, 2001.

Wasson, Haidee. *Museum Movies: The Museum of Modern Art and the Birth of Art Cinema*. Berkeley: University of California Press, 2005.

Weber, Katharine. *The Little Women*. New York: Farrar, Straus, Giroux, 2004.

Weiner, Jennifer. Review of *The Wonder Spot*, by Melissa Bank. *Entertainment Weekly*, May 30, 2005.

Weinraub, Bernard. "Mogul in Love with Winning." *New York Times*, March 15, 1999.

Weinstein, Arnold. *Recovering Your Story: Proust, Joyce, Woolf, Faulkner, Morrison*. New York: Random House, 2006.

Weinstein, Bob. "All Thanks to Max." *Vanity Fair*, April 2003.

Wicke, Jennifer. "Coterie Consumption: Bloomsbury, Keynes, and Modernism as Marketing." In *Marketing Modernism*. Ann Arbor: University of Michigan Press, 1996.

Wilinsky, Barbara. *Sure Seaters: Art House Cinema in the Fifties*. Minneapolis: University of Minnesota Press, 2001.

Willett, Jincy. *Winner of the National Book Award*. New York: St. Martin's Press, 2003.

Willison, Ian, Warwick Gould, and Warren Chernaik. *Modernist Writers and the Marketplace*. New York: St. Martin's Press, 1996.

Witchel, Alex. *Me Times Three*. New York: Knopf, 2002.

Wolitzer, Hilma. *Summer Reading*. New York: Ballantine, 2008.

Wood, Michael. *Literature and the Taste for Knowledge*. Cambridge: Cambridge University Press, 2005.

Wyatt, Justin. "The Formation of a Major Independent." In *Contemporary Hollywood Cinema*, ed. Steve Neale and Murray Smith. New York: Routledge, 1998.

Younis, Raymond. "Nationhood and De-colonialization in *The English Patient*." *Literature and Film Quarterly* 26, no. 4 (1998).

INDEX

Jim Collins is a professor of film studies and
English at the University of Notre Dame.

Library of Congress Cataloging-in-Publication Data
Collins, Jim
Bring on the books for everybody:
how literary culture became popular culture /
Jim Collins.
p. cm.
Includes bibliographical references and index.
ISBN 978-0-8223-4588-6 (cloth : alk. paper)
ISBN 978-0-8223-4606-7 (pbk. : alk. paper)
1. Popular culture and literature—United States.
2. Popular culture—United States.
3. Book clubs (Bookselling)—United States.
4. Book clubs (Discussion groups)—United States.
I. Title.
E169.12.C573 2010
306.0973—dc22   2009049951